FEATHER BRAINED

Feather Brained

My Bumbling Quest to
Become a Birder and
Find a Rare Bird on My Own

Bob Tarte

University of Michigan Press
Ann Arbor

Published in the United States of America by the
University of Michigan Press
Manufactured in the United States of America
♾ Printed on acid-free paper

2019   2018   2017   2016   4   3   2   1

Library of Congress Cataloging-in-Publication Data

Names: Tarte, Bob.
Title: Feather brained : my bumbling quest to become a birder and find a rare bird on my
    own / Bob Tarte.
Description: Ann Arbor : University of Michigan Press, 2016.
Identifiers: LCCN 2015048912 | ISBN 9780472119868 (hardcover : alk. paper) | ISBN
    9780472121885 (e-book)
Subjects: LCSH: Bird watchers—Anecdotes. | Bird watching—Anecdotes.
Classification: LCC QL677.5 .T285 2016 | DDC 598.072/34—dc23
LC record available at http://lccn.loc.gov/2015048912

ISBN 978-0-472-11986-8

To my friend Bill Holm,
discoverer of the special bird-attracting fluid

Also by Bob Tarte

Enslaved by Ducks
Fowl Weather
Kitty Cornered

CONTENTS

CHAPTER ONE

The Green Book and the Redhead

I should have listened to my parents. More than fifty years ago, they had warned me about associating with the wrong sorts of people for fear of what would happen to my priorities in life. First they had railed against cheats and liars, thieves, swindlers, braggarts, and the morally lax. When I got older, drug users and dropouts from society topped the list. Though they had never specifically mentioned birders, I should have had the common sense to steer clear of their influence, too.

Now look what had become of me. On a sunny June morning I had ducked out of work to skulk around a sewage pond.

It was pleasant as sewage ponds go. No foul odors, chemical or organic, assaulted my nostrils as I skulked. Mallards paddled across water that looked clear enough to sit inside a drinking glass, while a flock of sheep munched on bright green lawns. A bell jangled in the distance, bringing back not altogether fond memories of childhood as shrieking kids poured out of a school behind the facility toward a row of buses. A manicured housing development framed the south side of the property. A flooded field awash with swallows and red-winged blackbirds lay to the north. If you didn't know any better, you might consider it to be a prime spot for a picnic. But it was a sewage pond. There was no way around the fact. And I had spent an hour searching the sewage pond for birds.

As I scanned the pond edges through binoculars I kept an eye on the sheep, which were lumbering in my direction. I'd once had a narrow escape from a petting zoo where a sheep had tried to make a meal out of my pants, and I had no idea what twenty of them might do. Would sheep chase down and tackle a skinny man who tried to flee from them?

A facility employee waved as his truck scooted past, smiling—I was sure—at the idea that anyone would visit his workplace for fun. But the shorebird migration was in full swing, and I had hopes of finding a rare species. For reasons I didn't understand, sandpipers, plovers, and other waders gravitated toward sewage ponds on the way to their breeding grounds. My ability to tell those birds apart was virtually nonexistent. My only chance was shooting scads of photos and trying to identify them later by scouring three shorebird reference books, five general birding field guides, three iPad apps, and the Internet. So far I hadn't found any shorebirds at all. Just sheep.

Finding not just any bird but a rare bird of some kind in my little corner of West Michigan had been my obsession for about a decade. I'd seen rarities passing through the area, from cattle egrets to greater white-fronted geese, but only because reports from the birders who had discovered them told me exactly where to look. I had yet to find a noteworthy species on my own—a bird that other birders would want to see. Ferreting out a rare bird would indicate that I had finally arrived, achieving bona fide rather than bumbling birder status. It would jolt my sadsack soul with a surge of happiness like a bibliophile discovering a Dead Sea Scroll at a rummage sale or a fossil hunter finding a whale vertebrate poking out of a backyard boulder.

But there was more to it than that. Throughout my life, I'd always given up on any pursuit the instant that it turned into work—like playing a musical instrument more complicated than a pocket comb or making cute, blobby coffee cups on our potter's wheel. The only skills I'd mastered were dodging household chores and falling into a deathlike nap in the blink of an eye. By achieving a minimal degree of competency as a birder, I could prove to myself that I hadn't sputtered out a quarter of the way to every goal I'd set for myself and that I wasn't, in fact, the laziest mammal on the planet. While I'd never live long enough to evolve into an expert, I could finally say the words "yellow-bellied sapsucker" without sniggering and more or less knew what one looked like.

As I rounded the pond, the sheep changed direction and walked then trotted toward the back of the property. I was safe from depantsing for now. At the same time, three tiny sandpipers *peep-peep-peeped* and rocketed off, their pointy wingtips nearly brushing the water. I didn't have a clue what they were. They looked like every other sparrow-size sandpiper I'd ever seen. Identifying a rarity required learning all of the common birds first, then the uncommon but not necessarily rare species next, and finally having at least a passing familiarity with the good-luck-

My first rose-breasted grosbeak dumbfounded me by tricking out his tuxedo with a blazing red cravat.

seeing-any-of-these birds. The learning process seemed endless. The more I learned, the more I learned I didn't know. Hawks still looked alike to me. Sparrows merged into a streaky blur. Most thrushes and flycatchers needed to sing before I could pin a name on them, and the only shorebird I knew at a glance was the killdeer of ball field and parking lot fame.

Like a broken clock that wasn't even right twice a day because the hands had fallen off, I didn't have much chance of success. But I loved birds more than anything in the world, with the possible exception of my wife, Linda, and our cats. So even if I failed, there really wasn't a downside to doing what made me happy, other than the public humiliation of announcing yet another bogus identification to the online birding community and having to tearfully retract it. So I was determined to keep trying to find that rare bird that would change my life in a subtle yet meaningful way.

Birding would have come easier if I'd started as a child instead of taking it up in middle age when my memory, reflexes, and senses were sliding downhill like penguins on an iceberg.

I had given it a half-hearted go way earlier. Back in 1962 when I was nine years old, our neighbor Mrs. Glass lugged over a box heaped with toys that her sons had outgrown. Along with a plastic coin bank shaped like a pot of gold and an Uncle Wiggily Game with half of the cards missing, I fished out a small green book with a cartoon bird on the cover. It was a wood thrush, though I didn't know it at the time and can barely identify one today. But the aptly titled *Green Book of Birds of America* disappointed me once I peeked inside. Instead of the comic book story I had anticipated, there were lifelike drawings of birds accompanied by descriptions in tiny type. Not the sort of thing that appealed to me.

I forgot about the book until a few months later in the spring when I woke up to the Beach Boys singing "Surfin' Safari" on WGRD. I cranked up the volume of my brown plastic table radio until the bass notes buzzed. I had knocked it off my shelf a few days earlier and patched the case with cellophane tape. Convincing myself that the distortion made the song sound even "tougher," I decided that the time was right for transformation. Squinting and nodding my head to the drums, I brushed out my hair and moved the part from the left side to the right, which I imagined gave me the cool demeanor of a surfer.

My coolness didn't last. Pivoting at the stove and glaring at me through the steam of frying eggs, my mom doused the eggs with water and clapped a lid over the pan. "Go right back upstairs and fix your hair before you sit down for breakfast."

I wanted to tell her who I was and how my nine-year-old heart yearned for the thrill-packed life of a hotrodding beach bum. But with eggs sputtering and popping in greasy water, the kitchen radio droning the hopelessly square "The Syncopated Clock," and my dad breezing in wearing his Saturday white shirt and tie, the atmosphere wasn't conducive to disclosure. I slunk up to my room, readjusted my part, and reverted to the full measure of my never-to-be-anything-like-a-surfer, whiny, sulky self.

And sulk I did. Ignoring my sister Joan's exhortation to go bike riding with her and Terry Gray from down the block, I read a model car magazine instead. My bedroom door thumped as my mom emptied a basket of freshly laundered sheets into the hallway linen closet. "I thought you liked going to Aberdeen Creek," she said.

Aberdeen Creek? No one had said anything about going on our once-a-year ride to "the crick" to gape at the spectacle of flowing water that didn't come from a faucet.

I trotted out to the garage and wheeled out the bike that I never rode anywhere without a degree of shame. In order to save a few bucks, my genial dad had decided to scar me for life by attaching a painted broomstick bar to a blue hand-me-down girl's bike. I called up to my mom in the kitchen window that I was taking off after Joan and Terry. "You're not crossing Fuller Avenue by yourself," she said. "You'll have to find something to do around the house. You can help me with the dishes."

Contractually I wasn't obligated to dry dishes until after dinner, so I snuck back inside without answering and hatched a plan for showing everybody up. Rummaging through my dad's dresser, I fished out a small metal box resembling a woman's compact that snapped open into a pair of opera glasses. Armed with *The Green Book of Birds* and this two-power optical wonder that somehow managed to make distant objects seem even further away, I hurried to the closest approximation of a woods in our neighborhood: a scrubby string of trees behind the tennis courts at Aberdeen Park one block from our house.

I had no doubt that I would bag most of the birds in the field guide, even though I'd only ever laid eyes on one of them before. Joan and Terry wouldn't believe what they had missed, and my parents would admire me so much for taking up a grownup hobby that they'd let me wear my hair like a surfer.

For fear of becoming a target of the racquet wielders' aggression, I avoided setting foot anywhere near the asphalt. I willed myself into invisibility and whisked behind the chain link fence in back of the courts, which rang when a tennis ball walloped it. Though the term *birding* hadn't been invented yet, inside my head I sang my own version of the Beach Boys' "tough" new song, which I called "Birdin' Safari." Scanning the trees and bushes, I began searching for a vireo, warbler, or warbling vireo, which I fancied were as easily observed as the cardinals that sang from the telephone poles on our street.

Although I didn't realize it at the time, there was no better month than May for finding migrating birds in Michigan. But I also didn't know that out of the sixty-two species included in *The Green Book of Birds of America*, only the robin frequented my neighborhood. Barring the intervention of an inland hurricane or the defoliation of every other stick of wood in the state, I would have to bike to Aberdeen Creek for a reasonable shot at the vireos, warblers, or warbling vireo, and I'd have to mosey on down to Albuquerque to bag the verdin. Armed with that knowledge, an informed Bob would have rung Mrs. Glass's doorbell and insisted that she fork over *The Blue Book of Birds of America* if she had it—a companion guide to *The Green Book* that included the blue jay, European starling, brown-headed cowbird, northern cardinal, and common grackle, which were all commonplace on our block. But no informed version of Bob existed to make such a demand.

I followed the trail behind all four courts without discovering a single winged entity. Not even a fly dropped by. Eager to look at anything, I pressed the opera glasses to the bridge of my nose and tried to zero in on a pot-bellied squirrel scolding me from a tree branch. Having never used a pair of binoculars "out in the field" before, I couldn't find the *chuck-chucking* beast through the opera glasses, which I decided possessed sophisticated squirrel-avoidance lenses.

As I rounded the fence at the east side of the park, I decided to impress the tennis player in the mustard yellow t-shirt with my cool new hobby. With his wavy hair and perpetual grimace, he reminded me of Ron Westcott three doors down, who woke my dad revving up his souped-up car in the wee hours of the morning and was the closest thing to a surfing hotrodder on our street. Clutching *The Green Book* with its green cover conspicuously facing him, I stood in the grass next to his court and dramatically trained the opera glasses on the trees behind him.

Missing the bounce off the backboard, he shouted at me, using a two-word phrase I had never heard before and whose meaning I would ask Terry Gray about later.

It's probably safe to assume that many of the biggest names in birding had less than stellar results the first time they went out. Maybe they saw only a few of the most common species. Maybe, like me, they didn't see anything at all. But some sort of magic happened that took root and developed into a lifelong passion for birds.

I, too, fell under a spell when I returned to the wooded strip behind the tennis courts. As soon as my feet hit the path, an almost supernaturally powerful jolt of defeatism gripped me and pushed me toward home, dispersing my last fragile wisp of interest in any aspect of the great outdoors. I didn't even pause when I flushed a bright blue shape from a maple that might have been an errant indigo bunting.

I was over it. I hadn't succeeded in finding birds immediately. So behaving in accordance with principles that had already embedded themselves in the deepest fibers of my being, I whined bitterly to myself about the unfairness of life and gave up. I didn't just call it a day. I decided that bird watching was a fraud and threw the book back into the box with the Uncle Wiggily Game with half of the cards missing and a dried whelk egg case that the Glass boys had found on a Florida beach.

I didn't give wild birds another thought for the next twenty-five years. Then I met an unusual woman who combined the vivacity of Pippi Longstocking with the delicacy of Ma Kettle—or vice versa. My pigtailed, redheaded, wife-to-be Linda helped transform me from a useless lump of human clay into a semi-useless lump that began to fall in love with birds shortly after I had fallen in love with her.

Many unlikely things have happened to me over the decades—and most of them happened after I married Linda. But until recently if you would have told me that finding birds in the woods would bring me a shot of joy like few other activities in my life, I'd tell you that you were crazy. In fact, I might have used the phrase that I'd learned from the tennis player.

It wasn't entirely my fault that the first time I visited Linda's ramshackle trailer in the woods it shocked the bejeebers out of me. A lot had to do with my upbringing. I had never been nurtured to care about nature. I was born in the 1950s in the post–World War II era of technological hubris. Scientists hoped to control the weather by covering whole cities with huge inverted glass bowls and envisioned replacing snowplows with nuclear powered zappers. Although my dad never thirsted after climate manipulation, he followed the prevailing winds of the day by choosing urban leisure activities over countryside diversions. I don't recall my parents ever taking my sisters and me to anything resembling a woods, except for the occasional picnic—and on those occasions the hiking occurred strictly between picnic table and parking lot.

I was a Cub Scout for two years, but even though my *Boy Scout Hand-*

book with the happy Norman Rockwell cover bulged with outdoor lore pertaining to camping, woodcraft, and compass work, Blessed Sacrament Elementary School treated green spaces as if they were drenched in sin. We concentrated on learning to tie nineteenth-century sailor's knots instead of risking our immortal souls through proximity to wildlife.

I certainly didn't grow up caring about birds. I fought back against the house sparrows and the late-afternoon din they raised outside my bedroom window by banging on a saucepan with a spoon. It did little good. A few minutes after I had scattered them, they trickled back and returned to full volume. Annoyed at my mistreatment of birds, chimney-sitting mourning doves wreaked revenge upon me. Tiny, itchy bites began appearing on my skin. My dad tracked the cause to "pigeon lice" that he found crawling inside the bedroom windowsill. He didn't like mourning doves or any other birds that hung out in large flocks and complained about the grackles that pecked at our front lawn. He viewed them the same way that he viewed ants—as individually brainless members of a feeble-brained group.

Considering my dysfunctional relationship with the great outdoors, it was little wonder that Linda's trailer startled me. It probably would have startled Daniel Boone. The trailer crouched at the end of a rutted baked mud road near the village of Pierson. If I owned a Conestoga wagon, I wouldn't have risked its delicate undercarriage on such a rugged path. I parked my puny little gray Toyota Tercel at the entrance and hiked the rest of the way.

Linda lived without electricity, running water, or a telephone. We sat drinking tea in front of a wood-fired cooking stove listening to mice run a relay race behind the walls. I hadn't imagined that anyone outside of remotest Appalachia had such primitive digs, and I wasn't polite enough to resist asking, "Do you actually like living like this?"

"I'm a get-back-to-the-lander," she told me. "I wish I lived closer to nature. I'm thinking of putting up a teepee outside and moving in."

If any birds lurked within the shoulder-high weeds that tapped against the siding when breezes blew, I wasn't looking for them when she took me out on a tour. She had cut back the vegetation around her flowing well, a three-quarter-inch pipe that stuck out of the ground at an angle and constantly spurted water. While marveling at this hydro-engineering triumph, I jumped when a large bird dropped down from a tree. Within a minute or so I recovered enough to recognize it as a chicken.

"There's a rooster named Fletcher around here somewhere," Linda said. She stared up at the branches. "But I haven't seen him in a while."

The night was so black when I left that as soon as I had taken six steps I lost all sense of direction. I expected my eyes to adjust to the darkness and the hood of my Toyota to pop into view. Instead I saw a cluster of eerie blue-green phosphorescent mushrooms sprouting from a pile of firewood. This meant that in fifteen minutes of shuffling I had barely progressed past her outhouse. The situation terrified me. Once I identified a soft gurgling sound as the stream that ran alongside her driveway, I used it to grope my way back to the trailer. Emerging with a flashlight, she led me to my car.

I didn't see a future for us.

I had met Linda in 1985 after placing my fourth ad in a West Michigan singles publication. I liked her far better than the other women I had dated through the magazine, but we were just too different. I enjoyed living in downtown Grand Rapids and with my 1970s punk haircut tried miserably to be cool. Linda was the essence of the hippie earth mother and wore waist-length pigtails with colored rubber bands on the ends. Wide eyed with joy and effervescent, she talked in a rapidly flowing, bubbly stream of impressions about whatever had happened to her that day cleaning people's houses for a living, while I was so serious about the world I barely squeezed two syllables past my teeth without weighing them first on my tongue.

A country girl whose parents had come from rural Tennessee, Linda, with her first husband, Joe, had developed the utilities-free Pierson property to their liking after reading articles in *Mother Earth News* in the 1970s about getting back to the land, unhooking from the grid, and growing their own food. She spent much of her time outdoors not only tending their animals and fussing over their vegetable gardens but also operating their appliances, such as they were.

She did their cooking on a wood stove that made the trailer so sweltering, Joe had to relocate it to a tent. Her washing machine sat outside, too. It consisted of a tub of soapy water, a tub of rinse water, and a hand-cranked wringer. Water for the laundry was heated on a homemade barrel stove inside the trailer, which busied itself providing hot water for the outdoor shower, too. A clothesline served as dryer, though Linda had to watch their duds, because the goats nibbled on them if they managed to escape from their pen. The liberated goats' greatest pleasure, though, was barging into the trailer and hopping up onto the bed, since they preferred being up off the ground. A jailbreak by Mrs. Piggle-Wiggle the sow caused even more trouble. Too large to be hauled back to her enclosure on the end of a rope, she had to be painstakingly lured back from wherever she had ended up on their twenty-acre spread by waving a can of cat food under her nose.

Pleasures such as these struck me as horrors, and even with the addition of a modern house and the subtraction of hooved cotenants, I couldn't imagine a chain of circumstances that would take me out to the sticks. Linda had no intention of moving to the city. But we continued to see one another. She was beautiful, playful, naturally smart, and had a kind of fearlessness that I could only dream about. I couldn't figure out what she saw in me.

One morning after I'd known her for a while, as she was eating her strawberry shortcake and ice cream breakfast by herself at Jody's drive-in restaurant in Rockford, she spotted an ad in a weekly shopper for a two-room cabin. That same day, after she had cleaned two houses and a bakery, she zipped twenty miles north to look at the property, decided to buy it, and made plans to sell her land to friends Keith and Barbara—who would replace her trailer with a mouse-free house. Then she chose the first serious snowstorm of the season to move in, phoning to tell me what she had done only after she had finished. No wonder I was falling in love with her. While I agonized over whether or not to lower a window shade, she made major life decisions between bites of strawberry shortcake. And she didn't ask me to help her to move.

Every evening Linda would call me from the pay phone at Jody's after her last job of the day. She would also send me notes through the mail about whatever subject occurred to her at the time and using the materials at hand if she ran out of steno notebook paper. I tore open an envelope that had a curious bulge and fished out a folded rectangle snipped from a plastic McDonald's food container. "A beautiful turtle laid eggs in the sun all morning," the note said. "I hope she's nice to the swan babies."

I didn't understand how a turtle could raise swans, but when Linda phoned she cleared matters up by first telling me about a snapping turtle that had clambered up her bank and spent hours laying and burying eggs on the cliff. Then she mentioned a pair of swan parents. "They were so proud of their babies, they came to my dock to show them to me." In addition to keeping me up to date on the swans, she would also fill me in on whether the kingfisher was outside her cabin first thing in the morning or if she ran into it a couple of hours later on the Jefferson Road bridge. I hadn't a clue what a kingfisher looked like, but Linda infused her description with such enthusiasm that I could picture one plunging into the pond for minnows, though my mind's eye misrepresented it as a sort of pint-size pelican.

Fate must have brought us together. As a child she owned a pet parakeet named Bobby. Her real passion in those days was for garden snails, however. In the summer she would spend hours in the ditch across the street from her mom's house on the outskirts of Battle Creek, collecting snails in a Shedd's peanut butter bucket. She felt particularly lucky whenever she found a big one, which she considered to be the boy. Each morning she'd check on her little community to see who was on a rock, who was on a stick, and if they had eaten their lettuce. Her love of these sluggish creatures turned out to be prescient. In my better moments, with my nervous tics and oversize beak, I resembled a parakeet. Otherwise I was slow moving, lacking in industry, and able to sit contentedly for long periods of time in a space not much larger than a peanut butter pail.

When she visited me in my downtown Grand Rapids apartment, we'd take my car if we went out to eat, since I mistrusted the appallingly bad vehicles she drove. For months she struggled with an ultramarine blue Volkswagen Beetle that needed to roll downhill in order to start. She had found it at a used car dealer near Cedar Springs, and even though the owner couldn't get it the engine to turn over, she couldn't resist its cuteness. After the Beetle died, she treated herself to a brand-new Ford Escort. I took her to a Lebanese restaurant to celebrate and on the way back noticed that the driver's side sun visor was covered with phone numbers written in ballpoint pen.

"Why would you do that to a brand-new car?" I asked.

"Because I'm always losing things, and this way I'll have the numbers I need as long as I have the car."

A few weeks later I noticed her glove compartment dangling by one hinge. I decided not to ask about it for fearing of receiving another dose of unassailable logic.

Most of Linda's cleaning jobs were in the Grand Rapids area, and I didn't venture fifty miles north to her new cabin until spring. "I'll be there around three-thirty or so," I told her when she phoned me from a gas station. "Unless we get a blizzard. I don't drive long distances in the snow."

"In June?" she said.

I could always hope. My Heritage Hill neighborhood in Grand Rapids had gotten a little scary since a crack house opened down the street. I put two lamps on timers before leaving my apartment, though I was less nervous about a break-in than I was about spending the night in an isolated cabin. None of my fears were concrete. But as I drove north on US 131, I fought off images of rednecks from *Deliverance* slipping in and slitting our throats or a bear smashing down the door as we huddled in the dark. This was silly—she did have electricity at the cabin, but still no telephone. In place of indoor plumbing she had a hand-operated pump just outside her porch and an outhouse next to the driveway.

It's difficult to overstate how much her living situation frightened me—or even to explain why, except that I associated modern conveniences with civilization and the lack of them with danger. Wild spaces were even worse. People who spent too much time in them got lost, sick, injured, or went mad. I knew this from television, having been fed a steady diet of rural dystopia by *Rawhide, Bonanza,* and other westerns during my formative years.

Things weren't as I expected when I turned onto Linda's road. Instead of the desolate tract onto which she had plunked her trailer, I found myself cruising down a gravel road peppered with cozy-looking homes. The road took a bend, houses got sparser as the foliage thickened, and the next thing I knew I was parked behind Linda's car in front of a cheekpinchingly cute brown bungalow.

I heard Linda before I saw her. Though her cabin perched on the edge of a bluff above Morley Pond, the splashing and singing came from right out back. Wearing a one-piece burgundy bathing suit, she was hunkered down inside a child's plastic wading pool, slapping the water in time to a spirited rendition of "Sailing, Sailing Over the Bounding Main." I stopped dead in my tracks, as I always did. Jumping up, she gave me a wet hug and said, "Isn't it beautiful? It's so warm I couldn't resist." I nodded, but I was nodding to a closed door, because she had already zipped inside to change her clothes.

Despite being jarred by Linda's energy, I felt unusually calm as I surveyed the wilds of nature: the steep path that led downhill to the pond, the stream that ran alongside her cabin, and a dead tree studded with monstrous ear-shaped fungus. It took me a moment to figure out why I wasn't troubled by the setting. Then I realized that I could see a cabin on either side of hers. This was a significant discovery. It meant that instead of standing in a rambling stretch of woods, I was standing in a yard, with all of the ties to human civilization that the term implied. So while Linda changed into her purple floral dress, I leisurely explored the perimeter of her house without fear that I might disappear into the boondocks.

There may have been birds in the trees, but I wasn't seeing them until Linda invited me inside. As I bent over her inoperative kitchen faucet pondering the mysteries of half-completed plumbing, I glanced through her window and spotted the songbird that changed everything.

I had never imagined that such a spectacular creature existed. Bold and brilliant, the sharply patterned bird was nothing like the brown-and-olive smudges in the pages of *The Green Book of Birds*. You needed a mass spectrometer to tell them apart. But you could place this songbird in a police lineup with a hundred other North American species, and I would have been able to identify it instantly—once Linda told me what it was.

"Linda, quick, come here—*right away*," I said, sounding sterner than I had intended. I was afraid that the apparition might vanish before another set of mortal eyes took it in.

"What's wrong?" She followed my waggling finger to her brown plastic bird feeder.

Hogging the perch and grazing leisurely like a contented cow sat a graphic artist's conception of a bird. He had a jet-black head and back, white underparts, and a cream-colored bill. Tucked underneath his head was his most distinguishing feature—a fire engine–red triangular bib. This vivid addition to a crisp black-and-white body shocked me like a bolt of color in a grainy old silent movie. Imagine watching *The Gold Rush* and suddenly seeing Charlie Chaplin waddle into his cabin wearing a scarlet cravat.

In spite of my ignorance of everything natural, I had grown up more or less familiar with eight birds in our neighborhood—robin, cardinal, blue jay, mourning dove, grackle, starling, pigeon, and "sparrow." I also knew the red-winged blackbird, crow, Canada goose, and mallard. These were what Michigan birds were *supposed* to look like.

But not this bird, which would have fit right into a tropical rainforest alongside a cockatoo. I got wowed all over again when it flew off. A white patch near the end of each black wing appeared, giving its flight a flickering, transformative quality—turning the lazy sunflower-seed muncher into a mechanical whirligig rowing the air with flashing oars.

"What was that?"

"A rose-breasted grosbeak." My expression indicated that I expected something more. "He comes to the feeder all the time. His girlfriend is streaky brown and white, and she's just as pretty in her own way."

I doubted that. I doubted if another bird could equal him, but I had to ask. "Do you get anything else like that?"

I only had to wait a matter of seconds before a pair of birds lit on the feeder. Linda explained that one of them was a titmouse and the other was a nuthatch. "How do you tell them apart?" I asked. I was such a poor observer that I only noticed the gray feathers on both birds. The fact that the titmouse sported a cardinal-like crest was a distinction too minor to penetrate a brain that wasn't used to searching for differences between birds.

"The nuthatch walks upside-down," Linda said.

Sure enough, as a woodpecker walked up a tree, the nuthatch passed it walking down the tree headfirst. Ordinarily the woodpecker would have interested me, since I'd only seen the Saturday-morning-cartoon variety and considered the real item to be the stuff of legend. Instead I kept scanning the trees for the return of the rose-breasted grosbeak, which was the only bird that mattered to me.

I didn't realize it at the time, but this was the beginning of the mysterious hold that birds would have upon my life—a hold that I've never been able to figure out. But isn't love always like that? And by obsessing upon seeing the grosbeak again, I'd already taken the first step toward becoming a birder.

The birds and the cabin had a calming effect upon me, too. I no longer felt as if the differences between Linda and me were so vast that we couldn't vault over them together. And I started thinking differently not only about the non-city parts of the world but also about the non-city-dwellers who lived in them.

"Some farmer," my dad used to complain when we got stuck behind an old beater of a car on a two-lane road on the way to visit my grand-mother. Probably the only prejudice I ever heard him express was against what he saw as ignorant country folk, although there was that dislike of grackles. I was well on my way to embracing both. I certainly embraced Linda.

The next weekend, I saw the grosbeak a few more times. And another bird that Linda didn't know. It sang exuberantly from a tree on the bluff. I didn't think I had a chance of figuring out what it was, since Linda's *National Audubon Society Field Guide to Birds* seemed to be populated pri-marily by nondescript little brown birds. Even though I got extended looks at the singer through the open door of her bedroom–living room–furnace room, I couldn't recall what it looked like as soon as I looked away. That same lousy memory for visual detail would continue to plague me even when I got a whole lot better at identifying birds.

"Kind of drab," said Linda as I flipped through the pages. "Dark-and-light-colored striped head. Dark-and-light-colored striped chest." That narrowed it down to over a dozen birds, including the cactus wren, which barely made it out of Mexico into the southwestern states.

After studying photos of likely suspects and still not making any progress, I stumbled onto the back half of the book, which was packed with dense text descriptions somewhat reminiscent of *The Green Book of Birds*. I managed to find the song sparrow and under the heading "Voice" noticed a poetically licensed rendition of its song. "Madge-Madge-Madge, put-on-the-tea-kettle-ettle-ettle," is how the *Audubon* authors transcribed it.

"That's it!" said Linda. "I heard him say the 'tea kettle' part."

"This is easy," I said.

Between the visually unmistakable rose-breasted grosbeak and the vocally unique song sparrow—and aided by Linda, who knew upward of twenty birds, making her a near ornithologist—identifying birds seemed like a piece of cake. One thing bothered me. "I thought a sparrow was a sparrow," I told Linda. "I thought there was only the kind of sparrow that we had in our yard when I was growing up. But there are dozens of different sparrows in the index." I shook my head. It was almost too much to take in, yet the discovery seemed mildly exciting, although after perusing the sparrow photos again I reached the erroneous conclusion that none of the others visited our state.

"Maybe we can find the black-and-white ducks that I saw on the pond," Linda said. "I heard from someone they were buffleheads."

"They would have to be escaped farm ducks," I told her with a total lack of accuracy. "The only ducks that live in Michigan are mallards."

Within a few months all of my false confidence and pretense at instant expertise would come crashing down. Acting in accordance with chronic patterns of behavior, I would experience a minor setback trying to identify birds, and as a result I would abandon the hobby I had just taken up again. The urge to find a rare bird at that point was as remote as the hotrodding life of a surfer.

CHAPTER TWO

Twice Bitten

L iving in downtown Grand Rapids, I got tired of people breaking into my car. I could have understood the attraction if I'd owned a Lexus, Caddy, or even a vehicle that still had a rearview mirror. But the thieves weren't choosy about my crummy Tercel and absconded with such treasures as a stick-on dashboard clock that my father had received with his subscription to *Time* magazine, a notebook for recording mostly fabricated business mileage, and bright red plastic sunglasses, which I only wore to annoy family members.

As a result of the crime wave, I decided to move out of my neighborhood and buy a house. And because Linda had said yes when I asked her to marry me, I nixed the idea of living in the city or suburbs. I made up my mind to take the plunge and move out into the country, though not as much of a lover's leap as moving to Linda's little two-room cabin, which barely gave us room to turn around without smashing into one another. And where would all of the pets live that she was already threatening to bring home? Instead we looked at three houses in the country, all of which happened to be nearly the same shade of blue. The first house had a half-demolished basement wall with some massive, archaic machine lurking behind it. We crossed it off our list. The second house was downwind of a leather tannery. We crossed it off our list while plugging our noses. The third house was too close to a busy road. We loved it and bought it anyway.

The charming little one-hundred-year-old farmhouse a few miles outside of Grand Rapids sat on three and a half wooded acres near a big red barn that yearned to be filled with household junk and poultry. The Grand River puttered past the far side of the property. Just visible through the trees, our one and only neighbor's house linked us to civilization. We would later discover the added perks of spring flooding and clouds of mosquitoes in the summer.

At a wild bird supplies store I bought a feeder and asked, "What kind of seed do you have that will attract exotic species?"

The clerk sold me black oil sunflower seed and said, "Don't expect ostriches."

I was thinking more along the lines of rose-breasted grosbeaks. In hopes of seeing them better if and when they arrived, I bought a thirty-nine-dollar pair of impressively unwieldy binoculars. The packaging boasted "ruby red coated lenses," and when using them in daylight I was as conspicuous as a police cruiser with its flashers on. I set the binoculars on the dining room table for ready access whenever a bird landed on the feeder. But they wouldn't focus closer than fifteen feet and were useless for feeder watching unless I retreated into the kitchen and leaned back against the counter.

The feeder hung birdless for several days. Then the diners started to arrive. The yellow-and-black American goldfinches came first. I had no trouble recalling them from Linda's cabin, but she had to remind me how to distinguish a titmouse from a chickadee or nuthatch. I also had trouble telling two woodpeckers apart unless a big hairy deal of a hairy woodpecker hit the feeder at the same time as a comparatively down-sized downy woodpecker. However, the red-bellied woodpecker with its crimson head stripe was as unmistakable as a guy using binoculars with ruby red coated lens.

Next I chalked up the house finch, an otherwise dull streaky brown bird whose breast seemed to have been dipped in raspberry juice. I probably would have been more impressed by the house finch had I known that it didn't even exist in Michigan when I was growing up. According to author Jim Granlund in *Birds of Michigan*, the first reported sighting of a house finch in Michigan was in Berrien Springs on February 13, 1972. It had taken the species over thirty years to get here from New York State after breeders released their stock of house finches in 1940 following a government crackdown on illegally kept wild birds. The freed finches multiplied and spread from coast to coast, far expanding their range from their original digs in the southwestern United States.

On the ground beneath the house finch, a male cardinal pecked at

White-throated sparrow "Little Buddy" kept us company through a miserable Michigan winter.

fallen seed. He was significantly more spectacularly red than the house finch, but I barely noticed him. I had been seeing cardinals ever since I'd been old enough to look out a window, and I assumed that the species had been here since the Ice Age. But like the house finch, the cardinal was a relative newcomer. In the 1912 edition of his book *Michigan Bird Life*, Walter Bradford Barrows says, "The Cardinal appears to be a rather rare species [in Michigan], mainly confined to the southern half of the Lower Peninsula." It wasn't recorded in Ingham County (where state capital Lansing is located) until 1899. You can barely miss seeing one in Michigan today.

But I was waiting for a different bird. A few days later it showed up while I was changing the water bottle in the dining room for Linda's rabbit, Binky. I goggled, ogled, and gasped as a male grosbeak lit upon the feeder. Unlike the chickadees, titmice, and nuthatches that ran hit-and-run seed raids, the grosbeak stayed put, giving me time to study him as he shucked and chewed. His blacks seemed blacker, his whites whiter, and his red bib even more vividly red than the grosbeak I'd seen at

Linda's cabin—probably because I considered this one to be "my" grosbeak. When he stretched his neck forward, his big beak completed the downward curve of his forehead in an elegant, streamlined fashion. Everything about him was beautiful.

What could possibly top this? I asked myself the third time he came around.

It wasn't a rhetorical question. Within a week I started getting fidgety for the next magnificent species. I paged through the *Audubon Field Guide* wondering what kind of bird I might reasonably expect, but I had no more of a clue how to use it than I'd had with *The Green Book*. I hadn't discovered the hidden-in-plain-sight range maps yet, and as I flipped through the scads of photo pages over and over again, the white pelican was clearly laughing at me. I checked the feeder through the dining room window, willing Mr. Brand-New Pretty Bird to fly in. On my way to and from the car, I scanned the trees and bushes around the house. There had to be something shockingly, excitingly new, but only the usual suspects dropped in. Within a week, my discouragement turned into irritation.

"I can't believe it," I told Linda. "We've only lived here a month, and we've already seen all of the birds."

I wasn't incapable of reasoning out the fact that I might discover birds along the river that I wouldn't find in our immediate yard. Even I wasn't quite so simple. I knew that the kingfisher I'd seen working the pond behind Linda's cabin wasn't about to give up minnows for sunflower seed and that a mallard wouldn't install itself in our birdbath. But going out into the woods to search for birds was such an alien and borderline uncomfortable concept that I never even considered doing it. To my mind, birds were animated yard ornaments whose most important function was to beautify the space around our house. I wouldn't view them differently until I started living with parrots, doves, parakeets, canaries, ducks, geese, and chickens and discovered that each bird had its own unique personality.

Meanwhile, in an adult reprise of the tennis court incident, I swept our thirty-nine-dollar binoculars and *Audubon Field Guide* off the dining room table and gave up birding all over again. There wasn't anything to see.

It takes a special kind of person to go to one of the top birding spots in

North America and refuse to look at birds. I was that special person. The trip to Ontario had been my idea, but stopping at Point Pelee National Park hadn't been on the itinerary.

Toronto was our destination. I had enjoyed visiting Toronto ever since my parents took our family there for a vacation during my high school days. After living in our new house a year, I needed a break from the rural grind and talked Linda into going partly by bragging up the Henry Moore sculpture collection at the Art Gallery of Ontario. Linda had attended Kendall College of Art and Design in Grand Rapids and loved museums. When I told her about Toronto's Chinatown, that clinched the deal.

The trip turned out to be a disaster. Linda had seldom been out of Michigan and had never spent time in a big city. Downtown Toronto's crowded, closed-in atmosphere and the general lack of wooded ponds made her nervous.

"It'll be better once we start doing things," I said with misplaced optimism. "You'll love taking a streetcar to the art museum." But the lurching start-stop motion drained the blood from her face as the vehicle dropped off and picked up passengers. "They had a van Gogh show the last time I was in town," I said to cheer her up once we were back on solid ground. "It might have been a pain getting here, but this place is worth the whole trip." I was probably right, but we would never know. A wooden sign barricading the entrance informed us that the Art Gallery of Ontario was closed for renovation.

We stayed away from streetcars the next day and took the smooth-running subway to the Royal Ontario Museum. Linda seemed absorbed in the ride, and I congratulated myself for knowing enough about the city to whisk us to our destination by train. Then as we stepped out onto the platform, she sprinted to the nearest trash receptacle and threw up. I didn't want to jinx our afternoon by mentioning the splendors of natural history in store for us, but the museum might as well have been closed for all of the good we got out of it. Half the population of Canada had turned out. We couldn't see the huge slabs of dinosaur fossils any better than we could see the tiny Amazonian frogs. After admiring the backs of people's heads for two hours, we called it quits.

In the morning, we called Toronto quits, too. Linda had been having panic attacks in the middle of the night. She tipped me off by pacing back and forth in our hotel room and repeating the telling phrase, "I've got to get out of here." When I switched on the lights, she told me, "I need to be able to just walk out into a yard."

"That's pretty hard when you're on the ninth floor."

"That's the problem. It's way too claustrophobic."

We didn't want to return home immediately and put an end to our one and only vacation of the year. So we meandered along two-lane roads searching for rural attractions. When we ran into a string of tobacco-drying barns near Tilsonburg, I checked the map to assure myself that we hadn't somehow veered too far south and ended up in Tennessee. By the time we got to Leamington, the crop of choice had switched to tomatoes. The clerk at our motel told us that the area was located in a microclimate zone and had the second warmest temperatures in all of Canada. That shocked me, since we weren't much farther south than Grand Rapids with its notoriously long winters, short growing season, and almost total lack of sunlight.

"Most people come to Leamington because they have business at the Heinz factory or they want to see birds," the clerk said. We didn't have pressing tomato-related business, so she gave us directions to Point Pelee, a small national park that's hosted around 360 bird species over the years—342 more species than I had ever seen.

Linda wanted to go. From years of living in the woods, she loved birds, but not necessarily more than she loved anything in nature, from wildflowers to snapping turtles. If Point Pelee had been a porcupine sanctuary, her enthusiasm wouldn't have been diminished. I didn't care one way or the other. But I liked the shape of the park on the map. The peninsula came to a wickedly sharp point, and I wanted to see for myself if it narrowed down to a single grain of sand. Birds approved of the shape, too. Birds often follow geographical features like rivers and coastlines when they migrate, and a peninsula that juts five miles into Lake Erie makes a handy stopping-off point for rest and vittles when crossing the lake.

At the Point Pelee visitors center, I was delighted to discover that we could take a shuttle to "the tip" instead of having to trudge one and a quarter miles out in nature. About a dozen people shared the ride with us. Most were odd ducks wearing army-green vests decked out with colorful patches and either carrying binoculars or clutching tripods with small telescopes. I had never visited a birding hotspot before, and when we stepped off the bus I expected to run into something like the intense activity around our feeder, only on a massive scale. But as Linda and I headed toward the beach and our shuttle-mates lagged behind to squint at the greenery, my slim hopes of finding vast clouds of songbirds evaporated. I decided that the park's reputation was seriously overrated.

We took the West Beach Footpath to within a tomato's toss of the absolute tip of the point. The thin spit of land barely wider than a grocery store aisle delighted me until my shoes began getting wet. We turned around and squished back in the direction of the shuttle parking lot, passing birders in twos and threes. They were too focused on their optical devices to respond to Linda's greetings until a group of five green vests absorbed her as I strode past. I glanced back to see her in animated conversation, which was her usual state of being whenever she ran into strangers.

"They're seeing warblers, sweetie!" she called to me.

I looked up at the leafy branch that the people were pointing at. Nothing of interest jumped out at me. "We don't want to miss the shuttle and have to walk all the way," I said. I was crabby about having to leave Toronto early and felt more like the frustrated tennis player than nine-year-old birding Bob.

"They'll wait," said a woman in a dark blue cap. "They won't drive an empty bus back."

"Don't you want to see a black-and-white warbler?" Linda asked, passing me the woman's binoculars.

I couldn't refuse without appearing to be the sullen, self-centered spoilsport that I was, so I took the glasses and managed to locate a black-and-white bird skittering up the trunk of a sugar maple. Before I could take two seconds to convince myself it wasn't a downy woodpecker, it flew away.

"Thanks," I said in a tone of voice that meant *goodbye* as I handed the binoculars back to their owner. But Linda didn't budge.

I took a second look at the maple, shielding my eyes and trying to locate the source of a brief exuberant song. Concentrating on a movement in the leaves, I caught a flash of yellow that vanished instantly. "There's a magnolia warbler in the low branches and a chestnut-sided up in the canopy," Linda said, repeating what the Blue Cap had told her. So this is birding, I thought as I strained my eyes to pick out tiny, darting, distant, indistinct shapes. Only a nitpicker could possibly enjoy such an exercise in frustration.

"Do you want to see?" Linda offered me the binoculars.

I shook my head and edged away. Eventually my toe scuffing, wristwatch checking, and theatrical sighing pried her loose from the green vests.

We had the shuttle to ourselves as we rode back to the visitors center. Just inside the entrance was a logbook for recording birds that we had seen. "Nice beach," I wrote next to my name and address.

I hadn't really lost interest in birds. In fact, I found myself becoming increasingly involved with them—though not with the outdoor variety. Our dining room was filling up with birdcages. It started when Linda bought me a ring-necked dove named Howard for our first wedding anniversary. The gift perplexed me at first, but I quickly became attached to the goofy fellow, whose cousins undoubtedly moved gracefully under an open sky, while he hopped and plodded from place-to-place indoors. Chester the canary arrived as a birthday gift, and parakeets Reggie and Rossy soon followed. Living with them not only enhanced our love of all birds but also provided crucial experience that would come in handy a few years later when Linda began raising and releasing orphan songbirds for Wildlife Rehab Center in Grand Rapids.

I had expected pet birds to be colorless characters, but they dazzled us with their extroverted personalities. Chester would flare up in ecstatic song that was ear-splitting up close. He considered the whine of the vacuum cleaner to be a high-decibel challenge from a rival and tried to drown it out. Reggie enjoyed nothing better than lecturing his cage-mate, Rossy, and if she ignored him he would chatter to his toy bell instead. Howard was the clown of the group, flapping noisily in pursuit of the nimble parakeets. When he eventually caught up, he bowed and cooed in a display of supposed dominance. His posturing inexplicably appealed to Reggie. For reasons known only to himself, the little blue budgie had romantic feelings toward the dove and even tried to mate with him.

These things surprised us. But nothing that a pet bird did actually startled us until we bought a bright green "pocket parrot" named Ollie—a stubby-tailed, orange-chinned *Brotogeris jugularis* parakeet—

which a pet shop employee claimed was a peach faced lovebird. We learned later that the store owner had gone to a bird show and left Ollie behind due to his penchant for biting, which he shared with me at the shop when I tried to pick him up. We should have known better than to buy a bird that lacerated my skin mere moments into our relationship, but he immediately apologized with a series of self-deprecating chirps that were as impossible to resist as an ultramarine Volkswagen Beetle.

We had never imagined that any bird was capable of the exuberance that Ollie demonstrated. It bordered on mania. His constant squawking for attention and abrupt mood shifts from cooing baby to leather punch began to wear us down. The last straw came at dinner during his third day with us. The clerk who sold us Ollie told us to feed him "monkey chow" soaked in water, because it contained the protein that he needed. That evening when we presented the concoction to Ollie, he sat on the countertop happily eating alongside us. When he'd had enough, he punctuated the fact by flinging his dish onto the table, dousing us in soggy kibble.

"Do we really want a bird like this?" I asked.

"He's like a crabby little man in a bird suit," Linda said.

The next day I took him back to the store. Instead of feeling liberated by the loss of our tormenter, we couldn't stand the shroud of quiet that had fallen over the house. "I miss him," I blubbered at breakfast. I shot back to the pet store after work and retrieved him, much to the delight of the store owner, who had probably decided that she was doomed to endlessly selling him and taking him back. We made huge mental adjustments to accommodate him. Hardly a day passed that I didn't hear Linda yelp as he nailed her with his beak when I wasn't suffering the same fate myself. But I rarely found myself in a mood so dark that it couldn't be brightened by his incandescent personality, and we learned to take the better with the biter.

Ollie was constantly torn between reaping the benefits of getting along with us and aggressively installing himself at the top of the household pecking order. He loved oatmeal raisin cookies, but when presented with a morsel, he couldn't decide whether to take the treat or chomp the hand that fed him. When I was young, my dad had complained about the starlings and grackles that swooped down upon our lawn to peck for insects. I imagined growing up in Central America and having a flock of

boisterous orange chins like Ollie descend upon us instead. What if we were caught outdoors without cookies to bribe them with?

If we had lived 150 years earlier, my dad might have griped about the Carolina parakeet. America's only native parrot bore some similarities to Ollie and may have ranged as far north as southern Michigan. Flocks of them looted farmers' fields after the parakeets' beloved swamps had been drained and their favorite forests cleared to create open land for planting crops. Loss of habitat, slaughter by avenging farmers, and a flourishing feather trade for the ladies' hat industry doomed the bird by the middle of the nineteenth century. The Cincinnati Zoo possessed a mated pair of Carolina parakeets until 1917, when female parakeet Lady Jane died. Remarkably, the idea never seemed to have occurred to zoo officials—or to other individuals and institutions that still owned these birds in the early 1900s—that it might be nice to save the species via a breeding program. Maybe their caretakers had been bitten too often.

One afternoon as I was putting groceries away, for the very first time Ollie caught a glimpse of a new package of his beloved cookies. Even though they were stacked sideways in rows and he could only see the edges though the printed wrapper, he recognized them and paced back and forth on his perch making *chuck-chuck* "I want" sounds. This small feat impressed me. And it made me wonder if Howard didn't also possess more smarts than I had given him credit for. That evening as he was perched on the lamp above the dining room table, I told him, "Howard, time to go back." I didn't so much as even glance in the direction of his cage. He flew inside without hesitation. I never looked at mourning doves or pigeons the same way after that.

It took a deep-thinking African grey parrot to change my attitude about birds. Stanley Sue came to us as a male named Stanley from a nurse who was moving out of state. When a DNA test revealed Stanley's true gender, I borrowed the "Sue" from Linda's middle name.

Stanley Sue amazed us by being as shy as Ollie was bold. Adding a new perch to her cage meant first placing it on a table so that she could get used to seeing such a scary object without panicking. Then we put it unobtrusively at the bottom of her cage. Over a couple of weeks, we raised it slowly to the level of her other perch. Even then, she refused to set foot on it for months, climbing the bars to move around it instead.

She disappointed me in the beginning because she didn't talk as promised. But she was an expert at mimicking sounds, and this talent gave us a window into her impressive brain. Not only could she do a perfect imitation of our squeaky oven door, but she would do so as soon as Linda's fingers touched the handle—demonstrating that she associated the sound with the appropriate object. She went much further by producing the squeak when I grabbed the knob of the basement door. I thought she had made a mistake at first. Then I realized that she had correctly transferred the concept of "the thing that opens" from oven door to full-size door.

She also understood expressions of affection directed toward other creatures, including my wife. As Linda sat on my lap after dinner, we laughed as Stanley Sue made smacking sounds. "I can kiss my sweetie if I want to," I told her. A few days later, she repeated the imitation as I cuddled our little black bunny, Rollo. That was impressive enough, but later she mocked me with the kissing noise as I bent over Rollo's cage and said to him, "You're such a cutie-wootie."

More than any of our pets, Stanley Sue eroded my long-held feeling of separateness from birds and my diminution of them as "one-note" beings. When she sat on the arm of the dining room chair, I'd pet her head and get lost in whichever golden eye she turned toward me. She even changed my view of our pet ducks, whom I had considered to be the simpletons of the avian world. But they proved me wrong. Each evening, I would go out to their pen behind the barn, slosh the water out of their two wading pools with a push broom, and then shoo them inside for table scrap treats. After watching me a few times, they waited until I emptied the second pool, then filed inside on their own to await their cooked veggies. They had been watching, learning from my behavior, and remembering the pattern from night to night.

Like all of our pets, the ducks had mastered the intricacies of living captive lives. Wild birds faced much greater challenges. In the blink of an eye and the flicker of a wing, they had to make decisions that could determine whether they made it to their next meal or became somebody's meal. Far from depending solely on hard-wired instinct, as I'd assumed, they used their wits as much as people did to make it through a day.

Observing our birds also keyed me in on a simple yet far-reaching truth that would eventually help me identify wild birds. Behavior often provided a vital clue for determining the species of a bird. Under poor lighting conditions, the best way to tell a hermit thrush from a wood thrush is the hermit thrush's habit of pumping its tail up and down when perched. When searching a mudflat for food, a least sandpiper prefers to keep its feet dry while a similar-looking semi-palmated sandpiper will happily slosh around in the water. Different species acted differently. And I had the differences between finger-puncturing Ollie and retiring Stanley Sue to thank for helping to drive this point home.

As engaging as our pet birds were, it took an outdoor bird to cheer us up during a nasty winter. Linda shocked me with the news that the small flock of birds hanging out in our spirea bush and seemingly impervious to the blasting cold were American tree sparrows. I was unable to tell them apart from any other streaky-backed "little brown job" and couldn't figure out how she had worked the trick. "They're the only sparrow we get with a black smudge like that on the chest, and they don't come except during winter," she said. Her expertise dumbfounded me, and when she explained that she had found the bird in the Audubon guide while living at her cabin, my admiration multiplied.

Huddled with the tree sparrows was another obvious sparrow that stood out from any others I'd seen because of his white throat—an obvious tip-off to his identity. The pudgy little fellow also sported a white racing stripe just above the eye along with a bright little dab of yellow just above his beak on the stripe.

"That's one of the birds on our clock," Linda said—the clock my friend Bill Holm had given us as a housewarming gift. Instead of chiming the hour, it belted out the song of whichever bird the hour hand pointed to. "It's a white-throated sparrow."

"Only six hours, thirty-seven minutes until we find out what it sounds like."

Through howling winds and blowing snow, under gloomy skies, and in subzero temperatures, our sparrow—dubbed Little Buddy by Linda—made like the legendary mailman and never shirked his duty, and his duty seemed to be to bring us joy. More active than the tree sparrows, possibly because he should have high-tailed it a few hundred miles south with the other white-throated sparrows, he delighted us by unexpectedly popping up all over the yard.

"I saw Little Buddy twice this morning!" Linda told me when I came home from work. "Once in a bush next to the barn and once on the brush pile behind the fence."

My response to this good news was to sulk. I hadn't seen him in a couple of days. When I eventually found him scratching in the snow underneath the bird feeder, I actually became motivated to undertake the small amount of labor required to scrape the patch down to the ground and sprinkle it with sunflower seeds. The cardinals, blue jays, tufted titmice, and other winter birds enjoyed the dining spot so much that from that day on shoveling the snow beneath the feeder took priority over keeping the walkways clear.

Near the end of February, we heard a song that contrasted with the music-box tinkling of the tree sparrows. It attempted to carry a melody but fell short of pulling it off. "Didn't that sound sort of like our clock?"

Linda shushed me. Whispering as if Little Buddy might be able to hear, she said, "It's you-know-who, and he can't seem to get the tune quite right."

The lilting song of the white-throated sparrow is represented in field guides as "Old Sam Peabody, Peabody, Peabody," or "Oh, Canada, Canada, Canada." Little Buddy's Sam Peabody had turned too old to carry a tune, and his ode to Canada never made it to the border. He practiced his song from the spirea, but he never seemed to come up with the right notes. Appropriately, he kept the volume low.

"Maybe he got left behind by his flock because he never learned the whole song," Linda suggested, wincing as he wandered perilously off-key before truncating his effort. "Is there some way we could let him hear the clock?"

When March arrived and his hormones began their seasonal surge, he suddenly found his voice. He saluted Canada with a voice worthy of Gordon Lightfoot and made any member of the Peabody family within hearing distance proud. We stopped seeing him in mid-April. He presumably headed north to his breeding grounds, though he may have traveled east to the Carnegie Hall audience that he now deserved. We missed the cheer he'd brought us—though another peak experience with birds quickly approached.

On Saturday, May 17, 1997, after eight happy years of marriage and zero

years of birding, Linda and I blundered into one of the largest concentra-
tions of migrating warblers in the country. It changed my life.

Less life changing was our intended destination: the Toledo Museum
of Art. As we rolled into the parking lot at 3:15 p.m. on Friday, I discovered that that the facility had conspired with the Art Gallery of Ontario
and decided to shut its doors at 4:00 pm. Freeway construction snarls
had delayed our entrance into the city by over an hour—so, no master-
pieces for us.

"Why don't we go to Cleveland and see the zoo tomorrow?" Linda
suggested after I had finished banging my fists against the steering
wheel.

I was all for leaving Toledo, if we could. Since we wanted to get within
shooting distance of the animals before May 17, 1998, we ditched the in-
terstate and crawled east on State Route 2. I worried that I was suffering
from traffic fatigue when we hit the countryside and I spotted a huge
white bird perched on the roof of a tidy gray cottage. Linda pointed out
two more of them standing motionless in a ditch on the side of the road.
"They're egrets," she said. "Aren't they gorgeous?"

Although I rarely knew what day of the week it was, I vividly recalled
an episode of the television series *Lassie* called "The Egret" that I hadn't
seen since I was five years old in 1958. While out with the Audubon Ju-
nior Bird Club, Timmy finds an American egret (now known as the great
egret) and reports it to his birdwatcher teacher. The appropriately named
Mr. Bins (slang for binoculars) doubts him. "There hasn't been an egret
seen in these parts for over twenty years," he says. Lassie eventually ex-
onerates Timmy by leading them to the bird.

While enveloped in my rerun reverie, I obeyed Linda's instructions
and followed the car ahead of us into Ottawa National Wildlife Refuge.
Linda's back had tightened up from sitting in the car—a consequence of
years of hard work as a professional housecleaner—and she needed to
take a walk. I studied the map after we had parked. In one of life's little
ironies we were almost directly across Lake Erie from Point Pelee. As we
followed a path along the wooded wetlands, I was less impressed by the
egrets and great blue herons that popped up than by the morel mushrooms Linda plucked from the trailside. On our way back, she ran into
a park ranger who told us that a migrating Kirtland's warbler had been
found next door at Magee Marsh.

I was glad we were headed for Cleveland. Looking for the warbler sounded boring.

I knew that Kirtland's warblers were rare, but that was all I knew about them. To start with, I had no idea that their numbers were so small. Only about twelve hundred singing males existed in the entire world back in 1997. "Kirtland's warblers are persnickety creatures," Bill Rapai told me recently. And he should know, because he wrote the amazing book *The Kirtland's Warbler: The Story of a Bird's Fight against Extinction and the People Who Saved It.* "Because they nest on the ground, they want sandy soil that will drain water quickly. They also want to build their nests under the overlapping branches of young jack pine trees to give them protection from predators." No other tree will do. The warblers insist upon jack pines.

Bill told me that even though jack pines grow all across North America, the crucial combination of jack pines and sandy soil is limited to a small area ranging across Ontario, Michigan, and Wisconsin. Even more limited is the number of jack pines between seven and twenty years old. The warblers turn up their beaks at older or younger trees. "That shortage of habitat means that the population of the Kirtland's warbler will always be small," he said.

To provide these conditions in Michigan, where most of the breeding birds hang out, the Department of Natural Resources (DNR) manages nesting grounds though fire, clear-cutting, replanting, and reseeding. But the warblers have another big problem—brown-headed cowbird neighbors who don't bother building nests of their own. They lay their eggs in the nests of other birds. A baby cowbird, which dwarfs a Kirtland's tot, will hog the food and shove the little ones out of the nest. To restore a sense of fairness to the jack pines, the DNR sets up traps to catch the meddlers—thus preventing the warbler from going the way of the Carolina parakeet.

The first person to identify the threat to the Kirtland's warbler from the cowbird was amateur ornithologist Nathan Leopold. In October 1923, at the tender age of twenty, he presented an important paper to the American Ornithological Union on the subject. Less than a year later he would achieve a different type of fame. He became one of the most infamous murderers of the twentieth century. His name would be irrevocably linked to Richard Loeb's in one of the infamous American crimes of the twentieth century, the "Leopold and Loeb" thrill killing of fourteen-year-old Bobby Franks. It is horribly ironic that the man whose insights helped save the Kirtland's warbler from extinction cared so deeply about birds but so little about human life.

In appearance alone, the Kirtland's warbler is irresistible with its blue-gray, black-streaked face, back, and wings illuminated by a yellow throat, breast, and belly. Still, it's squarely in the middle of the warbler pack in terms of razzle-dazzle, competing with birds that sport color palettes fiery enough to make the gaudiest Mardi Gras costume seem drab. Their bold looks are as fleeting as they are arresting. The chance to see a large assortment of warblers in their full spring glory is limited to a few weeks—and you may only have a window of several days to overload your senses with over thirty species of a national total of fifty-four passing through places like Magee Marsh. Those few days enveloped by kaleidoscopic beauty and song are the moments that many birders live for throughout the rest of the year.

The following afternoon, after I'd worn down my shoes at the Cleveland Metroparks Zoo, I tried to telepathically block Linda from thinking about chasing warblers. In case my psychic powers failed, I popped in a cassette of an old Jack Benny radio show and yucked it up with exaggerated gusto as we puttered west on State Route 2. But Linda had been watching for the Magee Marsh Wildlife Area sign, and to the accompaniment of groans from the driver's seat she told me to hang a right.

"You like boardwalks," she insisted.

"I've done enough walking today."

"My back is bothering me. I have to get out and walk somewhere, and we might as well do it where there might be birds."

We drove down a ribbon of two-lane road flanked by impressive wetlands. Magee Marsh and Ottawa National Wildlife Area—along with Crane Creek State Park, which somehow slots in with the other two—preserve a small chunk of the old Great Black Swamp. In its heyday the swamp impeded human movement in an area approximately 120 miles long and 40 miles wide. Then in 1859, the federal government told the lumber industry to go ahead and drain the whole thing. Only a few patches of the Great Black Swamp remain, primarily in protected areas.

A Canada goose crossed the road in front of us with a dozen young-sters in tow. Herons, egrets, and mallards flapped placidly by. We passed a few vehicles that huddled in stubby turn-offs, and the visitors center displayed a healthy number of cars. But after our road swung left at the beach, I was surprised by the packed parking lot. It wasn't swimming weather by any means. "Maybe there's a flea market," I said.

As soon as we hit the marsh boardwalk, I understood why it had drawn a crowd. It was as if we had entered a botanical garden brimming with captive butterflies—but these were brilliantly colored birds flutter-ing at an arm's length away. I had never seen anything like it before. I had never even dreamed anything like it. One moment I had been stand-ing on asphalt, sunlight blinding me off the mirror of an SUV. The next moment I was immersed in a lost world of birds, closed in, buzzing with song, alive with leaves and boughs spun and bounced by wild beauty in constant motion.

I had to duck when a crazy cross between a goldfinch and a chickadee tried to part my hair. "Chestnut-sided warbler," said a woman's voice. A brown-backed bird with a spotted white breast and outrageously striped head popped up onto the railing, dropped down onto the boards, hopped into the undergrowth, and disappeared. "Ovenbird," said a man whose camera-laden companion was already nudging him to look somewhere else.

The whole woods seemed to be moving through and past us. A branch bent low as a blue-headed vireo snagged a caterpillar. A lemon-yellow bird showed off red stripes on his breast. A deeper yellow bird flicked blue-gray wings and probed a log with a needle beak. The boardwalk wound on and on, snaking and looping for almost a mile, though we only followed it as far as the ninth or tenth group of birders pressed against the railings and clustered around a hotspot. I followed the goggle-eyed stare of a woman in a green windbreaker to a black-backed bird with yel-low breast and black side stripes. I began to feel drunk on dazzle, like I'd just chugged a six-pack of rose-breasted grosbeaks.

"She says it's a magnolia warbler," Linda said.

"I wish we had birds like that in our yard," I told the Windbreaker.

"Where do you live?"

"In West Michigan. On a river."

"Trees and bushes? Then you probably have them."

We edged past a man whose monster telescope, camera, and tripod rig hogged the walkway. As he zeroed in on what looked to me like a red-winged blackbird with orange patches on the wings and tail, he shook his head. "I've got enough American redstart photos. If you want to see something, there's a Kirtland's warbler on the beach."

Searching for a single tiny warbler on a half-mile stretch of beach struck me as the ultimate exercise in futility. I harped upon that theme as I followed Linda across the parking lot. "Needle in a haystack" received an obligatory mention. But as we stepped onto the sand, we had no doubt whatsoever as to the whereabouts of the bird. It hopped and rested, rested and hopped in the approximate center of a thirty-foot-diameter circle formed by slack-jawed birders. I ventured close enough to take a couple of photos. It wasn't much of a challenge, because at one point the warbler skittered between the legs of an observer and then flew back to continue pecking at the ground.

I had no notion at the time how rare this sighting was. Years later, *Kirtland's Warbler* author Bill Rapai told me, "Since the species was discovered in 1851, there have been only a few hundred recorded sightings of Kirtland's warblers outside of northern lower Michigan. If a birder finds a Kirtland's warbler between Michigan and its winter home in the Bahamas, it's the equivalent of winning the PowerBall lottery."

A man in the circle of birders understood the significance and told his son, "You have now joined an elite group of birders."

I didn't feel elite, but I did feel excited and unusually optimistic about the world.

On our way back to the car, I heard a familiar song coming from the bushes. "Little Buddy!" Linda said.

"Not just one. There's another Sam Peabody with him. And they're both singing on key."

"Maybe he brought a friend with him."

I didn't know much about birds, but I was reasonably confident that northern Ohio had its own complement of white-throated sparrows without needing to steal our winter friend. I caught a glimpse of a chubby striped head as the bird dropped to the ground and then immediately jumped back up into the foliage as if he were on springs. I didn't get another look before he and the other little cannonball shot away, but it had been enough. Even though I'd been awed by the razzamatazz of the warblers, renewing my acquaintance with one of Little Buddy's cousins sealed the deal.

For the second time in my life, I had been bitten by the birding bug. Only our little green parrot, Ollie, could have bitten me harder.

CHAPTER THREE

A Song Soothes Mr. Crabby

The afternoon after we got back from Magee Marsh, I moved faster than I'd moved in thirty years. Linda pointed out the window and said, "There's a magnolia warbler on the evergreen." I saw a flash of black, white, and yellow, and then I was off like a flash, grabbing our thirty-nine-dollar binoculars from the broom closet and clomping out the basement door. The bird was long gone by the time my feet hit the grass.

It had been almost a year since I braved the iron fingers of shoulder-high weeds and fought my way through our woods to the Grand River. But thinking that the lesson of Magee Marsh had been "where's there's one bird, there's one thousand," I sloshed through the beginnings of our vernal pond and pushed up the hill through knotted brambles that were still only shin-high, green, and tender. A few small silhouettes in trees along the river faded west as I gained the clearing from the east. I chased after them, trying at first to hold the binoculars to my eyes as I trotted along the riverbank. Then I sprinted, stopped, and looked—sprinted, stumbled, and stopped.

A few minutes later as I trudged up the basement steps, Linda called, "Did you find any morels?"

"I didn't go out to find morels."

"Well, I want to look. If they were near water at Magee Marsh, they should be near water here. It's a similar climate, more or less. And your bird is probably still here."

I turned around and followed her back outside. She moved much too leisurely through the woods for my liking, using a stick to shove aside a fallen leaf or twig. I wanted to cover a lot of ground, not scrutinize the ground cover. But I considered her to be a warbler magnet and stayed close.

"What's that bird?" she asked.

I saw nothing. Then I noticed a loud song, quite close. "It's that song sparrow again. Remember, from your cabin?" She shook her head. "It just changed songs," I said. "A minute ago it was singing a song that ended in 'white turkey.' Now it's got a new song without the 'white turkey' ending." I kept listening and started hearing other birds. I hadn't noticed them when I went out earlier, having pushed them into the background along with the noise of passing traffic, but once I started tuning in, they seemed impossible to ignore. Something squeaked like an athletic shoe on a basketball court. Then a woodpecker drummed across the river.

As Linda soldiered on fruitlessly searching for fungal fruiting bodies, I stayed rooted to the spot and counted three more new songs from the sparrow. Each song repeated several times before the bird went back to calling me a white turkey. I also heard the rubber-on-gym-floor squeak again—the same squeak I'd heard in our yard just before a rose-breasted grosbeak whirligigged over to the feeder. I scanned the bushes and found the song sparrow, which responded to the glare of my ruby red lenses by diving for cover. Lifting my chin, I located the grosbeak tucked away in a mulberry tree. I followed my ears to find other birds flitting in the leaves, but even through binoculars they were too far off for me to misidentify.

As we ambled back toward the house, I thought, how great and mighty is my presence that my awareness fills the woods with birds.

"I think I'll look across the street, if you'll come with me, " Linda said.

Too bad my mighty presence didn't work with mushrooms.

Although I appreciated the repertoire of the song sparrow, I had underestimated the bird's virtuosity. According to F. Schuyler Mathews, who made multistave musical transcriptions of bird vocalizations in his 1904 book, *Field Book of Wild Birds and Their Music*, "The Song Sparrow has the ability to render a motive in both the major and minor keys, just exactly as Verdi has done in the ninth and eleventh bars of 'Di Provenza.'" I didn't know Verdi from vermicelli, but I nodded when Mathews added, "The Song Sparrow is also one of the very few birds who is able to sing half a dozen songs, each of which is constructively different from the other."

I didn't need musical training to single out the song sparrow from our other backyard birds. The dead giveaways were the general form of its song ("Madge-Madge-Madge, put-on-the-tea-kettle-ettle-ettle," as the *National Audubon Society Field Guide to Birds* and other sources put it), its pattern of repetition and change, and the bell-like yet buzzy tone of its voice. Having mastered this identification, I decided to expand my expertise beyond one species. I started stalking our yard birds. Whenever I heard a song I didn't know, which was almost all of the time, I tried to get a look at the singer.

I had no problem finding a robin or rose-breasted grosbeak erupting in full-throated song, but I couldn't tell the robin and grosbeak songs apart. The nuthatch with its nasal *enk-enk* was easy. The tufted titmouse drove me crazy. Though it only had two notes in its arsenal, it combined them in seemingly infinite variations, so I took solace in the predictable two-toned whistle of the chickadee. The cardinal with its sliding notes and hearty chirps I knew from my youth. But our Lowell cardinals had regional accents, as did cardinals in other places. It would be years before I ran into one on the other side of the state that sounded like a member of the old Dorroll Street gang.

One mystery singer resisted allowing me to glimpse his person. This tireless Caruso taunted me from various trees throughout the day, zipping unseen from the oak beside the barn to the front hackberry, and then to deep down in the swamp before launching an aria from the barn oak yet again. He sang a jingly, feverish phrase of staccato note pairs that could only be termed melodic by the generous of heart. So intent was he upon celebrating his existence that I figured he'd be oblivious to me. I couldn't get near him, though. When I approached him in the front yard, he suddenly sang from the next tree down the line. After I'd taken another dozen steps, he popped up across the street.

The following day I managed to get the briefest look at him—a small dark bird that didn't match up with anything in my field guide. "Was he way in the top of a tree?" Linda asked. "It's probably an indigo bunting. Unless the sun hits them right, they look almost black instead of blue." I looked up the indigo bunting in *Field Book of Wild Birds and Their Music*. Mathews's transliteration of "sip, swee, swee, chir, chir, wis wis wis sir sir sir" more or less described what I'd been hearing, though the bird didn't call me "sir."

"I want to see him," said Linda. "I love indigo buntings."

"You'll hear him, but you won't see him."

Linda lured the stunning wood ducks closer to the house by setting out heaps of scratch feed on our hill.

When I led her to the oak beside the barn, the bird was perched in plain sight on the top branch, blazing a brilliant lazuli blue.

Unlike the indigo bunting, which looks like the Twitter logo, the wood duck isn't easy to describe.

The females are the alarm-givers. The first time I ever heard one was shortly after we moved in. I was crashing through the underbrush gawking at the river when a reasonable imitation of a whistling teakettle trying to come to a boil greeted me as the duck fled for its life. *Ooh-eek! Ooh-eek!* Every spring, these skittish birds peppered our seasonal pond. All it took was my silhouette in the dining room window over a hundred feet away to send the flock flapping toward the river.

Hiding in the shadow of the refrigerator we would watch them through binoculars and gasp in disbelief. The pretty females wore brown and beige earth tones. But the males were stunning, awing us with their hand-painted intensity. Topping a chestnut-colored neck and throat, the iridescent green head with bold white pinstripes ended in a backward sweeping crest—a jaunty cap for a sleek Beau Brummel. The crisply patterned body flaunted metallic green, blue, and purple overtones, with a creamy white patch on the side that gave my overstimulated optic nerves a place to rest. I could imagine storybook emperors trading their gold and jewels for such a bird.

The old-school field guide authors dug deep into their poetic souls when describing the wood duck. "Woodland ponds and forest-bordered streams make a proper setting for the grace and beauty of these richly attired birds," wrote Frank M. Chapman in *Birds of Eastern North American* way back in 1895. "I know of no sight in the bird world which so fully satisfies the eye."

In *Michigan Bird Life,* from 1912, Walter Barrows says, "This is doubtlessly the most beautiful of American ducks, and the male in full plumage is probably without a superior in any part of the world."

Pioneering ornithologist Elliott Coues—who helped establish the modern taxonomic classification system in zoology—wrote the two-volume, 1,152-page *Key to North American Birds* in 1875. Dauntingly awash in scientific terms and Latin phrases, it's not a book for the dabbler. To call it dry denigrates run-of-the-mill dryness. But Coues can't resist calling the wood duck "exquisite" and lamenting the fact that "the pernicious spring shooting of the bird on its breeding grounds has made it rare in many places where it was once common."

Linda turned our own wood ducks into less elusive birds by luring them closer to the house shortly after we started keeping domesticated ducks as pets. Envious of the bounteous food that we gave our plump pet khaki Campbells, a pair of wild mallards flew in to beg. Linda dumped scratch feed on the hill for them. Within a week, the wood ducks joined them, marching up the slope like wind-up penguins for an al fresco meal of grains. No matter how many separate heaps Linda made, the males quarreled over the feed, charging one another with lowered heads and then returning to discover that another male had stolen their spot.

I told my friend Bill Holm about them a few days after my successful identification of the song sparrow, and he said, "I'll be over Friday for dinner and a duck show." He didn't particularly like birds, but he liked them more than he liked people—and he loved watching the Canadian Broadcasting Corporation's Inuit-language programming on our "big dish" satellite TV. I'd met Bill twenty years earlier at *Cadence* weekly newspaper in East Grand Rapids, where he may or may not have been my boss. He'd been too detached from everything for me to figure out what he did. Bill had been a witness to my strange transformation since marrying Linda from pet disdainer to fussy caretaker for scores of demanding animals. Early in my duck-keeping days, he had helped me build an extension to our backyard pen, astonishing me with the fact that there was indeed someone in the world more inept with hammer, nails, and a bent handsaw than me.

We didn't have dinner guests often. I accommodated Bill by putting our birds back in their cages so that they didn't land on his head while he ate. He still wasn't satisfied. "You might want to wipe the pigeon poop off my chair before I sit down," he said.

As Linda set a plate of veggie stir fry in front of him, she said, "I wish I had some morels to go with this, but our woods didn't have any. We'll have to take a trip up north."

"Didn't you listen to the news?" I asked. "They're saying there weren't any morels up north this year and don't bother looking."

"They did not. You just don't want to go." This was true. I always felt humiliated watching virile men, tiny children, and stooped-over grannies alike struggling with huge sacks of mushrooms, while all we ever managed to bring home was a record number of mosquito bites.

While shoveling stir fry into my mouth, I stared out the window waiting for the wood ducks to show up. It hadn't rained in over a week. Our once-mighty pond was but a murky shadow of its former self, and we had been getting fewer ducks each day.

"Your only friends in the world have abandoned you," Bill said.

"I'm seeing a few ripples."

"Fourteen, you said."

"Not every night. I said that we get *as many as* fourteen."

"None is less than fourteen, so I guess you were right."

I was scraping leftovers into a dish for our barn birds when a pair of wood ducks finally flew in through the trees and toddled up the hill. As the female pecked at the scratch feed, the male gallantly stood guard. We passed around the binoculars and oohed at them. When it was his turn, Bill announced, "There's something else in the water. What the heck's going on with his head? It's like a lady's fan." He lowered his voice two octaves. "Or a blacksmith's bellows."

It didn't take Linda long to find the black, white, and chestnut-colored male hooded merganser in our Audubon field guide. After his own fashion, he was as sensational as the wood duck. What he lacked in brilliant hues he made up for in high style with a huge disc of a crest that he erected and collapsed as his mood dictated. Instead of fleeing at the sight of us like a wood duck, he calmly steered behind a log and disappeared.

Before Bill had a chance to lose himself in an incomprehensible Inuit-language TV talk show from Iqaluit in the Canadian Arctic, I bragged about identifying yard birds by their songs. "I guess it makes sense that I'm good with my ears, since I write a music column." For ten years, I'd somehow managed to cobble together a CD review column for a reggae and world music magazine called *The Beat*. To hide my vast ignorance, I avoided covering styles like Celtic or Cuban that my readers might know about and instead stuck to obscure genres like Tuvan throat singing whenever I could. I got paid what I was worth—I did my column for free. To earn a living, I wrote sales copy for a mail order company that sold hi-fi gear, which theoretically added to my sonic expertise.

"You hear that?" I said, lowering the TV volume. "That's an indigo bunting."

"Show me," Bill said, setting down the remote after he had just grabbed it from me.

As we stepped outside into bright but waning sunlight, the slam of the front door silenced the bird. I picked up the song again across the yard and led Bill down the hill behind the barn to a large hackberry tree flanked by jewelweed. "This isn't an ideal spot," I said. "They like to perch way up high, and it'll be tough to see him."

"He sounds low to me."

"He might be, but I'm not finding him."

I passed the binoculars to Bill, but he didn't need them. "There." He pointed to a bird singing from a stunted bush. "If that's an indigo bunting, he's cleverly disguised as a goldfinch." Bill couldn't have sounded more delighted. "Maybe it's going to rain, and he's wearing a yellow slicker."

I shook my head. "There must have been two different birds."

"Maybe you can devote a column in that reggae magazine to your bird identification talent. You can call it 'Cool Runnings and Yellow Buntings.'"

"I know an indigo bunting is what I heard." And I also knew that I hadn't heard the last about my mistake from Bill.

To boost my auditory skills, Linda bought me the cassette tape *A Field Guide to Bird Songs* by the Cornell Laboratory of Ornithology and Roger Tory Peterson, the father of the modern field guide. In 1934, Peterson revolutionized birding with his *Guide to Birds* by inventing a system of identifying birds by the field marks that most readily separated species. So if the blue grosbeak and indigo bunting looked nearly identical in his illustrations, lines pointing to grosbeak's grossly large beak and the bars on its wings distinguished it from the bunting, which lacked these traits. He also broke new ground by urging his readers to study birds through binoculars instead of shooting them for carcasses to examine, as birders of his day liked to do. (When a pair of unspeakably rare and presumed extinct ivory-billed woodpeckers was discovered in Florida in the 1920s, museum reps rushed to the scene to shoot them for their collections.)

I didn't listen to cassettes at home, but I had a tape player in my car. And I'd have time to use it, since Linda had scheduled a morel-hunting trip at Newaygo State Park, about an hour north of us. Although I'd lost some of my resistance to tromping through the woods, I preferred to do so within sight of our back door. So I devoted the first ten minutes of our drive to complaining that we'd never find a single mushroom, that campers would have already scoured every inch of the park, and that Bill had phoned to ask if I'd ever heard a calypso called "Yellow Bird." Then, at Linda's urging, I popped in the Peterson cassette and leaned back to absorb a flock of brand-new songs.

Instead the vocalizations rolled off me like water off a loon's back as Tape One opened with "Loons, Grebes, Swans, and Geese," which didn't do much for my backyard birding skills. "Marsh Ducks" came next, followed by "Diving Ducks, Coots, and Gallinules." As we got into "Terns" I cranked down the volume and asked Linda, "Are you getting anything out of this?"

"We're not going to learn all of these in one trip," she said. This was a significant understatement.

Flipping the tape over, I grappled with hawk vocalizations, hooted at a selection of owl calls, and hit the eject button. "Let's concentrate on birds we might hear today."

"What would those be?"

I had no idea, and the fact that Linda didn't know either surprised me, since I still considered her to be something of a bird expert. "Well, we won't be all that far from your cabin, and since you had song sparrows in your yard, lets listen to some other sparrows."

We sat through the white-throated sparrow, white-crowned sparrow, chipping sparrow, field sparrow, swamp sparrow, American tree sparrow, lark sparrow, clay-colored sparrow, grasshopper sparrow, Bachman's sparrow, fox sparrow, song sparrow, vesper sparrow, Lincoln's sparrow, and savannah sparrow before Linda said, "Stop, I'm getting a headache." I felt overwhelmed as well. Out of all the sparrows that we'd heard, the only ones that I remembered after I'd switched off the tape were the song sparrow and the white-throated sparrow, which I already knew.

"The announcer has a nice voice," I said. "I'd probably recognize him if I heard him again."

My worst fears and best hopes came true when we climbed out of the car at Newaygo State Park. The bad news was that the place was over-run with morel hunters, which doomed us to another forlorn search. The good news was that the abundance of mushroomers meant that we could probably give up and go home early.

It was easy to tell the collectors from the weekend campers. When they weren't straining the canvas of their collapsible chairs, the campers wandered aimlessly around their RVs, hands in pockets and faces relaxed into a state of amiable boredom. Their eyes darted about in search of anyone new to talk to. But the collectors avoided contact with anyone outside their raiding party. They wore the hard, focused expressions of competitive athletes as they examined one small patch of ground after another with thoroughness that would shame a bloodhound.

Linda asked a heavy-set woman with a cloth bag looped around her belt, "Are you finding any morels?"

She stiffened at the impertinence, then realized she was dealing with greenhorns. "Not a thing," she claimed. "They're late this year."

"Sweetheart, I found one," Linda called a few minutes later. Like a deer switching to high alert at the snap of a twig, mushroom hunt-ers across the park's 257 acres all froze and twitched their ears. "Never mind," she said. "It's a false morel." As we climbed up and over the ridge, an elderly man glided over and plucked it.

Although the big, brown, brain-shaped false morel *Gyromitra esculenta* is classified as poisonous, Linda had a friend in Morley who had eaten them for years. They're considered to be delicacies in parts of Europe. Reactions to eating them range from a satisfied burp to death, with a full spectrum of ill effects in between, depending on one's sensitivity to the toxin gyromitrin. Symptoms of mild poisoning include lethargy, disorientation, dizziness, anxiety, and headaches—or just another typical day for me.

False morels and morel collectors dogged us in the wooded parts of the park. Knowing that true morels were fickle fungi that could pop up almost anywhere, we retreated to the park entrance to hunt for them in a field at the edge of the trees. As I took a swig from Linda's water bottle, the *conk-la-ree* of a red-winged blackbird reminded me that I'd been ignoring bird songs. I couldn't push them into the background now. All around us macho males of various species clamored for attention as they claimed territory and asserted their identities. Those identities eluded me.

"What do you think these are?" I asked Linda as I scanned the branches.

"Some of them could be the sparrows from the tape."

I could pick out our old familiar song sparrow easily enough, but he was just one player in a complex orchestra. The rest of the performers were complete unknowns. We got close looks through binoculars at a dark bird that resembled the eastern phoebe back home who helpfully announced his name by calling *fee-bee*. But this bird said *fitz-bew*. A mystery vocalist serenaded us with a strenuous bout of *wick-wick-wick*-ing. Another bird imitated a squeaky pump handle. Others peeped, chirped, or crafted rambling melodies.

Linda could appreciate the sounds and sights without worrying about who was doing what. Not me. I had gone from having only a casual interest in birds to suddenly needing to pin a name on them, and I didn't have a clue how to do it. Even when I was able to observe the singer, it usually registered in my brain as a complicated assemblage of gray-brown-and-beige parts that looked identical to every other assemblage of gray-brown-and-beige parts in our field guide. Who could keep track of the stripes, spots, speckles, wing-bars, caps, crowns, eye-rings, patches, and streaks that earned a bird its membership in one particular species instead of the species next door? It made me glum, and being glum made me even glummer with so much life bursting out around us. I tried consoling myself knowing that I was out in nature attempting to learn about birds, which was a giant leap forward for a fresh-air-ophobe like me. But it wasn't consolation enough.

"Let's go," I said. "I've had enough futility for one day."

"I want to find at least one morel," she said.

I had never found one. I didn't have the eye. But I threw myself into the hunt, because it was a relief to focus on the ground and see nothing but plants and grasses whose names I didn't expect myself to know. I couldn't even name the colors—so many shades of green with an occasional splash of white or yellow that nestled softly in my ignorance. Hoping for a mushroom miracle as I searched, I tried thinking like a fungus, which wasn't all that much of a stretch. I prayed to the spore-bearing gods that I might blunder into the morel mother lode and then call Linda over supposedly to admire some particular weed so that she could make the discovery. But I needed to keep my head down and concentrate.

A sudden commotion made me look up. A pair of red-headed woodpeckers thrashed the air fifteen feet above us, scolding us in unison before rocketing off. Most bird sightings this brief barely registered with me. But time froze as the pair hung overhead, crisscrossing, flicking one another with black-and-white wings and giving us holy heck. I didn't have a chance to even touch my binoculars much less raise them to my nose, but my impression of the birds was gigantic. No eagles or pterodactyls could have made a stronger impact. I had never seen one of these birds before, but I knew them immediately from having admired them in my field guide. As we traipsed toward the edge of the forest, they swooped over us again, flapping furiously to hold their positions. They harangued us with rattling *churr-churr* invectives expressing unprintable woodpecker expletives. Losing altitude, they swirled and veered away, only to come back once more. We changed course and moved our search to the opposite end of the field.

"We must have gotten too close to their nest," Linda said.

"Or too close to their secret morel spot."

I kept looking back for another glimpse and even considered invading their territory again in hopes of a fourth flyover. But I didn't have it in me to bother a bird. I didn't want to get my head hammered, either. Still, I was tempted to go back. Their red heads and snow-white bodies were right out of the book. But their blazing-eyed ferocity couldn't be found on any page. I hadn't simply seen two birds. I'd gotten a peek at a totally different world of grace and struggle that had little regard for us. We were pampered apes adrift in leisure time, searching the woods for food for fun, and we didn't have a particle of sense or seriousness compared to them. We were also lucky to have made it out of there without perforated skulls.

Learning songs seemed like the key to identifying the gray-brown-and-beige birds that had apparently taken over the world. At home I made another stab at improving myself via the *Field Guide to Bird Songs* cassettes. To avoid inundating my leaky bucket of a brain with far more information than it could contain, I decided to limit myself to learning a manageably small group of birds. Vireos seemed like an excellent place to start. I had read somewhere that the red-eyed vireo was dubbed "the preacher bird" due its gift for tireless repetition. No other bird sang its song up to twenty thousand times in a single day. The odds favored my hearing such a blabby bird, especially since the *Aubudon* guide referred to it as "abundant."

Its short, punchy song was easy to remember. *I've got this*, I thought. Then I listened to the Philadelphia vireo. It sounded exactly like the red-eyed. Next I gave the solitary vireo a whirl. I couldn't tell it from the first two. And the black-capped, black-whispered, and yellow-throated vireos were so similar to the others that I lost my last dwindling trace of vireo virility.

I complained about this to my buddy-since-kindergarten Brian O'Malley, who lived near Washington, DC. Brian wasn't a birder. But anything that interested me interested him, because it gave us more to talk about on the phone. Rooting around in local bookstores, he found a CD set and sent it to me. But this wasn't just a catalog of songs. *Birding by Ear* grouped similar-sounding birds together, and compiler Richard Walton provided helpful hints for telling them apart. So once I'd mastered the robin's song, which wasn't too hard, Walton explained that a scarlet tanager sounded like a robin with a sore throat, and he described a rose-breasted grosbeak as a robin that had taken singing lessons. This was brilliant. Even better, it was simple enough for me to understand.

Excited by the tapes, I met Linda at the door with my portable CD player.

"You'll never guess what I just found in the front yard," she told me. "Right under the lilac tree." She opened her hand to reveal a black morel. "Isn't it beautiful? Even though there's only one, I'm going to sauté it in butter with some garlic, and we can split it at dinner."

I followed her into the kitchen. As she plopped the mushroom into a bowl of cold water, I played the track that compared three mimics—the gray catbird, brown thrasher, and northern mockingbird—and explained how their songs were different.

"I always love hearing the catbird," she said. "Do you want to cook the morel for me? You do a better job than I do with mushrooms."

"But isn't it great that now we know which bird is which?"

"I'd have to hear that again to really get it."

Telling the birds apart wasn't difficult. All three were thieves who stole songs from other species. But the catbird sang each phrase just once. The thrasher usually sang phrases twice, and the mockingbird went whole hog with three or four repetitions.

The next day I brought the CD player into her study to demonstrate the differences again. Before I had a chance to punch the "play" button, she said, "You learn them first, and I'll listen to them later."

I slunk away muttering to myself that since I'd given Linda my half of the morel the night before, the least she could have done was indulge me with the bird songs. Then I brightened when it hit me that for the first time in our relationship, I was actually more interested than she was in some tiny aspect of a subject having to do with nature. Either that or I hadn't chased her around the house enough with the songs.

The weather turned hot a few weeks later, and Linda wanted to go to the beach. I dreaded this even more than morel hunting. When we searched for mushrooms, I could keep my clothes on. But I didn't have good options at the lake. Stripping down to bathing trunks transformed me into a white stick of chewing gum—and it seemed pointless exposing my pathetic physique when I had no intention of splashing around in sixty-five-degree water. Staying fully dressed surrounded by half-naked people wasn't much better. I felt wildly out of place at Ionia State Recreation Area in a long-sleeved shirt, jeans, socks, and shoes. I didn't want to be taken for a voyeur—especially by the lanky blond woman in the yellow bikini next to us. So I flopped down on my back and closed my eyes. As Linda stashed her watch inside her shoe, I pretended that the towel spread across the lumpy sand was our bed and tried to take a nap.

"Are you sure you don't want to come in with me?" she asked.

I wrote this off as a rhetorical question and didn't bother to respond. Seized by a fit of crabbiness, I briefly regretted having told her about this little lake just fifteen miles from home, but the alternative meant driving fifty miles to Lake Michigan to put me in the same antisocial mood. Not for the first time did I wonder why I had a congenital blockage that prevented me from having fun. The energy that should have flowed to the part of my brain that experienced joy jammed up and streamed into an overdeveloped complaint cortex instead. It baffled me that Linda had married such a droop. When I heard her holler, "Whee!" I propped myself up on one elbow to admire her ability to play with a couple of kids. Then I took another stab at a nap.

In the brilliant sun, I could see the blood pumping though my closed eyelids. I threw a towel over my face, but the dark green shirt and blue jeans hadn't been wise color choices. After roasting for a while, I stuck Linda's watch into my pocket and set off across the parking lot for my water bottle. As I neared the car I heard bird songs in the wooded field between the lake and the road. Grabbing my brand-new pair of ninety-nine-dollar binoculars, I searched for Linda to reassure myself that she would stay in the water for a while. Her shoes, our towels, and my Dashiell Hammett novel remained undisturbed a short distance from the woman in the yellow bikini, who had just turned over onto her back.

I followed a line of parking curbs to a clearing. Suddenly an unusual sensation lit me up from scalp to toe. I couldn't place it for a moment, and then I recognized it as delight. My ears unplugged. From behind me I heard waves of laughter from the beach. In front of me the world's greatest vocalists chipped away at my bad mood. I didn't even care that I was a fully dressed man loitering conspicuously in a beach parking lot with a pair of binoculars. Okay, I cared a little, so I waded into the brush hoping to get closer to the birds, but the wiry branches put the "thick" in thicket, and I had to stop.

I was treated to a selection of remarkably clear and distinctive songs. The *chiva-chiva* of the tufted titmouse dueled with the *pretty-pretty* of the cardinal, while the rhythm of a ping-pong ball speeding up as it bounced indicated a field sparrow. It was as if a bunch of birds with the most easily identifiable songs were having a little fun at my thick-headed expense, getting together just so I could have the pleasure of sorting them out. A scarlet tanager serenaded me with the hoarse version of a robin's song, and I beamed at the virtuosity of my friend the rose-breasted grosbeak. I heard the laconic musings of warbling vireo, a mewing gray catbird, and the *bubble-zee* of a brown-headed cowbird.

A door had burst open to reveal a secret world that had been hiding in plain sight. These birds were the mouthpieces for the seasons. They were what we had lost when we learned to speak. They were themselves and nothing more in the same way that we were ourselves and something less. Just by being, they made me happy. I didn't have to touch them. I didn't even have to see them, though my ego preferred that I could name them. They made me want to sprint down to the beach, grab the arms of the family playing volleyball, pull the laughing swimmers from the water, tug the yellow-suited sunbather to her feet, and tell them, *turn around, you don't realize what you're missing.* Then again, those people could say the same thing to me.

After Linda toweled off, she followed me across the parking lot. Feeling like *Birding by Ear*'s Richard Walton, I identified one singer after another—although by now they had been joined by birds I couldn't recognize.

"The water was the perfect temperature," she told me as we headed back to the car.

I heard myself reply, "We should come here more often," stunning both of us into silence.

As we avoided potholes on our way out of the park, she said, "I'm glad you found so many nice birds. You didn't happen to see any morels, did you?"

CHAPTER FOUR

A Duck Out of Water

I had come pretty far, considering that when I'd first met Linda I had only seen a woodpecker on Saturday-morning TV, and now I could identify four of them—or five, if you counted Woody. I could also point to any frequent visitor to our feeders and tell you what many of them were, though I might as well have leaped to another continent once I left our yard and ventured into the woods. Most remarkably, I hadn't given up, even though I was well past the point where I usually lost interest in a pursuit—like the year that I vowed to learn a new word from the dictionary every day and quit after *aardwolf*. But I still had a long way to go on the road to identifying most common birds. I ran smack dab into a major obstacle on the afternoon when I chased a pet duck through the weeds.

The ducks and geese had been out in the yard for an hour practicing their unique brand of insect control, which included eating every blade of grass down to the topsoil. When they had stuffed themselves so full that I marveled at their ability to still waddle around, I started to shoo them back into their pen. Then I spotted a duck pacing on the wrong side of our rusty backyard fence. She had apparently squeezed herself through a hole that had escaped my latest round of patching.

Fortunately, our ducks were so tubby that they either couldn't or wouldn't fly. Unfortunately, they could swim as well as the sleekest mallard, and at the bottom of the hill lay a seasonal pond—and not far beyond the pond stretched the Grand River. So I needed to act fast.

Straddling the fence, I talked sweetly to the pretty, pretty little girl while doing my best to conceal a trout net behind my back. When the net slipped as I hoisted my leg over the wire, she quacked and bolted. I staggered down the hill three steps to get between her and the water and chased her back and forth along the fence line. This agitated the ducks and geese inside the pen, who called out encouragement to their favorite—but I didn't have time to stop and thank them for their support.

Twice I would have caught her except for her sudden change of direction or the intervention of a clump of garlic mustard between duck and net. I ratcheted down my pursuit once it became clear that she was more interested in rejoining her flock than in making a break for the water. Panting from a few seconds of exertion, I stood and watched as she found the same opening in the wire that she had apparently used as her exit, but she had trouble squirming through it a second time. When she got stuck, I scooped her up in my hands, narrowly missing a sprig of poison ivy that waited for me among the creeping charlie.

I carried her back to the pen, petting her head as I told her what a naughty girl she had been. She complained about her mistreatment when I set her down with the others.

Back inside the house, I told Linda about my adventure, stressing the fact that I had already mended the escape hatch with chicken wire so that she didn't need to remind me. "How that fat duck ever made it through that little hole is a mystery," I said.

"Which one of Chloe's girls was it?" she asked, referring to the khaki Campbell mother who had refused to practice family planning. "Carla, Marla, or Darla?"

"I don't remember. I don't think I noticed."

"Then it must have been either Carla or Marla. You'd remember if it was Darla." Our two black-and-white ducks looked so much alike, we hadn't named them as individuals. Together they were Carla and Marla. But their sister, Darla, was our only brown-and-white female. I should have remembered her.

In my mind's eye I could clearly see a two-toned duck pacing at the top of the hill, yet I had no recollection whatsoever of her color. I had a solid yet at the same time vague sense of her, as if I'd encountered the idea of a duck rather than a duck in feathers and flesh. I had been so consumed with the idea of catching her before she bolted to the pond that my brain had skipped over this obvious physical detail if it had ever recorded it in the first place. It was like trying to sort out one of those dreams where one moment I was folding socks on the front sidewalk

A dazzling male rufous hummingbird like this one took a wide detour south from the Pacific Northwest to end up near Battle Creek, Michigan.

with Linda, and the next moment my sister Joan and I were searching the hallways of Catholic Central High School for my locker.

"It must have been Carla or Marla," I said. "I held her and petted her. I would have noticed if she was brown and white." I felt embarrassed and unnerved by this gaping hole in my perception. I loved our ducks and spoiled them with macaroni treats and lawn sprinklers to frolic through, so it wasn't a matter of failing to pay attention to them. "Isn't it crazy that I don't know?"

It didn't strike Linda as unusual. Every year she told me the names of her flowers, and every year I immediately forgot them. I had no trouble with the easily recognizable ones that I'd grown up with: snapdragons, tulips, lilies, daffodils, and roses. But I struggled with geraniums versus begonias, and I couldn't tell clematis from columbine, zinnias from marigolds, or mums from mum's-the-word. It wasn't that I recognized the flower but momentarily misplaced the names. I was a poor observer with an abysmal visual memory, and I blurred together flowers that shared structural similarities—such as having leaves and stems.

I had a similar problem with birds. If a bird flaunted some dramatically obvious difference from every other bird on earth, I might match up that single feature with a picture in a field guide. But if you were to ask me how I recognized an adult male American redstart, I'd reply that it was a black bird with bits of orange on it quite unlike the bits of orange on a red-winged blackbird. However, even today—even after seeing numerous redstarts up close, in books, and on the Internet—I'd probably have to consult a picture to jog my memory that it had two orange patches on each wing and an orange patch on either side of its tail.

It wasn't as if I walked around in an absentminded fog all of the time—at least not while I was birding. Out in the woods, my senses were in as much of a state of high alert as my sluggish self could muster. Linda could be tromping through the woods beside me, snapping sticks beneath her feet, snuffling, clearing her throat, and describing the terrible ingredients that the chefs were forced to cook with on this week's episode of *Chopped*. Then I'd touch her arm and say, "I just heard a red-eyed vireo in the crown of that tall tree on the river." But while I'd been slowly, steadily getting better at identifying birds by sound, my visual skills didn't seem to be improving.

To some degree, my brain actively filtered out what it considered to be superfluous visual information, and I had to work to get it back. So when I ran into a sparrow that was festooned with stripes, streaks, and speckles, I would describe out loud what I was seeing in order to make it stick. "Stripe through the eye," I'd say. "Streaked breast, streaked brown back, faint white bars on wings." One or two of these features might survive long enough in my head for me to write them down. But usually I had to make do with a smeary sense of pattern and color before both bird and memory flew away.

So the bottom line was that I could put names to maybe three dozen birds, especially if they were cooperative enough to open their beaks and sing on cue. But when I ran into an unfamiliar one that decided to keep its birdie lips zipped, too much subtlety or complexity to its appearance overloaded my simple brain. And so, apparently, did a completely familiar brown-and-white duck versus a black-and-white duck.

My only hope was to discover other identification methods beyond simply what a bird looked like and sounded like, though I doubted that any such methods existed.

Ever since I'd met Linda, she had cajoled me into joining her in what she called "nature walks"—long, rambling hikes through the woods that hadn't appealed to a city-bred lad like me. Finally, after a decade of marriage, these nature walks became a thing of the past. We went birding instead—which amounted to taking the exact same long, rambling hikes through the woods, except we now carried binoculars. That made all the difference to me. It didn't change much for Linda, although she enjoyed my newfound enthusiasm for our walks in place of my former grumbling.

One Saturday afternoon, Linda and I traipsed through a meadow at a local nature center where someone we knew had seen a barred owl. I had my ears cocked and ready for its *who-cooks-for-you?* song when a whoop from Linda spun me around. Her smile was so wide, she could hardly look through her binoculars. I jammed my field glasses into my face and moved directly behind her to get a bead on whatever had captured her attention. I couldn't locate the source of her delight. If she had found the owl, it was an expert at camouflage.

"Sweetheart, look at this squirrel with his bulging cheeks," she said. "I can't tell what he's eating, can you?"

I briefly reverted to my former grumbling self. I was there to search for birds, not to enjoy nature. A few minutes later, Linda called out again, but this time she said, "I see a bird!" I recognized him immediately from my want-to-see list. He was mostly black with an orange patch on each side, but I wasn't likely to confuse him with a redstart or a red-winged blackbird. He looked more like a robin sporting an orange-and-white vest. The perky fellow had an air of dignity. He cocked his tail when he saw us but otherwise didn't act flustered. He seemed politely embarrassed at our mutual surprise over running into one another.

"A rufous towhee," Linda said. I wholeheartedly agreed.

We could be forgiven for not having the name quite right, since the experts had gone back and forth about what to call the bird. For decades it wore the nondescript mantle "eastern towhee." Then ornithologists decided that the towhee of the eastern United States and the spotted towhee of the western states were subspecies of the same bird and lumped them both together as the "rufous-sided towhee." But the lumping didn't last. Recent hairsplitting split the birds a second time, and the "eastern towhee" fluttered back as a separate species.

For most Michiganders, the towhee is a go-out-and-look-for bird, but this wasn't always the case. In the 1912 edition of *Michigan Bird Life*, Walter Bradford Barrows says, "It is one of the commonest of roadside birds and one can hardly drive a mile along a country road anywhere in the Lower Peninsula without seeing several." In those days it was popularly known as the "chewink." In *Birds of Eastern North America*, Frank M. Chapman explains why. "He greets all passers with a brisk, inquiring *chewink, towhee,* and if you pause to reply, with a *fluff-fluff* of his short, rounded wings he flies to a nearby limb the better to inspect you."

Our bird retreated to the back of a winterberry bush, but we still had a clear view as he peered at us through the leaves. A *chewink* of joy rose up inside me, and I felt doubly gladdened when an outdoorsy couple with oscillating walking sticks appeared on the path. Holding my face in an open, excited expression, I unlooped the binoculars from my neck, preparing to share our find. The two quickened their pace and chugged past us. The snub offended me. Who wouldn't want to stop and see the object of a fellow hiker's scrutiny? Then it struck me like the bang of a red-headed woodpecker's beak. I had turned into the very same binoculars-toting bore that I had avoided years earlier at Point Pelee. Far from shaming me for past behavior, this realization puffed me up with pride. I'd never been mistaken for a knowledgeable nerd before.

It would have suited me if all birds were as easy to identify as the towhee with its big blocks of bold color. But as we followed the path along a creek, my least favorite bird to attach a name to appeared on the opposite side of a small pond—some kind of sparrow with indecipherable stripes and streaks.

"A song sparrow, I suppose."

"He doesn't act like a song sparrow," Linda said. If this had been a movie, the camera would have zoomed in on her face to a portentous swell of violins. She had said a mouthful, though the significance didn't sink in right away.

Instead of diving for cover at our approach as a song sparrow would have done, he ignored us altogether. Like a little sentry, he marched along the edge of the pond, weaving in and out of grasses and climbing over weeds. He flew off, only to return to his starting point and begin his patrol all over again. He was either hunting for insects or had ants in his pants. He never stopped moving, and he flicked his wings as he walked.

Back at home I sat on the bed trying to flip through my birding books as our black cat Agnes repeatedly thrust her head into my hand demanding to be petted. The first thing I did was study the range maps, which I had never paid much attention to until now. These immediately let me chuck out the rufous winged sparrow, rufous crowned sparrow, Bachman's sparrow, and a number of other sparrows that summer far west and/or south of Michigan. That narrowed things down a bit. I couldn't remember much about the plumage of the sparrow we had seen, but the lack of a confusing jumble of stripes on his face and the absence of streaks on his breast led me to a chipping sparrow. But something about the chipping sparrow didn't feel right.

The range maps and the descriptions for, of all things, the seaside sparrow gave me my next hint. As the name pointed out, the seaside sparrow is a sparrow of coastal areas. So not only geographical region but also habitat plays a huge role in identification, I realized. My field guides insisted that chipping sparrows stick to dry areas, so that probably wouldn't be our bird. Then I pondered what Linda had said about how the bird had acted. According to the experts, the swamp sparrow—which resembles a chipping sparrow—engages in just that kind of energetic obsessive-compulsive foraging behavior on the edges of marshes and ponds that we had witnessed.

I shut my books and petted Agnes. Thanks to Linda's observation, I had actually identified a bird by taking geography, habitat, and behavior into account, just like an actual birder would. Sometimes I amazed myself.

The amazing thing was that it had taken me so long to grasp the fact that birds that liked to hang out in fetid swamps wouldn't feel at home in undulating grasses. Another basic concept had yet to dawn on me. The *when* of seeing birds was every bit as important as the *where*—and when it came to making personal appearances, many birds were on stricter schedules than Thomas Pynchon. We learned this the hard way after driving 150 miles to see an attention-grabbing species that only nested in a few spots in Michigan. The most reliable place to find the bird was Saginaw Bay.

In past years we had traveled far from home to experience such splendors as a house shaped like a shoe in Hallam, Pennsylvania, Colonel Harland Sanders's first restaurant in Corbin, Kentucky, and a teapot museum in Trenton, Tennessee. But decades of cleaning houses for a living had taken a toll on Linda's back, and she couldn't sit for hours in a car now. Saginaw Bay still lay in reach.

Originally our primary destination had been the German-style village of Frankenmuth, which has acquired such power as a tourist attraction that it's a politically independent entity in Frankenmuth Township—sort of like Vatican City is to Italy. I wondered if we needed a passport. As I researched other places to visit in the area, I discovered Nayanquing Point State Wildlife Area with its fourteen hundred acres of coastal Lake Huron marshes and the largest colony of yellow-headed blackbirds in Michigan. Once I showed Linda a photo of this heart-stoppingly beautiful bird, it pushed Frankenmuth's gingerbread Bavarian architecture into the background.

In western states, where yellow-headed blackbirds outnumber red-winged blackbirds, residents yawn at the spectacle of a coal-black bird that's shockingly yellow from the neck up—just as Vatican City villagers inoculate themselves to St. Peter's. But this half-grackle, half-canary was a spectacle we had to see. Despite its scarcity in Michigan, my online sources assured me how easy the species was to find at Nayanquing Point. Just zero in on the distinctive song—which sounded to me like a red-winged blackbird coughing up a hairball—and you've got your bird.

We were long overdue for a vacation. Linda's parrot Dusty had perfected the art of prying his metal food dish loose from the clamp and throwing it to the floor—scattering seeds as far as the refrigerator. My parrot Stanley Sue had taken to scolding me with loud bell ringing if I made too much noise crinkling a package of tortilla chips when she was trying to sleep. So we revised our novella-length list of instructions, made arrangements with our faithful pet sitter, Jamie, and hit the road. Although fleeing from our birds at home to hunt for another bird across the state amounted to a unique form of masochism, we couldn't resist.

Pumped up by what I had read online, I expected to see the yellow-headed blackbird within minutes of arriving at Nayanquing Point. But we couldn't see much of anything. An impenetrable wall of cattails blocked a throng of singers as we hiked around a pond of unknowable size and shape. I couldn't depend on my ears to locate the blackbird, either. If you had plunked us down in the middle of a rainforest in Borneo, we wouldn't have been more astonished by the incredible musical din. From time to time a red-winged blackbird flitted to the top of a cattail and added its *conk-la-ree* to the noise level. But most of the song makers stayed hidden.

As we hobbled on, frying beneath a rare emergence of the Michigan sun, we caught a peek through the foliage at a black chicken-like bird with a bulbous red beak. Floating among the reeds, it clucked fearfully and paddled away. Mad avian laughter answered, though we could barely hear it above an understory of chatter resembling a cross between bubbly whistles and a finger drawn along the teeth of a plastic pocket comb. We had no idea that these were marsh wrens staking out their territory or that the common gallinule's clucks had been answered by a cackling American coot.

One of the few birds that wasn't busy singing dogged our steps. Linda recognized the black-and-white eastern kingbird by the white band on the end of its tail. He flew to a bush ahead of us, waited until we had almost caught up, then flew to the next bush, warily eyeing us the whole while. I checked to see if he was wearing a tiny earphone, but he didn't seem to be a member of a coordinated security team.

The path narrowed as it took us deeper into the wet. The cattails on our left grew denser as the brush on our right pressed in. Bright yellow balls of fluff with thin red streaks on their breasts sang from each thicket—unless ghosts that cried *witchity-witchity* had claimed it first. Wearing a sooty toupee, a professorial gray catbird lectured us with whistles and squeaks about the folly of vacationing without a machete. I jumped up on my toes to see where we were going and where we had been.

"Nayanquing sure lives up to its name," Linda said. "It's as exotic as it sounds."

We hadn't a clue how to pronounce *Nayanquing* and wrapped our tongues around it differently every time. I decided it meant "loud marsh birds you'll never see." Before leaving on our trip, I should have had brains enough to learn the songs of a few other likely suspects so that we wouldn't feel so disappointed if Mr. Yellow-Head turned out to be a no-show. I also hadn't bothered to investigate what his fellow wetland residents might look like.

"Is that a marsh wren or a sedge wren?" Linda asked when a bird hopped across the path.

"How do you know it's one or the other?"

"It was on the papers you printed out, and the tail stuck up like a wren."

I didn't see it. To ease my claustrophobia, I'd been staring at the sky. Gull-like birds that I assumed were terns cocked an eye at the ground as they sailed overhead. A lone gull rowed the air with short, stiff wing strokes. Scratchy-voiced swallows too quick for the retina zoomed and looped, while a pterodactyl disguised as a great blue heron croaked its displeasure at our intrusion.

When the trail took a bend, the cattails all at once opened up to a silver-surfaced pond. I scanned the edges with binoculars, confident I'd locate the blackbird, whose blazing head would surely leap right out of the background. But my spirits fell as I noticed how easily mallards with flashy green heads and red-winged blackbirds with orange shoulder patches melted into the complicated interface of weeds and water. I thought back to a few days earlier when we had traced the song of a scarlet tanager to a tree across the street from our house and had been mystified that we still couldn't find it. Scale was everything, and it only took a couple of leaves to smother the glory of one of the most brightly colored birds in the hemisphere.

"So much for the easily found yellow-headed blackbird," I said.

Linda put her arm around me. "We're still in a really beautiful place, and we're away from all of the animals."

"We should drop off the parrots here."

A swan with four chubby babies idled past us as we hugged. I couldn't think of anyone I'd rather cling to in the jungle heat than Linda. But the heat was beginning to get to us, and we decided to turn around.

Our friendly neighborhood eastern kingbird escorted us part of the way back. Then a second kingbird buzzed in to take his place, making sure that we didn't try anything funny as we headed for the parking lot. Not for nothing is this bold character a member of what's called the "tyrant flycatcher" family. In *Key to North American Birds*, Elliott Coues singles out the kingbird for its "irritability, pugnacity, intrepidity, and its inveterate enmity to Crows, Hawks, and Owls, which it does not hesitate to attack, either in defense of its nest or just to show its spunk; but in its turn it is attacked and sometimes worsened by the Hummingbird."

I was nowhere near as formidable as a hummingbird. I was wilting, and I jabbed the air conditioner when we got back inside the car.

It made no sense to me that we had visited Nayanquing Point at the height of summer when it teemed with birds, yet we hadn't managed to find its most famous resident. I searched the Web and discovered a posting about Nayanquing from an Ann Arbor–based birding listserv group. The idea of people emailing their sightings as they happened intrigued me. It meant that I could jump in the car, drive clear across the state, and narrowly miss seeing a bird that had flitted around in plain view hours earlier. I cursed the fates that denied West Michigan a similar email group and joined the Ann Arbor list anyway, though I didn't expect to get much out of it.

I read the first few batches of sightings with mild curiosity. Then as the observations continued to flow, a larger picture gradually came into focus. I'd been wondering where the orioles, grosbeaks, and finches had gone that had filled the woods with songs until recently. A poster noted that these birds were still around but they had become quieter and less visible because they had finished courting and claiming territory for nesting.

Although I'd been dimly aware that something called migration took place, I had no idea what a complex and orderly cycle it was. One species or another seemed to be on the move all year. Turkey vultures and sandhill cranes began returning to Michigan from warmer climes in the dreary winter depths of February, while American tree sparrows and juncoes showed up in late fall and stayed until early spring, preferring our deep freeze to the Arctic blast farther north. Even the spring migration was broken down into waves of birds, with red-winged blackbirds trickling back during the first part of March, some swallows, thrushes, and sparrows showing up in April, and the bulk of the warblers, vireos, and flycatchers popping in during May.

I didn't learn all of this from the listserv right away. But when I posted a question about the yellow-headed blackbird, I found out that we hadn't seen the bird at Nayanquing Point because the males had already begun leaving the breeding grounds in July. Linda and I had arrived a couple of weeks too late.

By sticking with the group, I began to learn which birds were winging through southern Michigan. And I would also have the chance to publicly embarrass myself on numerous occasions.

I was lucky to have found an online group whose members included several of the top birders in the state and professional ornithologists. Unlike other listservs that are tailored to experts in search of the rarest of rare species, birders@great-lakes.net welcomes people of all levels of accomplishment, and uninformed beginners of my ilk receive patient answers to the densest questions. Although the group officially describes itself as "a local/regional email list for discussing bird sightings in Ann Arbor, Washtenaw County, and southeast Michigan," I soon discovered it to be a congenial spot for conversing about sightings almost anywhere in the state.

At the center of the generous attitude and high level of civility is the affable and organizationally masterful Bruce Bowman, who has served as list administrator since 2000. Bruce is a retired research scientist from the University of Michigan working in the field of automotive safety. His academic background is physics, mathematics, and engineering. Bruce's website, www-personal.umich.edu/~bbowman/birds/index.html, is awash with scads of crucial information and resources for birding in Michigan.

One of the emails from Bruce's group reported that a rufous hummingbird was visiting a backyard feeder in Leroy Township. This was just outside of Battle Creek, where Linda's mom lived. It made no sense to me, since the range maps in my field guides showed only the ruby-throated hummingbird in the eastern United States—and the rufous hummingbird called the Pacific Northwest home. I was skeptical of finding any bird so far out of place. But we were visiting Linda's mom the following weekend, so we decided to loop over to Leroy and repeat our yellow-headed blackbird defeat.

It didn't feel like a Saturday on which anything out of the ordinary could happen. It felt like any other Saturday. We grabbed a couple of subs and ate them in the little town of Nashville on the way to Battle Creek so that Linda's mom wouldn't have to make us lunch. Keeping an eye out for the telltale pine trees, I still managed to overshoot her driveway. Then we took her to the bank and the supermarket. Back at her house we sat in the breezeway and ate confetti cake with pink icing and a rock-hard slab of ice cream from the garage freezer. Everything was exactly as usual.

"Don't run any water if you don't have to," her mom told us. This stricture had been in effect ever since her well pump had started running rough a year earlier.

"Didn't you finally get a new pump last week?" I asked.

"I don't want to take any chances with the well running dry," she said.

We played two games of Uno, stashed three bags of produce from her garden in our trunk, hugged her goodbye, and headed past Binder Park Zoo toward Leroy Township.

Magee Marsh and Nayanquing Point had been wild places that throbbed with the possibility of encountering rare birds, quite unlike a tidy ranch-style home with a bicycle leaning against the porch. None of the other houses on the street looked capable of concealing a rufous hummingbird, either. "Shouldn't there be a bunch of people here?" I asked Linda as our front tire bumped the curb.

"You'd think so to see such a rare bird."

We walked into a backyard sheltered by trees and a massive lilac. On a table next to the door lay a spiral-bound notebook. Nothing will happen in this ho-hum place, I thought. A nectar feeder hugged shadows near the house. A second feeder dangling from a shepherd's hook was identical to ours—way too ordinary to attract an exotic species. I flipped through the notebook. "Saw the bird four times," Steve from Jackson had written that morning. It was already ancient history, like reading Henry Stanley's dispatches from the Congo. Nothing was happening now. Near the feeder a metal sunflower sculpture basked in the attention as our eyes swept the yard.

Moments later, a burnished copper shape buzzed out from the lilac, tilted to greet a blazing glint of sunlight, sip, sip, sipped from the feeder, sip, sip, sipped again, turned to show us an orange throat, and then zoomed back to the lilac. It came back as a bee in gilded armor, once more as a bubble of molten glass, and finally as a ball lighting with a beak. We drank in long, close looks at the magnificent little guy with metallic red-brown upper parts, dark wings, and that fiery iridescent throat that only winked on like a neon sign when it caught the sun at the right angle.

"Saw the bird four times," I wrote in the notebook. I wanted to add, "Still no yellow-headed blackbird," but the comment seemed petty under the circumstances.

"I hope that bird's okay," Linda said as we left the neighborhood. "I hope he isn't lost and gets stranded here this winter."

I assured her that he wouldn't. I didn't know if I was telling the truth.

The idea of this gorgeous little bird stranded thousands of miles from home nagged me, so I emailed Allen Chartier, who had posted the Leroy Township sighting to the online group. I didn't know Allen from Adam at the time, but he turned out to be the author of *A Birder's Guide to Michigan* with Jerry Ziarno and also a nationally known hummingbird expert who wrote the introduction to the *National Geographic Field Guide to Birds: Michigan*.

Rufous hummingbirds are amazing flyers. They breed in the Pacific Northwest north to southern Alaska and then make the long flight all the way to southern Mexico every winter. Instead of migrating directly south, they jog east and move southbound along the Rocky Mountains. "A few thousand of them—a tiny percentage of the population—deviate even a bit farther east to end up spending the winter along the Gulf Coast," Allen told me. "Even smaller numbers make an even more easterly track, with the result that there are records of rufous hummingbirds from every eastern state."

So the birds that visit Michigan aren't lost. They're playing out a strategy that's only now becoming apparent to hummingbird researchers like Allen.

"What appears is happening, though we have no solid proof yet, is that they have a two-stage wintering strategy with two winter homes," Allen said. "This has been noted in the Deep South where most of the banding studies have been done, where birds arrive in August or September and spend until Christmas or New Year's at one site. Then they seem to move to a second site where they remain until March, when they begin their long migration back to the Pacific Northwest."

I asked Allen why the birds would bother with the two-stage migration instead of doing it all in one fell swoop. "It is my hypothesis—not even close to being proven—that these birds stop at the first site to complete a molt, up to a point when it is 'suspended,' and then they molt the last bit—their outer primary feathers—before they move northwest in March." Banding studies by Allen and other ornithologists have proven that birds that have lingered into late December during single-digit daytime Fahrenheit temperatures have returned in subsequent years, "solidifying the reputation of the rufous hummingbird as a very hardy species."

Exactly the kind of little bugger that could kick an eastern kingbird's butt.

My close encounter with the rufous had energized me more than any bird I'd seen since the rose-breasted grosbeak. It made up for my failure to find the scratchy-voiced yellow-head, and I didn't have to slog through a marsh under the broiling sun to find it. This was practically drive-up birding. But I still loved the yellow-head for leading me to experts like Bruce and Allen and their mindboggling depth of knowledge.

All of this new information about birds was a good news/bad news thing. The good news was that habitat, behavior, species migration dates, and thousand-mile detours all played major roles in birding, so that finding birds wasn't just a matter of blundering into them. The bad news was that habitat, behavior, species migration dates, and thousand-mile detours all played major roles in birding, and with so much to absorb, I was better off just hoping to blunder into birds.

Awash in a flash flood of complexity, I was like Carla/Marla/Darla standing at the top of the hill in view of the great waters beyond and choosing the familiar comfort of ye olde plastic wading pool instead. Not that respite awaited me inside our own four walls. Linda had embarked upon a project that brought wild birds closer than ever. She was busy raising orphaned baby birds for a local rehab center. If I'd known how much trouble they would be, I might have tried to talk her out of it. Not that I ever managed to talk her out of anything.

CHAPTER FIVE

Close to Home

N ot long after we were married, Linda called me into the basement to investigate a mysterious peeping sound, which we traced to the base of the chimney.

"There's something trapped inside," she said. "It sounds like baby birds."

Taking advantage of a state-of-the-art soot clean-out system dating back to 1917, I slid out two loose bricks, plunged my hand into darkness, and retrieved what Linda determined was a chimney swift nest with three featherless chicks. Her attempts to feed them canned cat food from a toothpick failed. The tiny things kept their beaks clamped shut except to cry for mom.

Acting the part of favorite auntie, Linda looped wire around the nest, crawled out the upstairs window, and scaled the roof. "Oops," she said, bracing herself with one arm against the slope to keep from falling. "This is slipperier than I thought it'd be."

"It's a metal roof," I told her as I watched through my fingers. Her hard-soled shoes hadn't been designed for daredevil climbs. Raising herself on tiptoes, she somehow managed to anchor the nest to the top of the chimney so that it hung down inside. A few minutes after her descent, the mother swooped down to the chicks.

A decade later, I thought back to the chimney swifts as we banged on Peg and Roger Markle's back door. Linda had volunteered to foster orphaned baby starlings, and I wondered if we were doomed to struggle with another clutch of recalcitrant birds. I needn't have worried. I shrank back with an audible gasp when Peg flipped open the lid of a pet carrier and I was greeted by shrieking yellow beaks that looked more like a bouquet of carnivorous flowers than eight individual chicks. She demonstrated the feeding technique by filling a syringe with ochre-colored goop, sliding it into the open mouth and down the crop of a gaping bird, pressing the plunger, then moving on to the next starling. She fed them with assembly-line precision as if syringe and crop were as closely associated as a car engine's piston and cylinder.

"What's the matter, Bob?" Roger asked with a chuckle when he saw my shock. I had expected the chicks to be charming, passive little creatures rather than raucous food-intake machines.

"Don't pretend you didn't just eat," Peg told the starlings after she had made a few more passes with the syringe. "Your new mom and dad just saw you."

Peggy and Roger treated us as if we'd been friends for years, even though we had just met them. They were trusting us with their babies, after all, which made us more than casual acquaintances. Peg and Linda were hardly strangers, though. They had spoken several times on the phone after a neighbor of ours had taken an orphaned baby squirrel to Peg. The neighbor had described Peg in such glowing terms that Linda called to ask if we could see her animals. Not only could we see them, but after gauging Linda's enthusiasm for critters, Peg also decided that Linda might make a good foster parent.

From the stately appearance of the Markle house just north of downtown Grand Rapids, we never would have suspected that it was the home of Wildlife Rehab Center, LLC. But once we had passed through the gate to the backyard, we slid into a parallel universe where the animals were clearly in charge. A squirrel raced down a tree to rest its front paws on my shoe in hopes that I had treats to dispense. A plump blue jay too young to have developed a crest assumed a wing-flapping begging posture next to Linda. Canada geese with hissing pink mouths tested our mettle, but we had pet geese of our own and weren't intimidated, so they left us alone. Inside the house, we found cages and containers holding songbirds, ducks, baby opossums, and more.

"How long have you been doing this?" I asked Peg.

"Legally or illegally?" She grinned. "I got my state license about fifteen years ago. That was for mammals. After that I took classes and passed the test for federal, which allowed me to do birds."

"It started when I was working on Dick Bennett's boat," Roger said, referring to Dr. Richard Bennett, the vet for the John Ball Park Zoo in Grand Rapids. "He was doing wildlife rescue with his assistant, Dr.

Durham, and we offered to take care of an adult squirrel that got hit by a car. We named him Davey, after Dr. Durham."

"If you'd come over you would have seen Dave Durham and Roger, two grown men, sobbing when that squirrel died," Peg said. "The whole thing just sort of snowballed from there." She told us that she and Roger plus a couple of volunteers care for fourteen hundred to sixteen hundred animals a year. During peak summer months they may wait until midnight to sit down for dinner before staggering off to bed.

"How often do I feed the babies again?" Linda asked.

"Every two hours. Just during daylight hours," she said. "Birds aren't like baby squirrels or opossums, which you need to feed twenty-four hours a day."

Linda only did two or three house-cleaning jobs a week because of worsening back problems, and she could take the carrier with her on the job. I worked away from home each morning and could help with the birds in the afternoon. So this seemed totally doable. I didn't realize how quickly it would wear us down.

Linda was every bit as heroic with the starlings as she had been with the chimney swifts. Even though their care didn't demand a death-defying climb up the roof, they did require constant fussing over. One of the fussiest aspects was temperature regulation.

"What are you doing?" I asked as she rifled through a cluttered bedroom shelf.

"Looking for more magazines. The babies are getting too hot."

I followed her into her study to solve the mystery of how copies of the *New Yorker* would cool off her birds.

Because the featherless starlings lacked a mother to sit on the nest and keep them warm, Linda followed Peg's advice and placed a heating pad underneath their carrier. Even with the thermostat set on "low," too much heat was building up. So she layered magazines and towels between the pad and carrier until the inside temperature felt right.

Feeding the babies was far more work intensive than she had imagined. Two hours feels like a long time if you're suffering from a migraine or watching network television. But if you're raising baby starlings, two hours between feedings barely gives you time to catch your breath. I marveled at the stamina of a mother starling, which needs to catch thou-

An orphaned Baltimore oriole raised by Linda came back often to eat grapes.

sands of insects a day for her chicks. Mom hunts for beetles, grasshoppers, crickets, weevils, and worms, while also stealing a few cherries and other cultivated fruits. She may visit the nest as often as twenty times an hour during morning hours when the babies are young. According to Christopher Feare's book, *The Starling*, these visits level off to around three hundred a day for chicks ten days old, then decline a bit until the babies hit the ripe old age of fifteen days and leave the nest.

In comparison, we didn't have it bad, especially since Linda wasn't forced to forage for bugs. She combined kitten chow, chicken baby food, a few drops of liquid vitamins, and water in a blender, sucked it into a syringe, and squirted it into the youngsters' mouths as Peg had demonstrated. She had to learn the finer points of feeding on her own, such as only delivering a small shot of the glop at a time. Otherwise, with a shake of the chick's head, our wall and Linda acquired a spattering of ochre polka dots.

Adult starlings eat up to one-third their body weight each day, and the proportion for the big fat chicks we raised was probably higher. We discovered that most of what went into the birds came out later.

Thankfully a degree of hygienic behavior was hard-wired into their tiny brains. When nature called they raised their rear ends up and over their margarine-dish nest and dropped a blob of poop, which held its shape due to a thick coating of mucus. This allowed mama bird to keep the area around the nest clean by neatly scooping up the ovoid dropping in her beak and depositing it elsewhere. We had some success duplicating this feat with deft fingers and a tissue, though it was easier simply to replace the newspapers that we were using by the bale.

In just over a week, the starlings made the startling transformation from digestive tracts with legs to fully feathered beings. Linda moved them from their carrier into a cage and arranged them neatly on a perch for feeding.

"Come and see how good they're being," she told me. "I've got them all in a row."

As soon as she poked the syringe through the door, the birds threw themselves at her hand, each vying to be the first one fed. She placed them on the perch a second time, but the lone bird that stayed in place wasn't any easier to deal with than the bouncers and flappers. He remained still with mouth wide open until her finger pressed the plunger, then he jerked his head and got striped with slurry. I retreated upstairs as she dabbed the squawking bird with a washcloth.

I had been looking forward to the next phase of the starlings' development, when they would begin eating live food on their own. I hadn't realized that their parents didn't simply teach them to hunt but also to recognize insects as food. That was Linda's job now. Peg had told us that crickets would be an excellent choice, since their movements would attract the hungry birds. She was right. The crickets from the bait shop fascinated the starlings as they hopped around inside the cage and then exited to spread chirping cheer throughout the porch. I threaded adding machine tape in and out of the bars at the bottom of the cage to stop them. But the crickets had all the time in the world to plot their escape under the beaks of the clueless birds and join their liberated compatriots.

"Maybe once they taste a cricket, they'll get the hint," Linda said. Overcoming her squeamishness over grabbing a living, legged creature with tweezers, she dropped one into the begging mouth of an adolescent.

"I think he likes it," she told me. "He isn't spitting it out." He didn't have to. The bird continued gaping as if it hadn't been fed and the insect jumped out again.

Complicating the feeding process, the starlings had tired of confinement, and at least one managed to shoot past her whenever she opened the cage door. "Can you help me get him?" she called upstairs. I didn't even have to ask where the bird had landed. As if drawn by a magnet, the starlings loved to hurl themselves into an inaccessible corner behind the exercise bike, which also appealed to our thriving expat cricket colony.

At Peg's urging, Linda switched to mealworms. "The babies are finally eating on their own," she told me. "Half of the worms I gave them are gone already."

She found the missing worms when she pulled up the topmost layer of newspaper. The starlings watched fascinated as the exposed worms wriggled their way to the edges of the cage to slide under the paper again, but they weren't tempted to peck at them. Because the worms weren't as agile as the crickets, Linda had an easier time snagging one with tweezers and keeping it down the hatch of a gaping bird. Once the first starling formed a favorable opinion of this new food, others followed suit. The next step was getting the birds to grab a worm from the tweezers—then from a jar lid that she held in front of their beaks, and finally from a lid on the floor of the cage.

After the birds were eating on their own, Linda released them in the yard. Four returned for handouts for several days, swooping down on us when we stepped outside. "Don't even go out there without the slurry," she advised. "I had one of them on each shoulder and another one on my head."

With a little help from me, Linda had spent almost a month on just this single batch of birds, and we wondered how Peg and Roger mustered the enthusiasm to care for hundreds of birds at a time, summer after summer. It also made us appreciate the struggles that both parent birds and chicks go through to survive. And Linda surprised me by immediately volunteering to take on a second batch.

Our bushy, wooded property didn't provide the ideal habitat for starlings. They prefer foraging on the ground in large open areas. Starlings did visit us occasionally, and the juveniles we'd raised lingered contentedly until literally moving on to greener pastures. Their tenure got me thinking about out-of-place birds in general and the rufous humming-bird in particular. If a nonbirder could come up with a stunning species in her backyard, a wannabe birder like myself ought to be able to discover something, too.

I combed our woods for rarities, but whenever I found a bird singing an unfamiliar song, it turned out to be the familiar tufted titmouse per-forming yet another variation of its two-tone repertoire. Hoards of mos-quitoes further discouraged me, so I took my search beyond our proper-ty to greener, less buggy pastures, ponds, and forests. While training my binoculars upon an uninhabited bush, trying to turn a striped leaf into a prairie warbler, the idea of my quest first revealed itself to me. Despite the odds against it happening, I vowed to find a "good bird" on my own, a rarity that other birders would want to see. And I would keep looking no matter how long it took, even if it meant interrupting a game of bingo to peer out through the slatted blinds at the old folks home.

Much to my surprise, within a month I seemed to have already found my bird.

It was September, and a huge migration was under way. Shorebirds that nested in the Arctic were leaving their breeding grounds for the long flight to their wintering digs on the bottom of the globe.

Some of the birds put pedal-to-the-metal on the trip. Bar-tailed godwits nesting in western Alaska flew over seven thousand miles to warm their tail feathers on New Zealand beaches. According to the *National Geographic Reference Atlas to the Birds of North America*, the god-wits are believed to make the trip nonstop. But the certified nonstop flight record belongs to a small shorebird called a red knot, which flew five thousand miles in six days and six nights to reach Southern Brazil from North Carolina. The International Wader Study Group—consisting of researchers from the United States, Canada, Argentina, Britain, and Australia—confirmed this by attaching a geo-location device to the bird and reporting about it in the organization's 2010 bulletin.

One of the prime spots in the state for seeing some of these endur-ance travelers turned out to be in West Michigan at a site that in its own way was every bit as exotic as Nayanquing Point. The Muskegon Waste-

water Treatment System attracted plovers, sandpipers, and all kinds of
aquatic birds to a pair of 850-acre "sewage lagoons" that were actually
cleaner than many small inland lakes.

I prepared for a visit by flipping through my field guides, which devoted page after page to shorebirds that looked discouragingly alike
with their brown-on-top-and-pale-underneath plumage. The sandpipers
had spindle-like beaks. The plovers had stubby ones, including the ball
field–loving killdeer. Those were the only differences I could see until
the whimbrel, godwits, and curlews caught my attention. They helpfully
sported monstrous beaks that were nearly as long as their bodies. My
plan was to keep an eye out for them or for any other bird that seemed
wildly out of place. Posts on the mailing list reported numerous rarities,
so Linda and I made the fifty-mile jaunt to the Muskegon Wastewater
facility, anticipating vast flocks of mud-probing waders that were sure to
contain at least a couple of penguins.

The place was different than we expected. "Where are we supposed to
walk?" I asked as we drove along narrow dikes, squinting through a wall
of weeds at the concrete-strewn pond edges below us. "There's nothing
like a shore to walk along to see shorebirds."

"Slow down, I think there's something down there," Linda said. A
half-dozen peeping birds flew off in a panic at the crunch of our tires on
the gravel. The few that remained took it on the wing as soon as I raised
my binoculars.

"There's got to be somewhere to walk," I said. "I can't see anything
from the car."

Near the entrance to the treatment ponds we found a paved dike
wide enough to stash our car and to wander along without the birds seeing us immediately. Except that there weren't any birds. On one side of
us stood walled storage cells filled with water whipped into a froth by
roaring machines. On the other side, a vast lagoon was peppered with
dots that tried to resolve themselves into distant ducks when I squinted
through binoculars.

"That smell is making my eyes water," Linda said.

The chemical stench grew more piercing at the west end, where we
discovered a cell that had been drained. Dozens of shorebirds wandered
the puddles pecking at the mud. Concealed behind the wall, we could

have gotten decent looks at them, but the smell became overpowering and pushed us back to our car. We wondered how the birds put up with it and why they didn't choose a deserted stretch of Lake Michigan beach instead.

Just as we started to drive away, Linda pointed out a large bird with a gray body and white-striped black head on the edge of the east lagoon. It allowed us leisurely looks as it preened. It wasn't a shorebird. It was something even better.

"A northern goshawk," I said. "They're really rare this far south."

"Are you sure that's what it is?"

Raptors can be notoriously difficult to identify because they have so many plumage variations depending on age, time of year, and other factors. *The Sibley Guide to Birds* devotes a two-page spread to the red-tailed hawk showing twenty-three color variations for this common bird. But I didn't make my identification lightly even though I had barely glanced at *Sibley*. I was piggybacking on an expert who had reported the Wastewater goshawk to our birding group a day earlier.

I couldn't claim the bird as our own since someone else had posted it first. But later that week on my way to work, I saw a raptor zip over the parking lot of a Meijer hypermarket and identified it to birders@great-lakes.net as a northern goshawk based on my poorly firing memory cells. I waited excitedly for the reaction to this "good bird." Polite silence ensued. Three days later near the same spot, I saw a raptor perched on a utility line and in the morning glare fancied that I'd seen the white rump patch diagnostic of a northern harrier. I reported my find and couldn't have been prouder of myself. Then I received an email gently informing me that harriers almost never perch up high and that the habitat was totally wrong for a bird that for decades had been know as a marsh hawk.

My two "good birds" were figments of bad observing, and I decided to take a few months off from posting until my skills improved. The northern harrier gaffe got me thinking about the degree to which light affected what I was seeing. Under certain conditions, the most familiar species could turn into an unknown. I noticed this particularly with crows in flight. If sunlight reflected off oily feathers at just the right angle, their wings might appear to be white. Ruminating on this, I sent the following message to the listserv on April 1.

"Have you every gotten tricked by a crow when you're trying to make a species identification? Today I was walking down a trail when I spotted a crow, who told me, 'There's a Kirtland's warbler in the field down by the river.' He was lying. It was actually a yellow-rumped warbler."

Thus I ushered in my new self-appointed role as clown of the birding group.

When spring rolled around Peg asked us if we would be willing to raise more birds. We hadn't needed a permit for the starlings. Like house sparrows and pigeons, starlings are considered introduced species and therefore aren't protected by the DNR, even though all three species have been here long enough to have earned their citizenship.

Pigeons came to our shores first. Colonists with a taste for squab brought the bird officially known as the rock pigeon to America at the turn of the seventeenth century. Considering the ratio of pigeons to Puritans today, the birds got the better deal.

House sparrows arrived next, released in New York City in 1851 by bird enthusiasts who wanted to populate Central Park with all of the birds mentioned in Shakespeare's plays. According to the *National Geographic Reference Atlas to the Birds of North America*, more house sparrows were introduced in San Francisco in 1871 and in Salt Lake City in 1873. By 1900 they had spread across the entire continental United States. I'm relieved that Shakespeare didn't write about the cassowary.

We don't merely know the year when the European starling was unleashed upon America. We also know the name of the man who unleashed it. Eugene Schieffelin was chairman of the American Acclimatization Society, an organization that followed the misguided notion of making immigrants from Europe feel at home by importing European plants and animals. In 1891 Schieffelin released a flock of starlings in Central Park, and they flourished. "These birds are resident throughout the year, and, as they have already endured our most severe winters, we may doubtless regard this species as thoroughly naturalized," notes Frank M. Chapman in *Birds of Eastern North America* in 1895. By 1930, Eugene's starlings had spread across the eastern United States, and by the 1960s they were California Dreamin' with the rest of us.

Although Linda and I were willing to scatter additional starlings across the landscape, Peg had different plans and obtained the paperwork for us to raise and release protected species. The two baby robins she gave us turned out to be so well mannered compared to the star-lings, I checked their wings to make sure that they were birds. Instead of throwing themselves around the cage screaming for food, they perched demurely, managing an occasional amiable chirp to remind us that it might be mealtime. When we unlatched the door to feed them, they kept beaks closed until the syringe was an inch away. Then they snapped open their mouths, flicking their wings and twittering engagingly as they ate.

The robins had come to us fully feathered and looked a lot like a smaller version of an adult, exaggerated upright posture and all. The main difference was a cream-colored, black-speckled breast instead of an adult's trademark brick red. We considered the kids to be every bit as attractive as the grown-ups.

Like the starlings, the birds needed convincing to switch from slurry to mealworms. Their placid demeanor made it less challenging for Linda to toss a worm into their mouths. After a few fumbles they got the hang of live food and hopped down to the floor of the cage to help themselves. They still considered themselves dependent upon Mom, which present-ed an unexpected problem once Linda released them into our yard.

"Sweetheart, I can't get the babies to come down from the hackberry tree," she told me. I had been cleaning parrot cages in the dining room and had witnessed the robins' stubbornness through the window.

"They'll come down when they're hungry, won't they?"

"They're hungry now. But they don't understand that I can't fly up to feed them. I put their dish of mealworms on the ground, but they don't seem to see it." She went back outside and started calling, "Babies! Babies!"

I ran down to the basement and stuck my head out the door. "That won't help. They don't know that word."

But it did help. Like starlings, robins are ground feeders, and Linda's urging gave them extra encouragement to swoop down onto the lawn for the syringe. She placed their mealworm dish where they had landed, and within a few days the mealworms became their main food. After they had emptied the dish, they would flip it upside down. We weren't sure whether this was clumsiness or a signal that they required a refill. As they became more independent, their attitude toward us changed. Though they still wanted squirts from the syringe, they exhibited a "come hither, go away" attitude, suddenly unhappy that the procedure involved a human hand. They would stay at arm's length on the grass or embed themselves deep inside our spirea bush.

"I can't reach you," Linda complained as she tried to keep her balance while leaning into the branches.

Soon they were dining exclusively on mealworms and flitting off at our approach. This rejection stung us a little, but we were thrilled at how well they were doing on their own. From time to time we'd see them pecking the dirt in Linda's vegetable garden or sprinting through a patch of groundcover and then pausing to listen for insects. Attendance at the mealworm bowl tapered off—and then the birds disappeared. They either retreated into woods or, following the lead of the starlings, left us in search of more luxurious lawns.

It had been a model orphan bird release, progressing smoothly from dependence to self-sufficiency. We missed them terribly.

Not every release went so well. After the robins, Peg gave us two Baltimore orioles and two common grackles. The orioles acted even more laid back than the robins. One of them was so indifferent at mealtime that Linda was upset but not surprised when she found it dead in its margarine tub. People brought birds to Wildlife Rehab Center for a variety of reasons. A whole nest of babies might arrive if mama house sparrow had the bad manners to raise a family under the tarp of a sailboat. Or kitty might have grabbed and dropped a blue jay. The orioles had come in with lots of other youngsters after a storm had ripped through the area and knocked them out of their nests.

"They might survive a day or two and everything seems fine, but they can have an internal injury," Peg told Linda. "That's probably what happened with your baby."

When raising wild birds we tried not to fall in love with them, because we had to let them go—and for their own well-being, we didn't want them to bond too closely with us, either. It was difficult to hold back from a little one like our oriole. He had no siblings to lean on and looked to us for everything—yet he was so undemanding the robins seemed like divas in comparison. No bird gave us less trouble switching diets. When it came time for a fruit-eating bird to begin eating fruit, he readily accepted diced blueberries and grapes. Soon he was scarfing them up on his own, though I couldn't resist letting him nibble from my fingers.

We considered all of the birds to be "Linda's birds," because she was the primary caregiver. But I was too attached to this oriole to think of him as hers. "I knew you were busy with the laundry, so I fed the little guy for you," I'd tell her. Or, "I needed to use up the last two grapes, so I gave him his food a little early."

After we released him, he didn't stray far. He spent hours in the hackberry tree just outside the basement door or in the spruce just west of the house. His plumage matched his sunny personality and made him easy to spot. Unlike a boldly patterned, blazing orange-and-black adult male Baltimore oriole, he wore muted shades of gold with an olive-colored back and dark wings. He was particularly hard to miss when he flew in for food and perched sedately upon our wooden gate. I'd leave diced fruit for him on the pickets but couldn't help myself from strolling out to hand feed him a few bites.

Seeing him frequently relieved me at first. But he seemed so dependent upon us that after a while I started to worry. "I hope he's able to live outside on his own," I told Linda.

"He'll have to learn. We can't keep him as a pet."

"Oh, no, definitely not," I said, though part of me wished that we could. "He's got to figure things out for himself. Otherwise I don't know what we'll do."

One day after work I saw him around one o'clock and again two hours later. At six o'clock as I headed out to the barn to shoo in the ducks, geese, and hens, I noticed that the last bits of fruit I'd put on the fence hadn't been touched. Taking a cue from Linda, I wandered through the yard and then the woods calling, "Baby!" But the only response I received was a scolding from a blue jay. I made another search the following afternoon, but I never saw him again.

It just went that way with some birds. They would arrive like clockwork day after day and then abruptly stop coming instead of tapering off. Had they ventured too far and gotten lost? Had they been grabbed by a predator? Occasionally a missing bird returned a day later, but not our oriole. We hoped that his instinct for independence had suddenly kicked in, and he'd gone off to succeed on his own.

A pair of orphaned grackles cheered us up. It didn't bother Linda that they were as demanding as starlings. With their bright red mouths and begging croak, their clownish aspects won her over. One bird was larger than the other, and during feedings he had the habit of opening his beak and begging from the smaller bird. Lazier than his brother, he was less inclined to learn to perch, preferring to stay in his margarine dish even after he had outgrown it.

Because of his sedentary nature, large size, and enormous appetite, Linda dubbed him Jabba the Hutt, after the *Star Wars* character. "He's too lazy to swallow a worm," she said. "His brother will eat them. But when I put one in his mouth with the tweezers, he stays there with his mouth wide open and his brother grabs it. So he begs from his brother, but his brother gets food from him."

He must have finally found satisfaction in the live food that surpassed the pleasure of idleness, because Linda got Jabba to snatch a dangling mealworm from the tweezers and later to pluck them from a bowl. He seemed well on his way to self-sufficiency until she released both birds.

"He's back to only eating from the syringe," she told me. "He lands on the gate right where the oriole used to go, and he begs for slurry."

"I thought he was eating mealworms off the ground."

"He started to. But now he only comes for worms when his brother is with him, and instead of eating the worms, he opens his mouth and begs. The other grackle gets every single worm."

Later in the week Linda urgently called me into the backyard. "Something's wrong with Jabba. He's only standing on one leg, and he's been doing it all day."

Sure enough, I found Jabba perched on the back gate with one foot clutching a picket and the other leg folded against his body. He ate from the syringe as if nothing was wrong. I closed my hands around him and picked up the protesting bird. Linda carefully flexed the leg and checked the bones but couldn't find anything wrong.

Jabba stayed away most of the day after that, afraid that the terrible medical procedure would be repeated. When he returned after dinner, he continued to stand on one leg. But the next day Linda greeted me in the driveway with the good news that he had turned into a two-legged bird again. We never knew what had happened. But being handled had instilled a reluctance to venture too close, because he avoided the gate now and ate mealworms from the ground instead.

The following spring, the usual sprinkling of grackles appeared in our woods. Most of them kept to the woods except for a virile-looking male with a sleek black body and iridescent blue head who didn't fly far when we stepped outside to see him.

"I'll bet that's Jabba," Linda said, and I couldn't argue with her.

While we were busy raising the robins, I nearly fell off my chair when I read a post from Darlene Friedman to the online birding group. She had driven clear across the state to find a couple of rare species on Pinckney Road. I took it as a personal humiliation that someone who lived 117 miles away had found these rarities a mere 7 miles from our house. Then I faced the fact that I probably would have missed them even if they'd been flitting around in clear view across the street from us.

Darlene is a southeastern Michigan veterinarian who has loved birds since she was a child, though she didn't start birding until she attended college in central Illinois. A passionate bird photographer, she came up with a novel way to help her get pictures. She birds by ear, by car. She picks out what looks like a promising road in her *DeLorme Michigan Atlas & Gazeteer* and then drives along that road with her windows open and ears on the alert for telltale songs. "It's a good way to cover lots of ground," Darlene told me. "I've seen birds in seventy-eight of Michigan's eighty-three counties."

One of Darlene's birding excursions led her to Pinckney Road in Ionia County, just east of Lowell, where Linda and I live. Cruising down this rural road she heard a Henslow's sparrow and a sedge wren singing in a field. Finding either of these rare and secretive birds would make me seriously giddy. Finding both would do a nitrous oxide number on my naturally depressed demeanor. So after getting detailed directions from Darlene, I hustled Linda out to the car.

Since Darlene had located the birds by ear, I listened to the appropriate recordings before we left but was treated to a completely different ditty as we pulled up alongside a mailbox across from an empty house. To a tinkling, rollicking song that one of my field guide compared to a broken music box, we watched a bird that appeared to be flying upside-down burst out from the grass and settle in a tree.

"Is that a bobolink?" Linda asked. Darlene had mentioned bobolinks, too, so I knew that Linda was right.

Songbirds that are more than one color tend to be darker on top and lighter underneath. This makes birds on the ground less visible to hawks and other predators who view them from above, while perched or flying birds seen from below are less visible against the sky. The male bobolink hadn't read the memo, though. It's the only American songbird that's solid black underneath and mostly white on top, and the upside-down plumage gives it a weird look in flight.

I'd never seen a bobolink before and was drinking it in through binoculars when I heard a clicking, buzzy sound that took me back several decades—dialing the number 1–1–7 with my ear pressed against the receiver of an old-fashioned rotary telephone.

"I'm hearing a sedge wren."

"I see it!" Linda said. "Straight ahead standing on top of that weed, singing." On top of two weeds, to be exact, straddling them in classic sedge wren style, though he dropped back into the underbrush before I could focus on him. As Linda wandered off to get a better look at the bobolink, I continued scanning the field, hoping to see Darlene's Henslow's sparrow. A minute or two later, I had my bird. With some fumbling I managed to grab my brand-new Canon Powershot, zoom into the smudge perched upon a stick, and click off five photos before the bird grew camera shy.

Back home I couldn't wait to post the photo on my birding group's photo-sharing site. The previous year's northern goshawk and northern harrier gaffes still heaped hot coals of embarrassment upon me, even if everyone else would have long forgotten them. Though Darlene had discovered the Pinckney Road birds, reporting that they remained for other birders to see would help restore my standing, I decided. Contributing to my redemption was a credible photo of this hard-to-find bird. It was blurry. It was grainy. It was poorly lit. But, by God, it was my own photo of a Henslow's sparrow.

Only it wasn't.

Allen Chartier broke the news in an email—informing me that I had just posted a nice photo of a sedge wren. If there's one thing that birders hate, it's publicly making a misidentification, and I had gone three in a row. Bruce Bowman tried smoothing things over for me by posting his hopelessly blurred picture of an ovenbird, which he joked was the worst photo ever taken of a sedge wren. Other members chimed in with anecdotes about their own wrong calls. It didn't make me feel better. It made me feel like the poster child for feeble-brained birders.

I'll never learn, I told myself, but I had actually learned a lot by watching Linda raise the baby birds. Although little of it had to do with identifying species without humiliation, I could recognize a begging starling, grackle, robin, or Baltimore oriole when I heard them in the woods. And to add a much-needed jolt of levity to my altogether too serious search for that one good bird, I soon enlisted the help of my friend Bill Holm, a nonbirder who had his own peculiar reasons for assisting me.

CHAPTER SIX

The Adversary

When Linda released our last birds of the summer, they didn't act like our other birds. All five cedar waxwings melted into the woods, never to return for a handout.

"I guess we give the rest of our mealworms to Peg," she said.

We suddenly understood the true meaning of "empty nest syndrome," though we had no shortage of demanding birds in our house. After ten years with us, my African grey Timneh parrot, Stanley Sue, had died of a tumor, and her absence left a hole in my life that could only be filled by another African grey. Eighteen-month-old Bella had an easygoing temperament—for a parrot—and she wasn't particularly noisy—for a parrot. Alongside her whistles and spoken self-assurances that she was a "big gray pretty pretty," she had perfected a squawk that didn't bother me. But Linda found it piercing and headache inducing. Discovering that the noise annoyed Linda, Bella made squawking a priority, because driving people crazy is how parrots amuse themselves.

Not even earplugs helped. "The sound goes right through my forehead," Linda said. So when Linda was in the kitchen/dining room area with the pet birds, if Bella got too noisy we hustled her to a "time out" cage at the other end of the house.

One Saturday morning while in transit through the living room, she launched herself from my hand and flew in circles. White cat Moobie high-tailed it into the bedroom as if pursued by a hawk. Imperious "diluted tabby" Lucy barely deigned to raise her eyes as she groomed herself on her chair. As I scooped her off the floor, a flutter of black and yellow passed the window. From its tiny size and blown-leaf flight as it headed for the woods, I recognized it as a warbler.

After putting Bella in her cage, I grabbed my camera and binoculars. "I'm going out to look for birds," I hollered. "Be back in a few minutes."

The screen door slammed behind me as my feet hit the grass. I heard a muffled response from Linda back in the house and kept on moving despite a pang of guilt. I should have asked if she wanted to come along. But I had been waiting for weeks for the warblers to arrive, and one small straggly flock might be all that we got this fall. I didn't want her to slow me down, which was ironic since one of my original attractions to birding was that it gave us something fun to do together. I had become altogether too serious, and the fun was dribbling away as I started to view the birds as my adversaries.

During the summer I had cut a path through the weeds with a grass whip. Though physical exertion didn't agree with me, I took satisfaction in laying waste to a swath of vegetation with each swing of an arm. As I scurried along my little avenue, I heard the *chick-a-dee-dee-dee* call and remembered that my friend Dirk Richardson had once told me that warblers like to hang out with black-capped chickadees, because the chickadees are skillful foragers that lead them to food.

Suddenly the birds were on both sides of me, close but eaten up by trees. I saw only parts and pieces. An olive back. The glint of a yellow breast, dissected by leaves. A black-and-white tail. An eye with a ring around it. Then the fully assembled birds tumbled through the air to the river, chickadees leading the way. One jiggled behind a leaf, teasing, shy about showing himself. I barely breathed, binoculars growing heavy, until the warbler broke out, perching in plain view, but as a silhouette against the sky.

I cursed the trees and all of their leaves. It seemed unwise to curse the sun. So I cursed the birds as they took flight. I cursed the thickets that prevent me from leaving the path. I cursed the world, the cause of my stupidity. And I cursed a bear, any bear. Where was a bear when I needed one to put me out of my misery?

I thought of my sister Joan and my childhood neighbor Terry Gray catching grasshoppers in the vacant lot next door while I hung back terrified of handling the bugs. Terry delighted in grossing me out by showing me his brown-streaked hands. "They spit tobacco on you when you catch them." This never troubled Linda, who was also a grasshopper grabber. One of her fondest memories of childhood was finding a spotted salamander in the pump house and enjoying the feel of its cold, damp skin when she picked it up. That wouldn't have been me.

When the long-eared owl like this opened its eyes, it stared right through me with haughty, spooky grandeur.

Even humorous images of animals scared me when I was little, including *Howdy Doody Show* puppet Flub-a-Dub, a doglike creature with a duck bill and parts from six other creatures. The Flub-a-Dub fear factor paled in comparison to Morrell Gipson's *Mr. Bear Squash-You-All-Flat*. This book about a bear who sits on and squashes woodland animals' homes gave me nightmares as a child and still evoked echoes of dread.

Unable to find a bear, I found another warbler on my trudge back toward the house. The drab-on-top, some-yellow-underneath bird zipped across our all-but-dried-up seasonal pond and embedded itself in a bush. I tracked it almost to the edge of the "finger puddles"—two spots that stayed wet all year due to water seepage from an underground spring. I needed to get closer, so I plunked down my foot on a mat of creeping Charlie.

I sank in mud up to the top of my left calf-high boot, pitching forward and catching myself on my right knee. The fall jolted me, but it didn't trouble me at first. I had avoided landing face down in the water, and my brand-new pair of $350 binoculars were safe. Although I'd lost my bird, I carried a mental image of two other warblers I'd glimpsed, and I'd look them up when I got home.

I tried to stand and couldn't budge my left boot. With rubber slip-ons it should have been easy to free my stocking foot, but the mud gripped so tightly, I might as well have been wearing lace-ups. I pulled and pulled, and the mud pulled back.

Our house stood at the top of the hill. Through the same leaves that had hidden the warbler, I could see Linda moving around as she put breakfast on the table. I considered screaming, but she would have the radio on, and I had left my cell phone in my dresser. This was justice— my punishment for bolting out into the woods without her. Surely I was panicking, I thought. I only needed to relax, and my foot would slide right out of the boot. No good. Millions of years from now, explorers would puzzle over my fossilized skeleton. On top of my bones they'd find the remains of Mr. Bear Squash-You-All-Flat.

Behind me was a tree. From the tree a branch conveniently hung down to the ground. Raising myself to a wobbly standing position, I swiveled and managed to catch hold of it. With a mighty two-handed heave that nearly pulled my arms out by the roots, I uprooted my foot from the vise of my boot. The boot wouldn't budge when I yanked at it, forcing me to hobble back to the house on one galosh and one mud-encrusted sock.

"Is that you, sweetie?" Linda asked when I slammed the basement door. No, it's Long John Silver, I wanted to say. But I thought it best to keep my mishap to myself until I could think of a valiant way to frame it.

"Breakfast will be a little late," she hollered down the stairs. "One of the eggs from the barn was bad, and I have to start all over."

Putting on a spare pair of galoshes, I grabbed a shovel. With difficulty and a protesting *thwack* from the mud, I succeeded in prying the boot loose. The underground current must have created a quicksand-like super suction effect, and I was fortunate not to have blundered into the muck with both feet.

Back at home I retrieved my mental photos of the two warblers and ran them through my reference books. I identified one as a Kirtland's warbler and the other as a Connecticut warbler. This was the same as a strikeout, since the odds against finding a Kirtland's in our woods were beyond astronomical, and the rare and secretive Connecticut would have skulked through the ground cover instead of flitting from tree to tree. I had mixed up the parts and pieces of several birds and combined them in Flub-a-Dub fashion.

Next time I'd go looking for salamanders instead.

Happy to take a break from misidentifying warblers, I discovered from my online group that the shorebird migration continued in full swing. In addition to the usual look-alike plovers and sandpipers, people were reporting species at Muskegon Wastewater that even a know-nothing like me could pick out of a birdie lineup. I had no intention of returning to that dismal spot, I told myself. If I wanted an exercise in futility in a location hazardous to my health, I could let my boots lead me back to our underground spring. My resolve wasn't exactly rock solid, though.

"My back isn't good enough to sit in the car for so long," Linda said when I asked her to take the fifty-minute drive with me again. "Didn't you tell me you'd never go back?"

"I just thought you might be interested. I absolutely don't want to go."

My friend Bill Holm's enthusiasm shocked me. "Birding at a wastewater facility? How can I say no?"

I didn't have any birding friends. I didn't have many friends, period, and out of desperation I had given Bill a call. "I have to warn you, it's ugly and stinky."

"When do we leave?"

"And you can't really get out and walk around. You pretty much have to do the whole thing from your car."

Bill insisted on driving. When he picked me up, he overflowed with merriment at the idea of what we were doing. Most shorebird enthusiasts use high-powered spotting scopes to identify the skittish birds at a distance. Bill laughed until his face turned red when I lugged out my Celestron astronomical telescope with its six-inch diameter tube and counterweighted tripod and dumped the assembly in the backseat.

"At least you'll be the first to log the constellation Cygnus," he said.

As we merged onto I-96 and he nudged his Volvo "Turbo" to ninety mph, I interrupted his chortling to read a list of reported birds that I wanted to see. "Black-bellied plover, American golden-plover, Wilson's phalarope, those are all pretty easy to identify."

"Let's do what all the other liars do and just pretend we saw them."

I was shocked. "Don't you want to actually see some birds? That's why we're going."

"I would consider it a bonus, yes. But I doubt that any of the birds you mentioned are there. I doubt that most of those birds even exist."

Bill was briefly speechless when we tooled up the incline to the dike system and he saw the first of two lake-size lagoons. We watched through binoculars as an employee in a rowboat took water samples several hundred feet offshore. "Has anyone else reported the Ty-D-Bol man?" he asked.

Not far from us a trio of birders took turns peering through a spotting scope at a shorebird perched on the end of an outflow pipe. "Want to see what they're looking at?"

"And leave the car?"

I strolled over and introduced myself, instantly forgetting everyone except Scott Manly, whose name I knew from the online group. Not only was Scott an excellent birder, but he was also the pastor of three churches in nearby Ionia. After getting a telescopic view of a nonbreeding plumage dunlin—which might as well have been a Stalin for all I knew about it—I told Bill that our best bet for seeing birds was to putter around in search of other birders. So we scanned the dike roads with binoculars and found what appeared to be a sizable crowd on the south side of the east lagoon.

As we got closer the black-coated birders turned into fence-sitting turkey vultures at the foot of an immense landfill. The number of crows and starlings scavenging along the fence line defied calculation. But on top of a steep hill, a bulldozer teetered and tottered, and in its wake the most gulls I'd ever seen in my life shrieked and fought each other for first dibs at the trash being dozed. Just as I was about to remark that we had arrived at a little corner of hell, Bill braked hard and asked, "Is there any way we can get closer to that?" He leaped out the door and snapped at least fifty photos of the seething flock.

"That's pretty smart," I said when he slid back in. "You can study your pictures later to find out if there are any rare gulls mixed in with the ring-bills."

He looked at me as if I were insane. "It's not a picture of the gulls. It's a picture of the guy in the bulldozer." After we had wrung the last dribble of charm from the setting, we drove along the east side of the lagoon, scattering birds ahead of us. "You did see all of those people by the cement thingies when we first came in," Bill said.

"No. They must have found something. We should go back there."

"Hang on." He increased our speed, raising a cloud of dust that could be seen in Ohio.

"I didn't tell you, but we're supposed to have a permit to be here. So we might not want to go so fast."

He jammed on the brakes, pitching my telescope against the backs of our seats. "It would make a nice shortcut if we could get to that road down there," he said.

"Unfortunately we're going the wrong way, and there isn't room to turn around."

"Watch me." I kept my eyes on the floor as he nosed his front tires to the edge of the drop-off, throwing his car into reverse when a wheel started to slide down. "Attaboy, Turbo." A backward thrust bottomed us out with a thump that should have taken out his exhaust system. "Almost got it!" he cried as he spun the wheel and skidded us forward. Gravel pinged against the undercarriage like buckshot. I gripped the seatbelt, wondering if I should lunge for the door handle if we went over. After two more jolts, we somehow avoided a plummet and zipped back to connect with the parallel road.

I couldn't remember the last time I'd been with Bill that he had expressed a desire to do anything. He was always perfectly happy/annoyed to do whatever I did. But as we approached the main service drive he asked, "Where was the area that smelled so bad that you and Linda couldn't stand it? That's what I want to see." When I described it, he said, "Yes, the cement thingies. That's where those people were."

I still hadn't seen any notable birds so far other than the dunlin. But the best and worst parts of the morning speedily approached as Bill cruised past the administration building and took us back up the ramp to the lagoon where we had started. Scott and the other two birders had left, and I didn't see anyone at what I'd learned were called the Rapid Infiltration Basins, where Linda and I had met our Waterloo. We'd found shorebirds there a few weeks ago, so I decided it was worth another look.

"There's no room to park down there," I said. "We'll have to park here and walk." I unbuckled my seatbelt. Bill didn't slow down.

"Turbo will make room. You don't want to carry the Hubble Telescope all that way."

The gulls that lined the concrete wall in front of churning water must have been used to vehicles. Only a few lazily flapped away as we slid by them into a turnoff. "I don't think we're supposed to park here," I said, but he was already out of the car and pointing at shorebirds below us.

After making a quick scan with binoculars, I lugged the Celestron out of the back seat. It was the first time I'd tried it as a spotting scope, and it fought me quite literally at every turn. The equatorial mount was designed for following the celestial arcs of stars and planets and not for up-down, right-left navigation. The optics presented another problem. Everything is upside down through an astronomical telescope. Lunar and planetary maps are printed that way for observers. So to view birds right side up I had to turn my back toward what I wanted to see while bending down over the scope. It was clumsy, but the image of a black-bellied plover was razor sharp.

Lucky for me, the bird was in breeding plumage and easy to distinguish from typical brown-on-top, white-underneath shorebirds thanks to its brown, black, and white-on-top, black-underneath coloration—and a crisp white dividing line between upper and lower parts. Nearby a similarly shaped bird stood around looking for something to do. I checked my field guide to verify that the white-speckled-brown-on-top, brown-speckled-white-underneath little beauty was a previously reported juvenile American golden-plover.

"Sure enough," said Bill without much caring what he was assenting to.

Both plovers nest so far up in the Arctic they have to fly south to visit Santa. They show up in Michigan each year on the way to or from the bottom of the globe. To catch a glimpse of them you have to pick just the right moment to be in just the right marsh, flooded field, or wastewater management cell. They're so striking that if either landed on your head, you'd take it as a sign from heaven. Not all admirers appreciated them for their physical beauty alone. Barrows in *Michigan Bird Life* says of the American golden-plover, "They are always good eating, and especially in autumn when they have fed for a few weeks on seeds, berries, and insects, at a distance from salt water."

Hearing footsteps on the gravel, I pretended to be so preoccupied with my viewing that I hadn't heard footsteps on the gravel.

"Seeing any good birds?" a man in a multipocketed jacket asked. Fifty feet away, a dusty SUV idled with its passenger door open.

"Black-bellied plover and American golden-plover," I said proudly, peering backward through my Celestron. I stepped aside and gestured that he was free to look.

He gave my fat-tube telescope a bug-eyed stare and with a quick up-down flick of his binoculars said, "You are correct. Black-bellied plover and American golden-plover." He pointedly rhymed "plover" with "hover," and not with "over," as I had done. He motioned the driver of the SUV over. "I've got a couple of nice plovers here."

We had been dismissed because of my mispronunciation and stargazer scope, and Bill wasn't having it. Reaching into Turbo's trunk, he fished out an empty Smirnoff's bottle, held it in the air, and said, "If you want to see even more *ploovers*, you should try our special bird-attracting fluid." He pretended to take a swig and offered the bottle to them.

Multipocket shook his head. He said to his driver, "I think Jim has the Wilson's phalarope at the south end of the center dike."

"I'm not surprised," Bill told him as they walked away. "This special bird-attracting fluid has been known to pull in the *floop-de-dope*."

So much for my introduction to the flesh-and-blood birder community. I only hoped that none of these guys was one of my virtual buddies. For all of ten seconds, I was furious at Bill. Then I found myself laughing so hard I could barely stagger back to his car. Unlike the rest of us, he knew how to have fun birding. And as we followed the SUV at a discreet distance, piggy-backing on their observations, he spotted a pair of birds on his own that turned out to be horned grebes. I had never seen one before.

Just before he left the property, he slammed Turbo to a halt and showed me a large brown raptor on the ground in a grassy field. Paging through my field guides, we both agreed that it could be nothing other than a golden eagle.

"We found a really good bird," I said. "And we don't even have snooty attitudes."

"We do have my special bird-attracting fluid."

"I know. But a golden eagle!"

Like a bowling ball rolled down the hill of a city street, this misidentification would have unexpected consequences.

I should have learned from my previous claims of having seen a "parking lot" northern goshawk and northern harrier. But after failing to find another all-brown raptor in my field guides, I felt sure enough about my find to write up my sighting and hit the send button. Even though the golden eagle is a western bird, a few make their way east, and I had read reports of them showing up at Muskegon Wastewater in previous years.

Almost immediately I received a congratulatory email from Scott Manly, who asked me where I'd found the bird. I described the place, and he wrote back that he had seen a rough-legged hawk with "dark morph" brown plumage variation at that same spot, and could this have been the bird I'd seen?

I dug in my heels. "No, it was definitely a golden eagle," I wrote. "It looked exactly like the pictures in my field guides."

Scott mentioned details about the plumage and the beak structure of the bird he'd seen and wondered if he could email me a photo that he had taken. I knew when I was licked, and after kicking several trees and hollering at our ducks, I sent an announcement to the group that I'd been wrong again. It had been a rough-legged hawk. "Sorry for yet another erroneous report."

"You can't be expected to know what that eagle looks like when you've never even seen it," Linda said—which didn't make me feel a whole lot better.

It was childish. It was petty. It was egocentric. But from then on I cringed whenever I saw a posting from Scott. The good pastor had gotten the goods on me. Someday I'd even the score, although I didn't know how. Months would pass before I got my chance.

Identifying warblers became much easier when October rolled around. There was only one species in our woods, the late-to-migrate yellow-rumped warbler. The "butter-butts" were so plentiful, they outnumbered our goldfinches and chickadees put together.

They bustled through the woods, cartwheeling through the crowns of trees and looping out to snag a bug in flight. They kept tabs on one another with sharp *tchep* call notes—and by flashing the big yellow rump patch above their tail. The males were easy to identify with their streaked sooty upperparts, streaked sides, and yellow patches on the sides, head, and rump. The females and juveniles were duller, but the yellow rump gave them away. We watched as they stuffed themselves on clusters of bright yellow berries.

"I don't know what kind of tree has berries like that," Linda said. She tried to grab a handful to take home, but she couldn't reach them. This turned out to be a good thing.

I posted a photo of a yellow-rump gorging himself and asked if anyone in the birding group could identify the tree.

"Those are poison ivy berries," Allen Chartier emailed me.

"They're not growing on the ground," I replied. "They're dangling from tree limbs."

Allen said that if I took a closer look I'd find woody-stemmed poison ivy plants climbing up the trees and spreading out to mimic branches. I thanked him for the information and thanked heaven that Linda wasn't two feet taller. As far as birding disasters went, poison ivy berries in the hand would have trumped a boot in the mud.

The yellow-rump is one warbler that warbler chasers may not be pleased to see. So many come through in the spring, they can be a distraction that causes birders to miss the less common species traveling with them. It's a different story in the fall, however. They are one of the last warblers to migrate, long after most of the choice species have come and gone, so they aren't such troublemakers. And unlike other autumn warblers that stay only hours as they pass through an area, yellow-rumps can linger for weeks as long as they can find something to eat. And we had a bumper crop of poison ivy.

They cheered us on our daily walk through our woods. We found as many as three dozen working the trees along 150 feet of riverfront. They were constantly in motion. It took patience to catch more than a glimpse of them, due to finely tuned instincts that sent them catapulting off a branch a nanosecond before we found them with binoculars. When they zipped from tree to tree, it didn't look like they were flying under their own power. It looked like they were being blasted by the wind. But I had no doubt about their motor control when it came to foraging. Within two weeks they had stripped the trees of berries, and their numbers dwindled.

Late one October afternoon in the slanted rays of a low sun we watched bees, wasps, and hoverflies gathering pollen from clumps of wild asters. In the shallow river water, whirligig beetles resembling animated sunflower seeds bumped into one another, going nowhere. Collisions were so frequent that we dubbed them the "excuse-me" bugs. The insects were our only companions now—the warblers had moved on.

"All of the other birds are back at the house," Linda said. She was right. Thanks to the titmice and finches there were so many seed hulls under our feeders, I had to break out the snow shovel to scoop them up. I should have used a different shovel, because its appearance was all the prompting it took to bring on the first snow. The woods seemed even quieter now, though countless tracks told us there was no shortage of animal life.

We met a hearty soul paddling a kayak. When Linda asked if he had been seeing any birds, he didn't act surprised by the question. "If you like ducks, winter is the time to see them on the river. You've got your mergansers, you've got your golden-eyes, you've got other ducks you don't get in the summer."

"Ducks in the winter?" she asked as the kayaker floated away. We could hardly believe it and vowed to keep taking our walks no matter how bad the weather got.

Winter chuckled at our vow. Heavy snow soon buried our path. A sudden thaw revealed its edges. Then a refreeze turned everything to ice. After that I confined my skating and falling to the immediate yard, content from a safety point of view to do my birding through the dining room picture window. We had several dozen American tree sparrows—which we identified by the smudgy spot on their otherwise clear breast—and a few dark-eyed juncos scratching the ground like hens. Nothing noteworthy showed up until the afternoon in January when the phone was ringing as I walked into the house.

"Sweetie, is that you?" Linda said. I wanted to ask whom she expected to find in our dining room, but I didn't bring that up because she sounded excited. "Your cell phone was turned off, so I've been calling and calling and calling to tell you that right now at this very moment I'm standing on Washington Street next to the cemetery looking at a long-eared owl. If you hurry, you can see it, too."

My initial response was panic. I was here—the owl was there. What if I didn't get from here to there in time? My second response was to wonder if this could even be true. "How did you find a long-eared owl?"

"Brian Drake called about an hour ago and said that he was out walking his dog and saw some bluebirds making a big fat fuss and going after something, so he looked to see what it was, and he found a long-eared owl in the tree, and it's still sitting there."

We barely knew Brian and Pat Drake except by their reputation as accomplished local birders, and it surprised me that he had phoned us about the owl. But I had left a message on their answering machine the previous summer about the Pinckney Road birds, so he was probably returning the favor. Well, a long-eared owl was a big hooting deal, easily worth Darlene's Henslow's sparrow, sedge wren, and bobolinks combined. I'd only seen one owl in my life, the barred owl that haunted our yard on summer nights asking anyone in earshot, "Who cooks for you?"—a question that had to have mystical significance, since owls were too busy being folkloric entities to waste their time on trivial matters.

I put on the winter jacket, boots, hat, scarf, and gloves that I had peeled off moments earlier and jumped into the car with camera and binoculars. A mere seven minutes of drive time separated me from Linda, but I cringed as each swipe of the wipers across the windshield suggested the beats of the owl's wings as it left its roost, never to be seen by me—or by anyone else.

As birds go, the long-eared owl isn't unusually secretive. Some sparrows and marsh birds are far more reclusive. But this owl is scarce in

Michigan, and just by nature of being an owl, the long-ear is difficult to find during the night hours when it's active. In the daytime it retreats to a hiding place inside thick foliage. When approached, the owl flattens and stretches its body to blend into a tree with such success that after I skidded to a halt and trudged through the snow to meet Linda, for the longest time I had no idea what she was pointing at.

"Right up there, under those branches, close to the trunk."

"I don't see a thing. Are you sure it didn't fly away?"

"I'm looking right at it," she told me. "You have to look up under those front branches that are in the way."

I shook my head. How frustrating to be within twenty feet of an owl and not be able to see it. "I see a bunch of green, I see branches, I see the trunk, and that's all I'm able to see." I was getting whiny. Linda grabbed me by the shoulders, walked me two paces forward, tipped my head back, and waved a finger toward an unremarkable brown shape that I had taken for a strip of bark. "Good grief," I said. "It's an owl." The rabbit-like "ear tufts" (which are really only feathers) gave it away. Then I noticed the orange face. The bird opened its eyes and stared right through me with haughty grandeur spooky enough to embarrass me as a gawking intruder. It seemed impossibly tall and wraith-like. Pete Dunne's *Essential Field Guide Companion* calls it "a Great Horned Owl drawn by El Greco."

The owl had embedded itself so deeply in the branches, my autofocus camera wouldn't focus. Only by contorting my body was I able to get a few clear shots. I watched the bird for a while, but it wasn't doing anything, and soon the thrill of observation gave way to discomfort at the January cold. I followed Linda home, and as I took off my jacket the curious notion hit me that I should call Scott Manly about the owl. Brian Drake had reached out to us out of the blue, and I felt that I should reach out to Scott. It would be my way of evening up the score—which had never meant getting back at him for my embarrassment over the golden eagle gaffe. It meant making up for my querulous emails disputing his ability to identify a rough-legged hawk.

"I'm definitely interested," he told me. "The long-eared owl has been my nemesis bird." I took this as an indication that Scott shared my view of birds as adversaries, but then he explained that "nemesis bird" is a term for a species that a birder repeatedly tries and repeatedly fails to find.

After spending the next thirty minutes congratulating myself for doing a good turn, I decided that it wouldn't be so good after all if Scott couldn't locate the bird, even though I had given him precise directions right down to the address of the house across the street. Linda hadn't seen the owl until Brian Drake had come outside and pointed it out, and I had been helpless until Linda played puppeteer with me. Suiting up one more time against the elements, I arrived back on Washington Street to see Scott wandering through the cemetery a block away from Mr. Long Ears.

Scott was thrilled to finally get to see the owl. But it wasn't until I received an email from him later that I realized this sighting had more significance than simply crossing a species off his "nemesis bird" list and adding it to his "life list" of observed species.

"I drove to Belding this morning to make sure some handbills were processed by the post office for some upcoming religious meetings I was conducting on science and faith," he wrote. "A bit anxious about that venture, I had been praying about it on my drive, and casually requested of the Lord some token of His presence—like an owl, because owls have always had special significance to me. So when you called, I couldn't believe it and wasted no time getting to Lowell to check it out."

I asked Scott what owls meant to him, and he said, "Owls pop up in profound moments in my life. I was driving to church one snowy Sabbath morning, having had quite a time wrestling in prayer with no apparent answer. To be honest, I was really struggling. And as we drove to Portland, I again thought, 'I really could use a hug from God right now, like an owl or something.' A minute or two later, I looked up through the windshield at a largish bird in the branches right over the road, and to my utter astonishment, it was a barred owl!"

Scott struck me as the epitome of a "scientific" birder who knew when and where to look for species, keenly tuned into time of year, habitat, and bird behavior. But obviously he brought a whole lot more than a bean-counting approach to his passion. It was all part of a grander context that had deep connections with his life and beliefs.

Even the smallest bird is large enough to hold the biggest notion of what it is about. I admired the austerity of the sandpipers and plovers that breed in the most barren and remote Arctic places only to fly thousands of miles south to winter at the bottom of the globe. As penance for shunning humanity, they forage along the way in wastewater treatment ponds, maintaining dignity as I ogle them and mispronounce their names. And the yellow-rumped warblers deserve praise for making lemonade out of life's poison fruits.

But owls occupy a far more portentous position. They turn our concept of what a bird is upside-down. They aren't fragile, puny, or timid, and unlike other raptors, they aren't night blind. They embrace the darkness in a death-defying, three-dimensional manner that seems to laugh at the idea of mortality. The fiercest wolf or jaguar that stalks and kills at night still clings desperately to the earth with its toes, while the owl risks its life each time that it leaves the safety of a roost and flings itself into the void. What must daytime with its garish cartoon contrasts look like to such a master of subtlety?

For a scientist's explanation of how an owl works its nighttime magic, I asked wildlife biologist and owl expert Stacey O'Brien, author of the *New York Times* bestseller *Wesley the Owl: The Remarkable Love Story of an Owl and His Girl*.

"Owls have excellent vision at night, but that is not what they use as their main tool for spotting and homing in on prey," Stacey told me. "Their entire physiology is set up for them to hunt using their sense of hearing, which is so sophisticated that it's almost beyond our ability to comprehend. The large area that our brains devote to visual processing is instead devoted to auditory processing in the owl. Literally, there are layers of neurons specific to processing different frequencies of sound. They have an auditory map of the world in their brains in the same way that we have a visual map of our world."

According to Stacey, when an owl is hunting and senses prey, as he homes in on it, he always keeps his face pointed directly at his target. "His face is like a satellite dish—perfectly set up to gather auditory data accurately and feed it to his beautifully adapted brain to create an elegant 3D sound picture of the exact location of his prey." The facial disk that collects this auditory data is so meticulously set up with each feather funneling the sound so precisely that if a small chunk of facial feathers goes missing, "the owl will over- or understrike the prey, missing it altogether. It's an astonishingly elegant system and stunningly accurate," she said.

An owl's ears aren't symmetrical like ours. One ear is placed low on his head and is angled upward. The other is high on his head and angled downward. This odd arrangement gives the owl an auditory advantage. "When we hear a sound, we have to turn our head to triangulate it because we hear it across only one plane, but owls don't have to do that extra step." Stacey told me that an owl can navigate a thick forest without flying into branches and twigs because not only can he see them with his excellent night vision, but he can also hear the way the air flows around them. "It's as good as a very clear image would be to us," she said.

In addition to studying owls in the lab and in the wild, Stacey had the privilege of adopting an injured barn owl named Wesley who was unable to be released to the wild. "When I was living in close quarters with Wesley, he often responded to what I thought was nothing. But whenever I investigated, I would find that there was something, such as a bug crawling along the ground or behind a wall. He was hearing the tiny footsteps!" Shortly after moving into a new apartment, Wesley heard the running water in the bathroom just once, drew an auditory map in his brain, and used it to fly directly to the room and land on the sink.

"He was constantly challenging my sense of how we know where something is or what it is," Stacey said. "It's hard to conceptualize how completely visual we are until we come across a creature who uses an entirely different sense as his main source of information."

While Stacey wowed me with the science of owl abilities, Scott made me think about the meaning of birds. He made me realize that in my teeth-gritting efforts to become a birder, I risked losing the sense of wonder that had once wrapped me around the little toe of a rose-breasted grosbeak. I had gone from gazing awestruck at the wildness of a pair of red-headed woodpeckers to wondering if it would be cheating to report the owl as my own find—I was the first member of the group to find it, after all—instead of enjoying a gorgeous owl for its own sake. Linda didn't keep a species list, and her delight in seeing her fourth, fifth, and sixth eastern towhee was every bit as profound as her first. Then there was Bill Holm, who just wanted to have fun. He had the right idea with his bottle of special bird-attracting fluid. The spirit of the thing was what really counted.

I could do better than trying to make birding into a contest pitting me against the birds and against other birders. But I didn't have to mend my ways immediately. Nobody but Linda, Brian Drake, and I knew that Brian had found the long-eared owl, and neither Brian nor Linda subscribed to the birding group. After wrestling with my conscience, I decided to grab some glory and report the owl to birders@great-lakes.net after all—giving Brian Drake full credit for the discovery, of course.

Although I hadn't moved an inch closer to finding my own "good bird," I took heart that even in winter one was nearby waiting to be seen. In fact, it was even closer than I suspected. Within a year, my dreams of a finding a rarity in my very own backyard would come to pass, but with a bittersweet twist.

CHAPTER SEVEN

Not in My Backyard

M onths had passed since the long-eared owl sighting. And now something else extraordinary was happening. As I stared out the window at our birdbath in disbelief, I tried thinking again about the significance that birds had in my life. But it was difficult to think with Linda laughing at what we were seeing. I couldn't help laughing, too.

The string of small events that led up to my slack-jawed wonder at the scene outdoors had begun a few days earlier indoors when Linda told me, "Howard isn't eating." I wasted no time getting our pet dove to the vet. It hardly seemed possible that Howard had turned seventeen. While he still seemed hale, hearty, and sassy overall, we knew that birds can hide an illness or injury in order to maintain their position in the pecking order. An obviously weak individual might get harassed by other birds who don't want a laggard threatening the well-being of the flock. Things like this made me glad I wasn't a bird, or I would have been driven from the neighborhood years ago.

Dr. Richard Bennett, veterinarian for the John Ball Zoo in Grand Rapids, examined Howard and told me that he had a crop infection. "Here's where it started," he told me, holding the squirming dove and pointing to pinkish spot on his beak. "It looks as if he's been bitten by another bird."

We always let Howard fly around the room with our parakeets before dinner. Mostly he chased the smaller birds, though in recent years he had spent time fending off his little blue-and-white admirer, Harvey, who amused us by trying to mate with him. In his ardor, Harvey must have nipped Howard's beak.

"The infection is his beak isn't serious, but it's caused a crop infection, and that can be reason for concern," Dr. Bennett said. He told me that unlike a parrot's or parakeet's beak, which has no more feeling than a fingernail, a dove's beak carries a supply of blood. "It's sensitive to pain, which is probably why he isn't eating, but it's very important that he eats. If there are any soft foods that he likes, give him those. And if he won't take them, you may need to tube-feed him."

I returned home with an oral antibiotic and a resolve to tempt Howard with all manner of delicacies, because I wanted to avoid force-feeding him at any cost. I'd been down that road years three earlier with our parrot Stanley Sue, and I didn't want to go there again. It's one thing squirting food into the crop of a gaping baby bird and quite another trying to get past the clamped beak of an uncooperative adult.

While I was busy rooting around in the refrigerator looking for leftovers, Linda chopped a few strands of cooked spaghetti into rice-size pieces, scattered them across the countertop, and opened the door of Howard's cage, and within seconds he was stuffing himself. I should have been ecstatic, but I wouldn't take yes for an answer. "We're not out of the woods until he's eating seeds," I said. Then I proceeded to worry about him every moment of the day, envisioning worst-case scenarios during waking hours and bouncing in and out of sleep throughout the night. Even when I managed to push Howard out of my mind, a nameless dread clung to me like the black cloud over Joe Btfsplk's head.

The next day was Labor Day. Instead of sitting around the house listening to me complain that the vet's office was closed and we couldn't rush Howard in if some obscure emergency materialized, Linda said, "Why don't we go to Hoffmaster Park? You can look for birds, and I'll look for stones on the beach."

Muskegon County's P. J. Hoffmaster State Park was one of our favorite spots, with its windswept dunes, three miles of Lake Michigan shoreline, and meandering paths through the woods—all great spots for finding different types of birds. As it turned out, we didn't need to traipse any of these for me to score a species that I'd been trying to see for years.

The white-breasted nuthatch was common in our yard and one of the first birds Linda had taught me to recognize due to its habit of perching on a tree trunk upside-down. I could barely bend over to tie a shoe without feeling woozy, so I appreciated the nuthatch's head-under-heels equilibrium. Then I learned that the white-breasted had a cousin

This highly unusual yellow-rumped warbler had been under my nose in
our backyard for weeks when top-gun birder Caleb Putnam noticed it.

in Michigan, the smaller, zippier, red-breasted nuthatch, which sports
a black racing stripe through the eye and orangish underparts. They're
year-round residents north and west of us, visiting southern and eastern
parts of the state in fall and winter but staying away from their pine forest haunts whenever I searched for them.

We rolled up to the visitors center at Hoffmaster Park and were
about to hit the trail when Linda darted inside the building to use the
bathroom. I followed as far as a wall of windows overlooking an artificial
pond and immediately spotted a red-breasted nuthatch at the water. Its
thereness made me doubt what I was seeing. The reality was somehow
both more and less than I had expected, pitting a flesh, blood, and feathers individual against an idea of the bird that I'd envisioned from my
field guides. It was more delicate of body than I'd imagined, less like a
white-breasted nuthatch and more like a wren in its darting movements.
It amazed me merely by existing, and that amazement knocked everything else out of my head—including my worries about Howard.

Linda joined me in time to see the nuthatch just before it shot back into the woods. My amazement lingered, contributing to a feeling of openness and calm as we followed the walkway up a dune, then down again to the beach. I puttered taking photos of tiny shorebirds called sanderlings as they played tag with waves on the sand. Linda became totally absorbed with her hunt for stones and beach glass, following the shoreline, sanderling-like, until she dwindled to a speck in the distance. For once, I didn't even check my watch. Hours, days, and maybe even weeks passed before the speck turned back into a person whose pockets were loaded with treasure.

Linda showed me her finds—a Petoskey Stone, a heart-shaped stone, a possible agate, a chip of polished green glass—but I was stuck in bird time with mental eyes still fixed upon the nuthatch, and I kept talking about the nuthatch on the hour-long drive home.

As I stashed my binoculars in the bottom drawer of the dresser, Linda hollered the excellent news that Howard was eating seed. Then she said, "Sweetheart, come quick. What's this bird that's splashing around in our birdbath?"

It was the same urgent voice I'd used so many years before when I called her to the window of her cabin to identify my first rose-breasted grosbeak. A red-breasted nuthatch flapped its wings in our birdbath. It stopped to fix me with what I took to be an ironic gaze. Then it flew off.

I wondered how this was possible. What did it mean that I saw a red-breasted nuthatch at home after seeing the first one in my life somewhere else on the same day?

"Maybe he'll stick around for the winter," Linda said. But we never saw him again.

Our hopes rose in December when a second red-breasted nuthatch appeared. He left after a couple of days. The only other interesting species to brave the snow was a yellow-rumped warbler who occasionally showed up at the suet feeder. Members of the birding group told me that while the vast majority of yellow-rumps migrate south, a very few may overwinter near rivers in Michigan. I posted a photo and didn't give the bird another thought for weeks.

I did keep thinking about what birds meant to me. I felt peaceful, totally dialed into the present moment while searching for them, and not nearly as alienated from the world. A flash of wings had sufficient power to derail my internal monologue, but unlike Scott I couldn't attach a transcendental meaning. The best I could do was to conclude that the significance of birds was that they had become significant in my life. If the reasoning seemed circular, the circularity followed the route of the red-breasted nuthatch species that first appeared fifty miles away and then looped back home for me.

I hadn't forgotten about my quest for a rare bird. I regularly scanned the bushes for an ostrich or albatross, but opportunities for finding new species seemed to diminish as winter took hold. In early January it heartened me to read a report of a flock of snow buntings that regularly descended upon a farmer's field near Lansing. The white-winged, white-breasted snow bunting would be a "life bird" for me. Even better, the poster noted that a few Lapland longspurs could be traveling with them, and Mr. Lapland was a fairly rare fellow. In my fervid imagination, other rarities might fall in with them, so I went through my reference books and boned up on northern birds known to visit the comparative sauna of southern Michigan during the winter.

The weather broke a few days later, skyrocketing the temperature up to 20 degrees Fahrenheit by 11:00 a.m. I probably wouldn't do better than this until spring, by which time the buntings would be a melting memory. So I bundled up, turning my car heater up to the Molten Lava setting. The backseat held a scarf, a ski mask, an extra sweater, and a pair of Linda's snow pants. I almost had enough raw material to construct a second Bob.

Following the instructions I'd printed out from an email, I piled into a snowdrift near the corner of Desolate Tundra Avenue and Impoverished Farm Road a few miles south of Lansing. In front of me stood a boarded-up house that leaned so far to one side, I expected Buster Keaton to rise from the grave just in time for it to fall on him. Twenty feet from the back door, a television antenna rested its limbs on two short stacks of cinder blocks. Guided by this landmark, I trudged through glittering sun and deepening snow until I reached the designated metal fence.

In hand and over my shoulder I carried my secret weapon, a compact birding telescope with 20–60X zoom eyepiece fixed to a collapsible tripod that permitted me to pan left and right, up and down, instead of locking me into equatorial arcs like my far heavier and ridiculously cumbersome astronomical rig. Best of all, the new scope let me face what I wanted to look at.

Shivering, I directed my attention toward an ice-encrusted field dotted by weed stubble. A plume of black smoke rose from the Lansing Consolidated Power and Pollution plant. Scanning the frozen wastes with binocs I caught a ripple of brown and white on the ground. Gotta be a bunting, I decided. Switching to the scope, I twiddled with the focus knob to sharpen the view of a Snickers wrapper impaled on a twig.

I had vastly underestimated the vastness of the fields that I needed to survey for the presence of a sparrow-size bird that could easily disappear into any of a few thousand ploughed furrows. I grappled with a surge of optimism when I brushed across an extremely distant flock with my binoculars, but my telescope turned the prospective buntings into a gaggle of Canada geese.

I knew that patience was the key to birding and resolved to stay put no matter how long it took. Surely the bunting flock would be visible soon, swollen as it had to be with the cold weather companions that I'd researched in my field guides. In addition to the Lapland longspur, I expected the pine siskin, common redpoll, hoary redpoll, white-winged crossbill, red crossbill, pine grosbeak, and evening grosbeak. I should have paid attention to habitat. These are finches of northern forests, while buntings and longspurs are ground birds of the tundra. According to Chapman, Lapland longspurs have the habit of "squatting just behind some clod, and, as their colors are nearly matched to the soil, they are not easily observed, nor will they move until you are within a few feet."

I didn't move from my spot because there was nothing to move forward toward. As one of the biggest clods in the area, I hoped to attract them if I waited quietly. The temperature had turned pleasant, thanks to the bunting-esque absence of the usual clouds in the Michigan sky. The warm sunlight convinced me to unzip my jacket, relying on a cocoon of body heat to keep me comfortable. The bubble of warmth clung to me like my hopes of still seeing my grail birds until a stiff wind rose up from nowhere and turned the world back into an icebox.

The freezing gusts blasted me broken kite–style back to my Ford Focus. I barely pried the door loose from the grip of winter and with difficulty pulled it shut behind me. As I glanced at the boarded-up farmhouse, I could have sworn it was leaning in the opposite direction now.

Driving past an adjacent woodlot and spotting a *No Hunting* sign tacked to a tree, I fought a moral battle with myself, only deciding not to alter it to read *No Buntings* for want of a marking pen.

I hadn't really expected to find the longspurs and other rarities, but I naively never doubted that I'd find the buntings. Chilled not just to the bone but chilled for all time, I wrapped myself in a blanket at home as I checked the birding group, hoping to revive my spirits with accounts of other birds pursued but never seen. Instead I read bunting and longspur reports on the eastern side of the state.

How far would I have to drive to find a decent bird? As it turned out, I wouldn't have to drive anywhere at all. I received an email a few days later informing me that I might be hosting a very rare bird in my own backyard.

"Do you have more photos of the yellow-rumped warbler that's visiting your yard?" Caleb Putnam asked me in the email. "The photo you posted seems to be showing a bird with a yellow throat. That would suggest the western Audubon's subspecies, and there are only two accepted records of Audubon's warbler in the state."

I knew Caleb mainly by reputation as one of the top birders in this part of the country and as the Michigan Important Bird Areas program coordinator for Audubon, in charge of identifying and conserving designated sites that provide essential bird habitats. One of these areas is the Muskegon Wastewater Management System, where I once ran into a very helpful Caleb and peered through his scope at a peregrine falcon perched on top of a field irrigation rig. In 2005, he had participated in the Cornell Lab of Ornithology's search for the reported but presumed extinct ivory bill woodpecker in eastern Arkansas. So I figured that if he was interested in my bird, it had to be something special.

Torn between excitement at having a rarity on our property and humiliation at failing to recognize it as such, I sent three more photos to Caleb. He confirmed that it looked like an Audubon's and asked, "Is the bird chaseable?" I said that it might show up numerous times in one day—or it might not appear for several days. To Caleb this meant that the warbler was somewhere in the area. It could be chased and, with a little luck, found.

On Sunday morning, he rolled up in his Honda Civic wearing knee-high boots designed for serious slogging and a parka Sir Edmund Hillary would have envied. I soon discovered why he dressed so warmly. After staring at the suet feeder with me for fifteen minutes with no sign of the warbler, he hefted a spotting scope to his shoulder and strode off into the woods. Trying to find the bird away from the house struck me as a fool's errand. It could be any direction and distance away, including on the other side of the river. Where would he even start to look?

When more than an hour had passed with no sign of Caleb, I started glancing out the window. His vehicle in our driveway indicated that he was still at large. I didn't imagine that a veteran of trackless Arkansas swamps would lose his way in our narrow patch of woods. But he could have gotten caught in the same groundwater muck that had stolen my boot during warmer weather, or he might have fallen victim to Mr. Bear Squash-You-All-Flat. It was cold enough outside that his absence worried me. A full two hours after I'd last seen him, he finally reappeared, looking every bit as fresh as when he'd arrived.

I was sure that his extended time away indicated bad news. Linda made him a sandwich, and between mouthfuls he told us, "I found the bird about a quarter mile east of here near the river. It was all by itself—there were no other yellow-rumps—but there were titmice, chickadees, creepers, and nuthatches. It was very high in the treetop. And this is a frustratingly quiet bird, so I couldn't go by the call."

"How did you even know what it was if it was so high up?" asked Linda.

"I called it down using an iPod and Audubon's warbler chip notes." He shook his head as he drank some water. "If it hadn't been for the iPod and speakers, I wouldn't have been able to get a respectable look at this bird. I managed to get two photos, but I need much better detail. Most of the time, it looked very plain-faced. But at other times I noticed a very slight suggestion of an outline to the auricular—the ear—that suggested a myrtle and Audubon's intergrade."

"A cross between the eastern and western yellow-rumps?"

He nodded as he finished his sandwich and then asked if he might try again later in the week. Before leaving he dropped the little bombshell that he'd also run into a yellow-bellied sapsucker and a common redpoll. In two hours, he had located two species in our woods that I hadn't managed to find in eighteen years.

This was birding on a different plane, wrapped in subtleties of avian anatomy that I knew zilch about. Caleb wasn't alone at this level of expertise. Other top-gun birders tried to get diagnostic photos of the yellow-rump. A few days later Caleb waited in the side yard with Adam Byrne, who held the record for seeing the greatest number of bird species in Michigan—a stunning 389 at the time. They caught glimpses of the warbler high in the trees and nothing more. Next, the two men huddled in our basement behind a half-open door staking out the suet feeder, but Linda had to roust them when she dragged out the hose to fill the goose pen wading pools. As a consolation for casting them out into the cold, she warmed them with cups of hot chocolate.

On Sunday Adam joined Caleb again along with area birders Rick Brigham and Curtis Dykstra. Skye Haas, who lives in Marquette, in the Upper Peninsula, detoured to Lowell after visiting his family in Detroit. All received hot chocolate from Linda, and at 2:23 p.m., Caleb, Adam, Curtis, and I were treated to a close encounter with the warbler. We held our breaths as the yellow-rump zoomed into the yard and perched upon a chicken-wire fence just long enough for a photo opportunity. Caleb showed me the smooth trick of holding his point-and-shoot digital camera against the eyepiece of his spotting scope, using a homemade plastic adapter to position the camera perfectly for clear shots of the bird. This was my first encounter with a technique called digiscoping, which proved to be too complicated for fumble-fingered me when I tried it later.

After this appearance, word spread about our unusual warbler, and we never knew when we might look out the window to find strangers looking in at us. Early one morning as the sun barely peeped above the horizon, Linda sprinted out the basement door with a jacket thrown over her nightgown to do her usual wake-up jog around our redbud tree and almost collided with two birders in the gloom.

"They scared me," Linda told me when I arrived home from work. "I didn't expect to see anyone there that early."

Nearly as frightening were the two men and a woman from Kalamazoo who materialized on our front porch to ask if I would take them to the warbler, as if I were keeping it in a cage. When I left them on well-trodden ground across from the suet feeder, they took the news well that the bird had been AWOL for the past three days. Twenty minutes later they traipsed back to the door beaming with their good luck at having seen it.

I felt lucky, too, to be hosting such a noteworthy bird—but less lucky when Caleb emailed me later that he couldn't verify it as the third record of an Audubon's warbler in Michigan. "My final decision is that I don't know what the bird is," he said. "My best guess is that it is probably within range for a pure Audubon's warbler, but that's only a guess. All of the field marks seem to add up, *except* the presence of a slight supercilium behind the eye, which could indicate that the bird is an introgressed Audubon's x myrtle warbler. So I didn't submit it to the MBRC [Michigan Bird Records Committee] for that reason." No amount of nagging or tears from me would change his mind. The faintest hint of an "eyebrow" kept the bird—and me—out of the record books.

Whether it was actually a pure Audubon's warbler or merely a 99.999 percent Audubon's, I had still succeeded in finding a "good bird." Unfortunately, finding took a backseat to identifying, and in the end this was Caleb's bird, not mine. I reported it as such to the birding group and girded my loins for an avalanche of replies. The post received less interest than I expected. It didn't receive a single response. The warbler wasn't a rare species, but a rare subspecies or subspecies intergrade, and few birders who kept life lists pursued anything so esoteric. Still, this seemed pretty exciting to me. And it hadn't taken a trip to Hoffmaster Park to bring the warbler to our yard.

The Audubon's warbler may have been a fluke, but, reliably if irregularly, an occurrence known as an irruption takes place every few winters, and it has nothing to do with my sensitive skin. Due to a shortage of native seeds, fruits, and—in the case of owls—small mammals, bird species that normally spend the frigid months in the far north venture south in search of eats. Overpopulation might drive them southward, too. Except for my miscalculation with the no-show Lansing snow bunting flock, I had never expected to have the chance to see crossbills, redpolls, and pine siskins. But these "winter finches" were suddenly showing up not only in southern Michigan but also as far south as Virginia, Kentucky, and Kansas.

The crossbill is unique among birds in having a simultaneous overbite and underbite. The weirdly shaped beak somehow gives it expertise in extracting seeds from pinecones. Having gone through life suffering from an inability to use the simplest tool, I envied the crossbill and started scanning conifers for the bird whenever I was unfortunate enough to find myself outdoors in freezing temperatures. Report after report of crossbills in southeastern Michigan cropped up in the birding group, but they either consisted of brief, one-time appearances or demanded long hikes through the snow.

Then birding group member Dave Sing starting posting about a mixed group of crossbills, redpolls, and pine siskins that hung out in his side yard in the artsy little city of Chelsea. Side-yard birding was only one step removed from birding from the car. So I contacted Bill Holm, who agreed to drive.

"But you have to buy me lunch at some crummy Chinese buffet," he said.

As well loved for his insights about meteorology as for his detailed reports of birds, Dave was my go-to guy when I had questions about groundwater seepage, tree fungus, ice-crystal precipitation, and other natural phenomena. He didn't hesitate to give two people he had never met permission to tromp around his yard while he and his wife, Cheri, were away at work. "We have two large outdoor cats, a black Maine coon named Perry and Voltaire, a huge fluffy Norwegian forest cat, that are very gregarious and may join you," he told me. "They have little interest in the birds. Rabbits, voles, and mice are their forte."

Not being one of those people who drive to the ends of the earth to see a bird, I felt daunted by the 210-mile round-trip distance to Chelsea. Bill pooh-poohed it, though. He and his wife, Marcia, had just returned from Cuba, where they had been handing out donated medical supplies to hospitals for a Grand Rapids–based relief organization. As we shot down the highway into blowing snow, Bill described some of the shockingly bad conditions in the country. "They have ration cards for basic needs, and it's getting so awful there, the government just removed soap," he said. "And Cubans only make like eight dollars a month. It's a good thing I'd been coming to your house for years. It sort of helped prepare me."

"Since you're Mr. Intrepid, this should appeal to you." I quoted Dave Sing's email. *"If you don't find crossbills near the house and you guys are adventurous, walk down the hill past the spruces and there will be a deer-worn path down the hill angling north."*

"Down the hill. I don't know. I may be slow if we have to do any walking. I injured my knee at Bahía de Cochinos. You probably know it as the Bay of Pigs."

"Was this while you were delivering medicine?"

"Just after. We had a free afternoon, so we went to a park at the Bay of Pigs—the real-life Bay of Pigs, for God's sake—where we could eat and drink all day for twelve dollars each. It was surreal. Some Cubans had brought baseballs, bats, and gloves to the park, and we were just starting to play catch with them."

"You played baseball with Cubans at the site of one of the worst foreign policy disasters in American history?"

"Yeah, and at the same time I managed to compound the humiliation of our great country. I made a heroic leap for a bad toss by one of the Cubans, but it sailed just over my glove. I turned to run after it, but my old knee twisted the wrong way and I collapsed in a heap. It's still bugging me. It's as if I have assumed the burden of American guilt. And I have to ask, 'Why me?'"

Keeping one hand on the steering wheel, Bill fished around in the backseat with the other until he had retrieved his phone. "We did have time for birding when I wasn't busy writhing in pain." He flipped through the photos as he drove.

"I got a good photo of a *tocororo*, their national bird. It's a trogon. The Cubans we were with were fascinated, because none of them had ever seen one, even though we were in a park where they go all the time with us Americans. Guess they're not birders. They're always focused on us Americans, making sure we don't do something stupid."

"Maybe we'll find a trogon in Chelsea," I said.

The pine siskin was a cinch. As we slid to a stop on Dave's snowy street and Bill flung open his door, we were greeted by a buzzy *zzreeee* ascending trill from high up in the trees. It got better when we strolled up his driveway and found siskins squabbling over perches at a pair of thistle seed feeders. Though I'd seldom seen reports of crossbills before this season, siskins, like red-breasted nuthatches, popped up here and there across the state each winter—though never in our yard. Suddenly a decade's worth of the striped little finches chattered within fifteen feet of us. Another feeder slot was occupied by a streaky brown bird resembling a female house finch, but with the added adornments of black around the beak and throat, a white breast dipped in strawberry juice, and a jaunty red cap that a bellhop would have envied. Three more of them flew in and unselfconsciously chowed down alongside the siskins as if they were the most commonplace birds on earth.

"Redpolls!" said Bill.

"That's two new birds for me in two minutes."

"Find the crossbills and we can leave."

I thought I had. Birds hung from pinecones in trees around the yard, but my binoculars exposed them as siskins. Trudging past the house, I sized up the path down the hill as easily manageable, but on the pretext of needing to examine Dave's instruction, I let Bill slip ahead of me to break trail. *"Head north past the huge, downed, split ancient silver maple, and you'll see a more substantial stand of spruce set around past the base of the hill. The crossbills seem to love this stand,"* I said, quoting the email.

Bill acted as if he knew where he was going. I followed until deepening snow bogged us down and he turned to confirm that we were heading in the right direction.

"We're okay if that's the downed, split silver maple," I said. "Do you know what a silver maple looks like, downed, split, or otherwise?"

"It has silver leaves. But if the tree is downed and split, they'd be on the ground under the snow. There's probably a shovel back at the house if you want to dig them up."

"How about a stand of spruce?" I asked as we resumed our slog. "Is a spruce the same as a pine? And what's an evergreen? Linda says that holly is an evergreen."

"Maybe crossbills are eating holly berries under the snow."

I was grateful when a broken tree limb blocked our path. In warm weather I would have lumbered over it, but a lifetime sitting in chairs had ill prepared me for plowing my legs through drifts, and it was so cold I could barely speak without stuttering. "I th-th-think those are the s-s-spruces," I said wobbling a heavily gloved hand toward a clump of distant trees. Neither of us moved. Behind us, Dave's house towered on top of a hill that seemed to grow steeper the longer I gawked at it.

Bill saved the day by giving the spruces a glance through his underpowered binoculars and proclaiming, "There aren't any birds over there anyway."

It would have been difficult making out condors at such a distance, but I agreed. "Let's try the d-d-driveway again."

The climb sapped what little strength that the cold hadn't knocked out of me. I shook and shivered as I scanned the trees in Dave's yard. "What's this bird on the wire?" Bill asked. "Sort of a dirty yellowish gray—black wings and white wing bars. Are you looking at this?"

"F-f-female goldfinch." I was busy tracking a silhouette that turned into a pine siskin.

"That was no goldfinch. It was one of your crossbills, and it just flew away."

"Which way did it go?"

"Up."

Whenever the bug hit me to pursue a particular bird, I would be obsessed with it for days. But when the fever broke, due usually to a shock of physical discomfort, my interest level would drop like a rock. That's how it was with the crossbill. The triple whammy of weakness, an 18-degree Fahrenheit air temperature, and missing a target bird that had perched in plain sight kept me lingering in Dave's driveway just long enough to satisfy myself with a quick glimpse of another yellowish first-year white-winged crossbill. A brilliant red adult bird would have to wait for another opportunity—perhaps in another decade. The important thing now was having lunch in some crummy, overheated Chinese restaurant with gallons of piping hot jasmine tea.

Forty minutes later, as we wolfed down our food, I told Bill, "I know why I look for birds. It puts me the closest that I get to anything like a meditative state."

"I didn't know that Zen monks whined."

"But why do you do it? You don't call yourself a birder. Yet you go out and look for birds." I didn't expect more than a shrug as he poked at his plate of almond chicken. Then he set down his fork and stared at the red paper lantern above our table.

"Birding is a creative act," he said. "It's a way of not only being in nature, but also of being more in the creative flow of nature: you stop, listen, watch, shiver. Most creative pursuits are fundamentally solitary activities. But seeing unusual and beautiful birds—or any bird, really— is a form of expression, like pottery or painting. It's not easy to bird well. The bird symbolizes you, and you're closer to nature than the usual idiot. It's got to be good for you. The trouble is, the usual human flaws end up making birders insufferable snobs whose sense of wonder and connection is foiled by competitiveness, bad social skills, and anger. Maybe that's too harsh."

I shrugged as I shoveled shrimp fried rice into my mouth. The mysteries of birding had just deepened.

Linda ran out to meet us in the driveway. I knew that something had to be up, because she was wearing her slippers in the snow. Bill rolled down the window.

"Hurry, come into the house and look out at the feeder. There's a brown-striped bird with a little flash of yellow on its wing, and I think it might be a pine siskin."

Tracking snow into the house, I clomped down the hallway and into the dining room. Bill was right behind me, but he'd had the sense to leave his boots on the porch.

It couldn't be happening, but it was happening again. Sharing our sunflower feeder with goldfinches and a chickadee, a pine siskin treated me to a witheringly condescending stare. "How is this possible?" I asked.

"How far did we just drive?" said Bill. "Better keep an eye out for crossbills."

I just shook my head. I was flabbergasted. "Why today, why this exact moment, rather than tomorrow or yesterday?"

"I think you know."

Unlike the "loop-back" red-breasted nuthatch that disappeared shortly after splashing around in our birdbath, the siskin and a few of its friends stuck around to frequent our feeder. Meanwhile, crossbill fever struck again as I read continuing accounts of them in southern Michigan. Most of the reports came from the eastern side of the state. Then Scott Manly found a flock of white-winged crossbills at a Christmas tree farm near Ionia—a mere thirty-minute drive from our place. He had watched them from his vehicle, which meant I didn't have to brave the single-digit temperatures that had just arrived.

Santa didn't smile upon me. I drove up and down the road bordering the tree farm without a sign of any bird. Ignoring admonishments from my new GPS unit, Gypsy, to "make a legal U-turn when possible," I meandered along gravel roads for miles in every direction, slowing whenever I passed a stand of trees or a house that looked vaguely like Dave Sing's. I should have gritted my teeth against the cold and stayed in Chelsea until I'd seen my adult male bird. Now it appeared I had lost my chance. I checked our yard when I got home, but I didn't even find a siskin.

The next day I trudged out of the building where I worked at my morning job. While buckling my seatbelt, I glanced up at a row of spruces. At the very tiptop of a tree, a red bird sang his heart out in unfamiliar song.

My old fifty-dollar binoculars huddled underneath the passenger seat. Keeping an eye on the bird, I grappled for them and despaired when the strap caught on a spring. Crouching on the floor, I wrestled the binoculars loose and raised them to my face, expecting the bird to be long gone. Instead he waited patiently as I brought him into view. He looked like a white-winged crossbill. In order to be sure, I needed to see his side to distinguish him from the male house finches that loved that line of trees. Right on cue, the bird rotated to show me a black wing festooned with two bold white stripes. As soon as I lowered the glass, he flew away.

I sat in the parking lot with my heart thumping wildly, realizing I was on the cusp of a major breakthrough. I may not have found a Lapland longspur, let alone a snow bunting. I may have failed to identify an introgressed Audubon's x myrtle warbler when it flitted around in my own backyard. And I may not have been cut from the proper heavy cloth to succeed at winter birding. None of that mattered. I had discovered the "loop-back" phenomenon, and I had penetrated its deepest meaning, which boiled down to this: in birding, as in life, we don't so much find things as things find us.

In that vein, I decided to avoid further birding excursions, electing instead to stay snug and warm inside hoping for another rare bird to appear outside the window. But once spring arrived and birding fever struck again, I made slightly more ambitious plans with Bill.

CHAPTER EIGHT

A Crash Course in Warblers

Strange things continued to happen in the yard, making me wonder if birding wasn't moving into the metaphysical realm. We seemed to have a ghost bird. A phantom woodpecker, to be exact. I heard it on a cold April morning as I headed toward the barn. The drumming grew louder with each step and didn't diminish after I jolted open the big red door and bumped my bones inside. I could even hear the tap-tap-tapping above the honking, quacking, and squealing of the ducks and geese. The hammering was sharpest at the east wall as I leaned over a stack of empty grain sacks, but when I hustled back outside I couldn't find the bird.

Our barn, like our house, was built upon a slope with one ground-level entrance downhill and one ground-level entrance uphill. I trudged uphill this time and plunged myself into gloom that resolved into bales of straw and piles of household junk as my eyes adjusted. The huge space was woodpecker-less, unless the bird was invisible. Then in a small storage room I put my ear to the wall and solved the mystery. The woodpecker had squeezed into the barn through one of the numerous knotholes that also let in circles of light. After that it had made its way to the only part of the building with a double wall. For reasons known only to the bird's concussive-resistant brain, it had slipped between the walls and imprisoned itself.

Outdoors again I stared up at the boards wondering if there wasn't something I could do short of scrounging an extension ladder, a recip-rocating saw, and someone to operate them. And then I saw the beak. It flashed in and out of a freshly excavated pea-sized hole at the vertical seam where two boards met. From the shape of the short, sharp beak, the woodpecker had to be a downy.

I trotted back to the house and told Linda. A few minutes later she came out in her robe, and we watched in amazement. "That's one determined little guy," she said.

He paused to catch his second wind. The boards on the barn had been exposed to the ravages of the world for even longer than I had. They had survived baking summers, freezing rain, drought, and near monsoons, and I didn't expect that they would yield easily to the tiny beak of a bird. "At this rate, it will take him the rest of the day to get out, if he ever gets out."

"I'll bet you a horse it only takes him an hour," she said as he started up again.

Both of us underestimated the power of the peck. After a quick breakfast with Linda and the parrots, I stuck my head outside the basement door but couldn't hear the drumming. Worried that the bird had given up, I hurried back to the barn and discovered that the hole had been enlarged to the profile of a peach pit large enough for the woodpecker to squirm through and fly away. Not far from the barn, a male downy clung to a tree trunk. If he was the ex-prisoner, he didn't seem the least bit ruffled. What had seemed to be a life-or-death struggle from my vantage point may have been just another day of wood chiseling to him.

Linda had rehabbed downies before. I'd held one in my hand, and it was like holding a puff of smoke. I couldn't imagine how a creature that weighed less than ounce could carve a hole through wooden planks using a toothpick-tip of a tool that was made out of bone, not steel. It was incredible, miraculous, and far more impressive than anything a ghost woodpecker could have done. So I was glad that we hadn't been haunted after all.

I was also happy to have been treated to a symbolically loaded encounter that felt like a scene from a dream, though my dreams were never so imaginative. Since I interpreted the world through the lens of me, I wondered about the significance of the event. Maybe after ineptly pursuing birds for years, I was finally on the verge of a real breakthrough. Either that or it just meant that our barn hosted some particularly tasteful beetles that woodpeckers couldn't resist.

Still, I was feeling pleased about my progress as a birder. I could now reliably identify ninety-seven species by ear and at least another dozen unreliably. Add my eyes, and I turned into a finely tuned instrument capable of slapping the correct label on any bird common to city lots, rural

A charcoal black, triangular patch across a fiery orange face contributes to the blackburnian warbler's black, burning appearance.

yards, woods, and riparian settings, with the emphasis on "common" and as long as the settings were within a few hundred miles east or west of home—and half that distance north or south.

Exceptions were thrushes, which I could identify only if the bird sat in clear view while I fumbled through a field guide, and sparrows, which I had a fifty-fifty shot at getting right if they kept to their proper habitat. I played it safe with raptors by lumping anything large under the heading of "probably a red-tail" and anything smaller as "I'm thinking sharp-shin" due to the bewildering degree of plumage variation that can exist within raptor species. For the same reason I avoided places where gulls or shorebirds hung out, unless experienced birders were hanging out with them.

All in all, I had done quite well for myself in a decade or so of seriously bumbling around, and I felt confident that I'd eventually bring more unknowns into the "likely" column if only I had a chance to see them more often than fleetingly once a year. For this reason, I decided that I needed to take a crash course in warblers, and Magee Marsh provided the obvious classroom.

Linda wasn't able to go with me. Because of her worsening back problems, she couldn't sit for more than a few minutes at a time. She felt okay if she kept moving, which worked out well for her in daily life, since she was generally in motion. But her condition ruled out long rides in a car. Unless I wanted to visit the marsh by myself, I had to find another genial traveling companion.

"So just because you want to see this Connecticut warbler, you're going to subject me to being around birders?"

"I don't know how many people will be there," I told Bill as we hurtled toward Ohio in his Volvo. "The boardwalk is big enough that we should be able to keep to ourselves."

"It's not the people I mind. It's the birders."

We flashed through an underpass. A blink and it was gone. "I'm having trouble with birders, too," I said. "I keep finding birds and reporting them to the group, but apparently I'm not finding the right ones. I got zero responses for a bald eagle and nothing for a Carolina wren, except for stories from people who've had them nesting in their garage."

"They just want to one-up you. Birders use bragging to compensate for their lack of social skills."

"Most of the birders I've met have been great. I learned a lot from Caleb when we had the Audubon's warbler in our yard, and you couldn't find a nicer person."

Bill took a perfectly timed sip of his coffee. "What did Caleb say about that indigo bunting of yours that looks like a goldfinch?"

"You've got a long memory."

"I need one to keep birders honest. That's one of my unachievable goals."

I reached down to check and recheck my nylon bag to make sure I hadn't forgotten anything. Binoculars, camera, field guide, iPod. I rearranged my maps for Metzger Marsh and Magee Marsh, stuck them inside the front cover of the road atlas, and then pulled them out again. This didn't feel like a typical birding trip. Something else was in the air— either in my head or in the atmosphere. I couldn't sit still.

"Why do you keep doing that?" Bill asked. "Tapping the dashboard with your finger."

"I'm a determined woodpecker." I described the weird scene at our barn a few weeks earlier. "I must have assimilated the breakthrough tap-tap-tapping behavior. I feel like I'm speeding toward my destiny."

"And the 'Welcome to Ohio' sign. There it is."

For once I'd prepared for a trip. I'd been smart enough to make up for a whole lot of dumb in the past by studying warblers in my field guides and by learning as many songs as my Swiss cheese of a brain could hold via the *More Birding by Ear* CDs and a couple of iPod birding apps. I'd also looked back at the previous year's reports and determined which warblers were particularly coveted—Connecticut, Kentucky, mourning, and worm-eating—and set my sights on them.

"How do you know we'll see even one warbler?" Bill asked. "Or are you just going to claim to see them, and you want me to back you up for a price?"

"For fifteen years, Bruce Bowman has been keeping track of warbler numbers during his trips to Magee Marsh. He's figured out that May 10 to May 17 is the statistical peak period for them. So we're right on the money for a crash course in warblers."

He winced. "Don't ever say 'crash' when you're riding in Gus." Gus was the successor to Bill's Volvo, Turbo, which had been totaled the previous summer—t-boned one half-mile south of his house in Lakewood Township, Allegan County, by a teenager. Bill was lucky not to have been killed. Within twenty-four hours of picking up Turbo's first successor, Bill was celebrating the new purchase inside the Kopper Top bar in Grand Rapids with Marcia when a drug addict slammed into the parked car, totaling it. So he was understandably nervous about Gus, which he'd named after his father, Alf Gustaf Holm, who was 100 percent Swedish—just like the Volvo.

"Hey, if this is a peak period for warblers, it'll be a peak period for birders, too," he told me.

"Don't worry, I've got it all worked out. Species, places, dates, days of the week—the whole ball of suet. We'd be trampled if we went to Magee Marsh on a weekend, but a Wednesday definitely won't be a problem. And I thought we'd start out at Metzger Marsh, which is much smaller and out of the way."

"As long as I don't have to talk to anyone or otherwise suffer any unpleasantness. I've been through enough already."

I was itching to see birds as we streaked along the access road to Metzger Marsh. To our left was a fishing canal dotted with small boats. On our right a group of birders huddled on the edge of the Lake Erie marsh, peering at waterfowl through their scopes. I unrolled my window to ask if they had found anything special when Bill sped up and shot past them. "Oh, did you wish to stop?" he asked.

By then we had already hit the parking lot, and I didn't want to go back. The stand of trees between the lot and the beach was famed as a "migrant trap" for spring and fall birds. In three spasmodic jerks I was out of the car with my camera, binoculars, and iPod. But Bill, a state table tennis doubles runner-up, could sometimes be as slow moving on land as he was speedy behind the wheel. I watched in nervous pain as he looped his water-bottle-and-field-guide belt around his waist, dropped belt, bottle, and book when the clasp refused to catch, rehitched the rig, and recovered it from the asphalt a second time before we finally moved toward the trees.

The wooded patch didn't look like much, but as soon as we entered I heard a confusing mix of bird songs. I did my best to try to turn a heavily shadowed dark brown bird that was flitting around the ground cover into a blue-gray hooded, olive green–backed, yellow-underneath Connecticut warbler—but I grudgingly recognized it as a house wren. Bill made a theatrical gasp as five more birders straggled through the brush. I was about to try to shush him into polite behavior when a middle-aged woman loaded down with optical gear reprimanded a heavy-set man in a knit hat.

"Sir. You're trampling the violets. Yoo-hoo. Don't you ever watch where you're stepping? You. Stay on the path. That's what it's there for." The man jumped back as if he'd been bitten by a snake. "Great," she snapped. "Now you're crushing a trillium." Staring at us staring back at her, she said, "He still can't find the path."

Neither could I. I could make out faint suggestions of a route through alternating clumps of bare ground and vegetation, but nothing as orderly as a path. Sniggering as he walked toward us, he took off his knit hat as if he wanted to tell us something but continued on his way. I avoided Bill's triumphant eyes as Flower Scold continued muttering complaints. As the man trained his binoculars on the middle branches of a large tree, I scanned the high weeds of a marshy area. Although I easily picked out the *witchety-witchety* call of a common yellow-throat, my hours of listening to *More Birding by Ear* came to naught when I confronted a song that could have been a yellow, magnolia, or chestnut-sided warbler. I couldn't see a thing through the vegetation.

"What have you got?" asked a newcomer.

"Had a magnolia," said Flower Scold. She pointed at me. "But that guy flushed it."

I hadn't been anywhere near her, but I moved further away, joining the man in the knit hat. A drab olive-yellow bird bounced around a lower branch. Failing to recognize it from my warbler studies, I decided it must be a vireo and pointed it out to Knit Hat.

"That's an orange-crowned warbler," he said with mild interest. "Pretty good bird. It's better than a Tennessee, but not as good as a Kentucky."

"I didn't realize there were state rankings," Bill said. "It sounds like basketball."

His sarcasm was lost on Knit Hat. "I won't even look at yellow-rumps and magnolias. Garbage birds," he said.

After he headed for the beach, I stayed with the warbler long enough to hand it over to the man who'd been told I'd flushed the magnolia. He called to his companion, "This guy found an orange-crown." But had I? For all I knew, it was Knit Hat's bird.

"I saw it first," Bill said.

I continued hearing birds and continued not seeing most of them as they popped in and out of the canopy far above our heads. Tired of squinting up at silhouettes, we broke free of the woods to trudge along a dike that followed the beach. In the 1920s, the dike kept Lake Erie from flooding Metzger Farms. Then in 1929 the waves broke through, and the once-prosperous truck farm literally went under. The dike was completely gone by the 1950s. In 1995, the US Fish and Wildlife Service, Ducks Unlimited, local conservation groups, and the Ohio Division of Wildlife brought it back to the benefit of fishermen and hunters—and to the detriment of individual fish and ducks.

I puzzled over a distant flock of very large black birds on the ground. I could barely make out their shapes through binoculars. Had they been sitting in a dry field, I would have quickly identified them, but it took me forever because the habitat seemed wrong. "Who expects to find turkey vultures in a marsh on a lake?" I asked Bill.

"I never expect anything. Nowhere, nohow, and I'm never disappointed."

I hoped things would be livelier at Magee Marsh. Just before we turned back toward the car, a birder climbed up onto the dike from the beach and strode toward us with lowered head. "Hello," I said as a preface to asking whether he was having any luck. He didn't stop or nod but uttered something like "ugh" as he passed us.

"Be glad you're not that guy," Bill said.

"I don't know that I'm not. The bounce is going out of my life."

En route to the car, we cut through the wooded patch again and right into Flower Scold's clutches. "Do you like Kit-Kat candy bars?" she asked me. The out-of-the-blue question took me aback. Thinking I had run into her during a rare non-nagging moment, I told her that I did, and I happened to have a couple in my jacket pocket if she wanted one. "So you're the one leaving candy wrappers all over," she said. My protests that I hadn't enjoyed the chocolately wafer treat since a rest stop near Toledo sailed right over her head. I could hear her denouncing me to the world as I crawled into Bill's Volvo.

If we hadn't been cruising in Gus, Bill would have had to hoist me across his shoulders and lug me to Magee Marsh. I was that disheartened by the elusiveness of the birds at Metzger and the negativity of the birders who should have been celebrating the world instead of cursing it. Bill knew and tried to joke me out of my black mood.

"Aren't you going to write down your orange-wedge warbler in your little notebook? You'd better squeeze it in while there's still room on the page."

"Well, at least I proved my point about birders."

"Yes, you did. They make you look somewhat saner in comparison."

Bill had always been a placid pond of a friend with a few boulders of madness lurking beneath the surface, but unlike me he knew how to keep the jagged edges out of sight. Since the accident in his Volvo from which he had miraculously escaped with only bumps and bruises—and following his sessions with a shrink to address the resulting post-traumatic stress disorder—a few ripples of anxiety had begun to appear. But nothing as trivial as failing to find birds would ever have disturbed him.

"I don't have anything against games," he said, "but it seems odd to keep a species list, like you're reducing your interactions with nature to numbers."

"What about you and Dick placing bets on what the outside temperature will be when you drive to Monday-night ping pong?"

"That's different. That's sibling rivalry. And I'm not competing against every other driver like you're competing against every other birder. As long as that loud woman doesn't show up, I'm sure you'll find the Connecticut Avenue warbler and Boardwalk warbler and Park Place warbler at Magee."

I started to get excited again. I remembered a low, scrubby area near the beginning of the boardwalk where I imagined the Connecticut might skulk. I played its song for Bill on my iPod—a robust, repeating *chip-chup-eee*. "I figure if there are other birders there—and we have to assume there will be, because the birds are coming through—they'll mostly be looking up at the trees, while we'll be looking down at the ground for the Connecticut and find it first."

"I'm banking on more birds and less birders," said Bill.

We noticed an unusual number of vehicles at the Black Swamp Bird Observatory building just inside the Magee Marsh park entrance, but nothing struck us as remarkable until we rounded the final curve and discovered a sea of metal at the end. Hundreds of cars, trucks, and RVs packed the parking lot from end to end. It reminded me of a big day at the beach. People sat in folding chairs next to their vehicles, some of them grilling food. Others had set up scopes on the asphalt and were surveying the trees that bordered the marsh. I couldn't figure out why they didn't just haul themselves over to the boardwalk until we slid into a parking space and noticed the crowd jamming the entrance.

I couldn't conceive of worse conditions for finding birds. Surely the throngs of people would scare them away. But as soon as we filtered through the first clutch of boardwalk gawkers, it was as if we had stepped through a door into a rainforest. I believed I could hear thirty songs at once, some high-pitched and stuttering, others sweet and sustained—some complex and multiparted, others simple and repeating—crisscrossing their notes and rhythms in a bopping natural jazz.

I understood why so few people were moving. The birds were coming to us. As fast as I could find them by looking where other people were looking, I saw Nashville, chestnut-sided, magnolia, palm, black-and-white, and yellow-rumped warblers, along with warbling, red-eyed, and blue-headed vireos. If I didn't recognize a bird, I seldom had to ask. The murmur of its name rippled from person to person. We were all in awe together, an astounded harmonic whole. Then a woman poked Bill in the back with two fingers until he retreated from the railing and let her take his place.

We were ready to wander away anyway after a soprano *sweet-sweet-sweet* call knifed through the marsh. We followed it to a disintegrating stump where a golden sundrop of a prothonotary warbler climbed the bark like a dandified woodpecker, flicked his blue-gray wings, and stuck his black dagger beak into a crack in search of a bug. Flipping upside-down he probed another fissure in the wood, so bright in the shaded swampy woods he seemed to throw off light.

His appreciative audience scattered as a three-legged monstrosity lurched forward, pushed by a grunting, red-faced birder and dangling a DSLR camera from a monster of a telephoto lens that was larger than any scope I'd ever seen. The tripod legs nearly spanned the width of the boardwalk. The photographer acted as if hogging valuable observational real estate was his due. Though Bill and I grumbled, the intrusion didn't faze the self-obsessed prothon, who posed like a runway model as galactic flashes exploded from the camera rig and lesser lights popped from several point-and-shoots.

On our way to see the little ball of sunshine we had passed an observation tower. "Let's go back and see what's up," Bill quipped.

Working our way back toward the entrance against the human tide proved difficult, but vertical progress came even more fitfully. Everyone wanted to climb the stairs, but no one wanted to come down. A woman ahead of me in wide khaki pants pushed into a void. I filled half of her former spot and Bill jiggled in beside me. Every thirty seconds or so, we gained another step. How we continued to ascend in the absence of a reciprocal descent confounded my meager grasp of basic physics, though as a consequence of the crowding I found myself shoved against the railing. Below me nervous red-winged blackbirds churned in the wet weeds. A gray catbird flicked its tail. A squirrel and earth-bound birders stared up at me.

Finally we squeezed onto the platform eyeball-to-eyeball at treetop level with Baltimore orioles and scarlet tanagers—plus a leaf-obscured bird whose foraging commanded the attention of all binoculars. He came out into the open.

"Jeez, what is that?" I blurted out, startled by a face so fiery orange, it might have been painted with a fluorescent highlighter pen. Two birders told me its name. A charcoal black, triangular patch across the eyes contributed to the blackburnian warbler's black, burning appearance. At that moment I understood why I'd really come. Not so much for the numerical exercise of adding species to my list—though there was that undeniable pleasure—but for fleeting encounters with beings too splendid to exist. My mouth was so wide open with wonder, I worried I might swallow the bird when he zipped away.

I floated back to solid ground and meandered down the boardwalk with Bill, shouldering through clogs of spectators and stopping whenever we reached a crowd whose faces wore the same amazement as ours. In between we experienced improbably named epiphanies of our own— gnatcatcher, kinglet, waterthrush, ovenbird, northern parula—set to appropriately wheezing, nattering, bubbling, hectoring, or buzzing soundtracks. When we finally left the marsh, the absence of bird songs struck my ears so oddly I traipsed down to the beach and decompressed to the whoosh of Lake Erie waves.

Later I tabulated my species list in a hotel room forty miles away, which I'd reserved to save us thirty dollars compared to Toledo-area prices. I told Bill that between Metzger and Magee, we'd racked up an impressive eighteen warbler species—including the highly desirable orange-crown—plus twenty-one species of other birds.

"I'm more impressed by the amenities in our room. It even has a desk lamp. And these." He sniffed the curtains and pulled them apart to let in more light. "But don't you notice the flaw in your perfectly thought-out birding plan? There's no way to report your orange-slush warbler. No Internet connection. Definitely no wi-fi. And nothing to connect with, since I didn't bring my laptop, and both of us have dumb-phones."

"It's way too late, anyway. Someone else would have jumped on it by now."

"Your research missed another item, too. The reason why there were so many people in the middle of the week, contrary to what you claimed." He retrieved a brochure from his jacket pocket. "This was outside in the parking lot, almost right under my car."

So much for a quiet getaway in search of the Connecticut warbler. The brochure described an event at Magee Marsh, Metzger Marsh, and Ottawa National Wildlife Refuge that we just happened to drop in on. I read the name out loud. "The Biggest Week in American Birding."

"Well," Bill said. "They were right."

We returned to Magee Marsh the next morning for more of the same, but things were different. Without understanding how or why it had happened, Bill and I discovered that we'd been magically transformed from know-nothings to know-it-alls. It started just inside the boardwalk entrance when Bill announced, "Bee-yoo-ti-ful magnolia."

"What did you say it was?" asked a woman whose husband kept flipping a laminated warbler identification card over and over in his hands.

"Magnolia warbler," said Bill. "And a prothonotary. The yellow bird on the broken branch." He looked at me and shrugged as if he'd been a birding docent for years.

After we edged closer to the prothon and ogled it for a while, Bill suggested that we make a beeline for a large constellation of birders. "They must have found something pretty good," he said.

I slowed to a stop on the way, following three women's eyes to a leafy bough that hung directly overhead. Over the years I hadn't gotten any better at memorizing complex plumage, and in poor lighting even simple, blocky patterns caused me trouble. Backlit, the olive-green back and blue-gray head of the bird above us weren't immediately obvious, so I couldn't distinguish him from other dark-on-top, light-underneath birds. Then I focused on the face. Not only did he have a white ring around his eye, but he also had a white line that formed the "nose bridge" to his pair of "spectacles."

"Blue-headed vireo," I told the women.

Sweater Around the Waist told Rapid Blinker. "It's some kind of vireo."

"Blue-headed," I repeated. Bill kept his jaws clamped shut.

"He's gray like a warbling vireo," Rapid Blinker said to her friend.

The bird sang softly as he foraged. Listening to my CDs back home, I had tried in vain to differentiate the red-eyed vireo from the less common blue-headed. But this bird was a patient teacher. "He's repeating his two-note phrases slowly. Then pausing a few seconds in between," I said. "Definitely a blue-headed vireo."

For some reason this description convinced them. Once we had wandered out of earshot, Bill explained, "You don't look credible. Now *that's* what an expert looks like."

Ahead of us, a man in a sleeveless khaki vest with birding hotspot badges and a nametag danced a green laser light into the gloom of the marsh. "Straight back from this oak about twenty-five feet and low in the bushes," he told the big group of birders we had noticed earlier. A short man with curly red hair said to me, "Someone saw a mourning warbler, but I wouldn't get too excited. That was twenty minutes ago."

Bill and I moved on. Whenever we glanced back, the same crowd was waiting for the same mourning warbler in the same spot.

A man my age, whose existence reminded me how old I had become, stared at a dark-on-top, yellow-underneath bird and shook his head when he saw me. "Nashville warbler," I told him. "The eye-ring is the giveaway, plus the lack of bars on the wings. Some female common yellow-throats look like Nashvilles, but they tend to stay near the ground, while this guy's fairly high up." I recalled the "staying low" part from having seen most yellow-throats in bushes. Just like with the blue-headed vireo, details of the plumage had slipped by me—a Nashville has a gray back, and a yellow-throat, an olive-brown back. Nevertheless, a couple of "tells" had allowed me to clinch the ID.

Bill kept finding birds that the rest of us walked past, including a robin-size fellow with a reddish-brown back idling in a clump of weeds. "Wow, nice veery," a woman told us. "I've never seen one this close." I hadn't recognized it as a cousin to the wood, hermit, and Swainson's thrush. The speckles on its breast were as faint as my knowledge of thrushes. But by a process of elimination I might have eventually come up with the name. The bird's size and placid demeanor on the ground would have eliminated lots of other migrants. Bill's discovery caused a minor stir, and he pointed it out to a few newcomers before his resistance to birders kicked back in.

By the end of the morning, after having racked up seventeen warbler species—for a total of twenty-one in two days—I put a little swagger in my stride as we headed back to the entrance. Like our little downy woodpecker, I'd finally made my breakthrough. Yesterday, I'd been a shrinking violet downtrodden by life, life lists, and the Flower Scold. Today I had blossomed into a fertilizer of would-be birders.

As I was congratulating myself, thunder clattered in the distance and a murmur of concern swept through the crowd.

"And away we go!" said Bill in Jackie Gleason's voice.

I didn't get a clear view of the sky until we stepped off the boardwalk and into the parking lot. God's thumb was pressing down on us, the leading edge of an immense black cloud. Instead of racing for the Volvo, I turned toward a woman with lively eyes who was jotting in a notebook. To demonstrate my membership in the fraternity of birders who knew a rare warbler from a "garbage bird," I asked, "Has anyone seen a Connecticut warbler yet?" I knew the answer. The place was too crowded for expert-level birding.

"I found one yesterday morning, not too far from here on the stretch just past the tower," she said. "He was right out in the open for a while."

I thanked her for the information and kicked myself back to Bill's car. I brooded that I'd been so busy having fun seeing birds, I hadn't bothered looking for birds. "I probably walked right by the Connecticut," I told Bill. I considered turning around and asking the woman to show me where she'd last seen the warbler, but the bad weather rescued me.

"You probably did walk right by it," Bill agreed. "But it's not your fault you only saw 700 warblers instead of 701. It's my fault."

"Why is that?" I asked.

"I should have brought a bottle of my special bird-attracting fluid."

Rain hammered on the windshield as I dumped my binoculars and camera in Gus's backseat. People poured from the boardwalk, shrieking, huddled, stretching jackets over their heads as they ran. Switching on his *Benny Goodman Live at Carnegie Hall* CD, Bill nosed through them. Once we hit the main drive, I asked him about his reprise of the birding fluid joke. "Is your memory this good when it comes to important things?"

"I have no idea," he said. "If anything important ever happens, I'll put it to a test."

I thought about my crash course a month later as I marveled at a woodpecker through our dining room window. The trip to Magee Marsh had definitely paid off. I could now identify many more spring warblers by voice or plumage than before, plus a couple of vireos and Bill's veery. Although I gave myself a failing grade in finding anything rare, the crow-sized pileated woodpecker swinging back and forth from our suet feeder made me consider that one person's rarity was another's backyard bird.

The maniacal laugh and prehistoric look of a pileated impressed us whenever we found one in our woods. My birder/photographer friend Alan Ryff told me that in pre-Christian Rome, a *pileum* was a pointed felt cap, fitting close to the head, worn at feasts—so it's an apt name for a bird with a conical red crest. The beak is equally impressive. After seeing the rectangular cavities they excavated in trees, I felt lucky that one of these woodpeckers had never gotten trapped in our barn.

We rarely got within a hundred feet of them. They had a habit of loudly announcing their presence—which seemed rather counterproductive to me—then flapping off to a distant tree with a showy flash of white underwings. So it surprised us when a male began visiting the suet feeder just outside our house.

The feeder was a shallow cage about four inches square that hung from a wire I'd stretched between our house and the milk house shed to keep it out of the reach of squirrels. It had been designed to accommodate downy woodpeckers, nuthatches, and other small birds. A hairy or red-bellied woodpecker could also use it, though their bulk threw the feeder off balance. It was preposterously small for a pileated. But all of a sudden the massive bird would just be *there*, clinging to a rocking and bucking cage. The landing couldn't have been easy—like setting down a fighter jet on the roof of a motel—but he managed it somehow.

On a tree, a pileated has an imperial bearing. Dangling from the feeder, ours was a textbook example of awkwardness. His stiffened tail angled in toward his body. His neck arched up to pound his beak against the suet. Great shards fell to the ground as he mined himself a mouthful with a mad look in his eye, as if he couldn't believe a meal could be obtained from such a ridiculous contraption. He jolted the cage, sending shockwaves down the wire. Then, with the concluding twang of a bass string he was gone. I was sure each visit would be his last, but he returned for six days.

On day seven Linda and I stood outside the basement door watching the darkening sky, when a gust of wind swept in. "Here it comes," she said. Our huge spruce hissed and shook its limbs. Then with the smallest sigh our electricity winked out. After an hour I wheeled out a portable gas generator from the barn. Against all odds, I got it running and connected it to the switch box a few feet away from the suet feeder. For three days we relied on the noisy, sputtering machine for lights, water, heat, and satellite TV. It wasn't to the pileated's liking. He didn't return.

I posted to my birding group about the woodpecker's visits and received more emails than any other report of mine had ever garnered. A check of the range map for the bird in Ted Black and George Kennedy's *Birds of Michigan* indicated why. In West Michigan where I lived, nearly every rural yokel I knew had seen a pileated, but the woodpecker was rare in the southeastern part of the state, where most of the listserv members lived.

This caused me to experience an "aha moment" about the locality of rarities.

A couple of weeks earlier, Bill Holm and I had zipped over to Nayanquing Point to look for the yellow-headed blackbird and a few more coveted species. We didn't have hundreds of birders helping us this time. We didn't need them. Just as we stepped out of Gus—and Bill dropped his water-bottle-and-field-guide belt—our ears were assaulted by the red-winged-blackbird-coughing-up-a-hairball song.

"Yellow-headed blackbird," I gasped. It was shockingly beautiful, grafting the brilliant head of a yellow warbler onto the body of a cowbird.

"Isn't that one?" asked Bill pointing to a second patch of weeds less than twenty feet from the car. "Sitting with a female?"

We gaped at them for a while. Then we climbed the observation tower and were rewarded by the emergence of an American bittern from the cattails. A few minutes later, a much smaller black, white, and rusty-brown least bittern broke cover and flew past us. I was thrilled to see these secretive and uncommon members of the heron family, though much more impressive to Bill was my misidentification of a pair of bulky, slow-flying black-crowned night herons as slim and agile Forster's terns.

Back home, I submitted my species list to the birding group and waited for plaudits that never came. What I didn't realize then, and what my "aha moment" taught me later, was that locality means everything. Bitterns and yellow-headed blackbirds may be unusual finds in most places, but they're fixtures at Nayanquing Point. Similarly, the birding group members who responded to my email about the pileated woodpecker at our suet feeder either didn't know I lived in the western half of the estate or didn't realize that a pileated was fairly ho-hum in my area.

So I needed to find a bird that was rare throughout the state, not just here and there. But if the downy woodpecker in our barn had promised a birding breakthrough, I wondered if the incident with the pileated woodpecker and our generator indicated a loss of birding power on my part. I also wondered if Scott Manly could tell me how to stop seeing birds as symbols.

CHAPTER NINE

Learning from Babies

Back when Bill and I had been gawking at warblers on the Magee Marsh boardwalk, two guys stuck out from the crowd. Instead of watching birds, they argued about them.

"How can you dispute what I've got right here on my camera?" one guy asked.

"My points is, you can't rule out a backcross," said the other. "Your photos don't have enough detail to show the distribution of white at the primary bases distal to the primary coverts."

I had no idea what they were talking about or which species they were disputing, but I did know one thing. If I lived as long as Dracula, I'd never reach that level of expertise. I didn't have a corpuscle of scientific rigor in my body, and far from keying in on subtle feather features, I felt lucky to be able to remember the most basic plumage patterns, such as "heavily striped face." On good days it stuck with me that *supercilium* indicated a stripe above the eye, a *loral* stripe went through the eye, and *malar* referred to a mustache stripe at lower beak level that dipped down the throat. On bad days I stayed in the house and avoided glancing out at the feeder. Even so, I soon found lots of opportunities to learn about birds—though what I picked up had little to do with memorizing field marks and everything to do with getting deeply involved with the personalities of birds.

This was thanks to Linda, who said yes when Peg Markle, executive director of Wildlife Rehab Center, asked, "How would you guys like some baby dinosaurs?"

When I visited Peg to pick them up, I discovered that by *some* she meant *six* and that by *dinosaurs* she was referring to the gangliest northern flicker woodpeckers imaginable. Far from being chicks, they had full juvenile plumage including a dark mustache stripe that curved back from the mouth. Unlike adults, they lurched around making begging grunts that didn't get on my nerves until just after I had backed out of her driveway.

The grunting droned on, muted only when I got them home and Linda started sticking a syringe into their mouths. "They're sure not difficult to feed," she said as her hand darted from one bird to another. "They remind me of the way starlings act at mealtime, only crazier." As she was squirting slurry into one flicker's crop, a sibling muscled in front, while another jumped on her wrist and pounded her knuckles until she shook him loose. They had inquisitive and penetrating eyes, as if daring us to try and put something past them. And while they greedily embraced the syringe with beak, throat, and crop, they possessed an underlying wildness that we hadn't seen in other birds their age.

I enjoyed the chance to see these great speckled birds up close. We seldom ran into flickers in our woods, though in spring and early summer we'd hear their monotonous *wick-wick-wick* call—sounding like a pileated woodpecker reciting the terms of an insurance policy. Due to their fondness for ants, we were as likely to see them feeding on the ground as on the trunk of a tree. In the northern and eastern United States, the yellow-shafted subspecies has yellow underwings, but males sport a black mustache and accessorize with a red crescent on the nape of the neck. The mainly western red-shafted flickers have red underwings, and the males are allowed the extravagance of a snappy red mustache. Neither sex has the nape crescent.

The mealtime squabbles intensified, and so did the juveniles' urge to access the world outside their cage. No feeding was complete without a bird climbing up Linda's arm and flinging itself into the narrow slit between her desk and the wall. When Linda wasn't squirting food into their mouths or mixing up batches of slurry, she was tearing off yards of paper towel, cleaning up their quarters. "These guys need to go outside," she said. "They're wild and woolly. It's killing my back leaning down all the time."

Taking advantage of a rare placid moment after a feeding, I shot a group photo and posted it to the birding group. Then we transferred the birds to an outdoor flight cage that a college kid had built for us, since I didn't know which end of a saw to hold. The cage was twice the width of an old-fashioned phone booth with a full-size door that allowed Linda to walk inside and share a full-body experience with all six woodpeckers at once.

The interactions went smoothly at first. Pleased by their spacious quarters, the juvies perched on sticks or clung to the sides, allowing her to feed each in turn. Then a flicker decided that he wasn't receiving his fair share, so he landed on Linda's shoulder and sought her attention by pecking her neck. Brushing him away had the same effect as exciting a swarm of hornets, and she found herself enveloped by a flurry of wings and a hammering of beaks. She had to peel off four birds to make her escape.

"They are definitely ready to feed themselves," she told me. But they refused to give mealworms a try even when I managed to paste a worm to the end of a syringe using their beloved slurry as glue. Food in a dish—offered by hand or set down on the floor—was out of the question, and they ignored the suet feeder that I hung in a corner.

Peg was right to call them dinosaurs. With their powerful legs, alert eyes, and probing beaks, they looked like hunters that would be perfectly at home in a Cretaceous-period swamp hectoring a triceratops. I loved their coiled-spring energy and profound innocence of human expectations, which I experienced up close when I took a turn feeding them. One of the six immediately knocked the syringe to the floor. Another landed on the plastic cup in my other hand, catapulting mealworms throughout the cage.

Help was on the way. In response to the photo I'd posted, I received an email from Sherri Smith, an Ann Arbor bird rehabber with the Bird Center of Washtenaw County. In addition to her work with nonmigratory songbirds, Sherri undertakes the hazardous work of rescuing sandhill cranes, great blue herons, and other large birds. So flickers didn't daunt her. She shared feeding tips with us, and we agreed to take a flicker she'd been raising, since she was soon to leave for Canopy Tower in Panama on a birding trip.

I couldn't wait for the expert to arrive.

Feeling restless and energized by lingering sunlight at 9:00 p.m., I marched down the neighbor's driveway toward the river. Just before I reached our path through the woods, something hissed at me. Stopping dead, I scanned the ground to assess what manner of reptile or mammal

Orphan red-bellied woodpecker Big Boy enjoyed taking walks with us to the river.

threatened my life. I didn't find anyone and assumed I had misheard, when the hiss came again. Staring up at a tennis ball–diameter hole in a dead tree, I was amazed to find it filled by an excited little face staring back at me.

"What do you mean, 'a little face'?" Linda asked when I burst back into the house.

Laughing, I told her to come see for herself. I raced ahead. The light was fading, but we could still see the baby screech owl peering out and hissing like a grumpy cartoon character. The rounded edge of the hole was ringed in gold, framing the face in a kind of halo. Then the face disappeared. We exchanged questioning glances, but before we could discuss the wonder that we'd witnessed, a silhouette buzzed us, uttering an unhappy single-note *hoo* before returning to the dark branches of a tree. Mama wanted us to leave.

Not ten feet above our heads she watched us and her nest. I thought how splendid it would be if this devoted mother would take over the flickers. One by one I'd slide them into the hollow space inside the trunk, slowly enough so that she could keep an inventory. Then she'd initiate her new charges into the mysteries of hunting moths and mice on inky moonless nights. If only it could be. Turning back toward the lights of the house, we crunched along the gravel driveway, chorus frogs singing on both sides of us. From deep inside the barn, a duck heard our scraping footsteps and quacked.

When Sherri arrived in the morning, I decided not to share my plan about a screech owl surrogate mother. She was carrying a laundry basket, and since she wouldn't lug her washing all the way from Ann Arbor, I knew it contained the juvenile flicker.

"Cages cause lots of feather damage in frightened, frantic wild birds," she told me. "Netted laundry baskets can seldom do any harm to feathers, except to the truly self-destructive. They're fine for transporting woodpeckers. But they aren't good for woodpecker babies that we want to learn to eat, because a baby woodpecker wants to go to the highest possible place and then peck around for food."

"Maybe that's why our flickers aren't eating on their own," I said. "They're clinging to the sides of the flight cage near the top, and there isn't any food for them there."

I'd been an avid follower of Sherri's posts, and it was great soaking up her knowledge and enthusiasm in person. She loved our six flickers, and as soon as she stepped inside the flight cage with number seven, she made a great suggestion. "If you hang a sheet of plastic just inside the door, the birds won't be able to fly out when you open the door. And you can slip past the sheet."

We watched her flicker hop around assessing his new digs. "He seems to be doing well," she said. He looked so much like the others, I lost him in the crowd after the birds had played a few rounds of musical perches.

Making a quick trip to her car, she returned with two shield-shaped pieces of bark to hang inside the cage for the flickers to grip while feeding. I had extra seed dishes from our indoor birds. I fastened them to the bark and filled them with the food that Sherri had suggested in an email: one cup of peanuts mixed with sunflower hearts, one cup of "Original" Science Diet cat kibble, plus a dash of calcium carbonate and powdered bird vitamins, all ground up in a blender.

The fun came when Sherri led me down our hill into the woods to search for natural nutrition for the flickers. Poor Linda, sitting at a piano at Ionia Free Methodist Church that Sunday morning, missed our treasure hunt for insect-infested hunks of wood. We poked through tangles of weeds and braved the boot-stealing edges of sneaky seeping groundwater. Sherri shamed me with her assured and agile movements, as if she were guided by an inner topographical map, while I puttered along distracted by the chiming repetitions of a song sparrow. The trick was finding wood in an advanced enough state of deterioration that in addition to housing creepy crawlies it had nooks and crannies for holding the ground-up food.

"The best ones are dried out and so lightweight, you can carry them with one hand," she said when she saw me dragging a wet log.

After we arranged our finds in a tidy pile, she pulled out the buggiest, most dilapidated piece—a prize-winner that she had discovered on the hill behind our goose pen. A daddy longlegs hopped off while a nematode hung on for dear life. That fine specimen of natural disintegration would serve double duty as a buffet table and perch. As Sherri stood inside the cage holding the featherweight log above her head, I balanced on a plastic chair outside, fishing loops of wire through the ceiling. She was totally unperturbed as the raucous woodpeckers flapped and cried and clung with steely toes on and around her throughout the operation. The female screech owl would have been proud of her motherly devotion.

"I think that's very lovely," she said when we had finished. Judging by their interest, the flickers concurred.

Ideally you would never want to release wild birds until they're eating completely on their own. You would also want to sock away vast sums of money for retirement and remember to buy your favorite calendar in August while it's still available. Unfortunately, few things in life measure up to the ideal.

Three of the flickers busied themselves chiseling away at the insect condo. When they weren't eating, they joined the others literally climbing the walls or jumping from branch to bark. The confinement was stressing them. Linda felt certain that the leader of the successful foragers was Sherri's bird, due to the immaculate condition of a tail that had never scuffed up against the bars of an indoor cage. She decided to release him and the other two eager beavers in hopes of reducing tensions. It worked for about a day. Then the remaining four birds grew more frantic.

"I can hardly feed them anymore," she said. "We should probably let them go, and if they get hungry, they'll come back like the starlings and robins."

Over the years, some of the orphan birds that Linda had raised became so attached to their cushy lifestyle, she had to gently toss them out of the flight cage to get them to leave. Not the flickers, though. Once she opened the door and freedom beckoned, they launched themselves into space. I fretted that they wouldn't be able to find their way back if they got hungry. I needn't have feared. I had never been good at recognizing the one-syllable call note of a flicker, but I quickly learned the *kleer* when they began summoning us for food—meeting us on the hackberry tree and perching just out of reach.

A few days after the big release, Linda was standing on a chair refueling them with a syringe when a dark shape cut across the roof of the milk house and powered into the woods. It must have been a hawk. Panicking, the flickers scattered. Instead of flying up, up, and away like the other three, one shot straight out from the tree at high velocity and hit the hardware cloth wall of the goose pen. He didn't fall but clung to the wire mesh, breathing heavily with open beak. Linda pried his toes loose and set him upon a piece of wood at the bottom of the flight cage. He didn't move, except to breathe.

She made an appointment for me to take him Dr. Bennett, but I soon acquired a second flicker patient. Balancing on the chair to feed the little dinosaurs, I only found two of them. I heard the third calling as if from a distance, but whenever I strayed from the backyard, his *kleer* became unclear. Oddly, the call was loudest when I stood close to the house, but there was no way he could have pulled a downy and pecked his way into our walls. Acting on a weird hunch, I opened the tiny clean-out door at the base of a chimney for a basement wood furnace that we hadn't used in over a decade. I discovered the bird coated in soot, blacker than the blackest crow. For reasons that would only make sense to a woodpecker, he had located the chimney opening and decided to plunge deep into the unknown.

Dr. Bennett handled the bird that had collided with the goose cage with exquisite tenderness. Shining a light into its red-brown eyes, he told me, "He's got a concussion, but nothing appears to be broken. I'd let him sit quietly for a day or two, and as long as you're able to keep some nourishment in him, he should be okay." Already the flicker seemed a little livelier. It might have been my imagination, but I thought he appeared more reassured than discomfited by the zoo vet's poking and prodding.

After examining the sooty bird, Dr. Bennett pronounced him "fine but filthy." All hopes vanished that he'd whisk the flicker into a backroom and return him good as new when he prescribed a thorough bath with a dishwashing detergent that's often used for cleaning oil-contaminated seabirds. "He definitely needs to be washed, because he'll try to groom himself, and the soot can be carcinogenic," he said. "Be very careful of his eyes. And keep him warm once his feathers are wet, or he could get a deadly chill."

I told him, "No problem." But back at home the procedure turned scary as I soaked the bird in the shower. The recognizable shape of the flicker faded and the underlying anatomy emerged—a lollipop head attached to a shivering lollipop body with pipe cleaner legs. The feathers had turned so mushy, I couldn't imagine how they would ever spring back to life. I feared that I had irreparably injured him. Dialing down Linda's blow dryer to the lowest setting, I gradually succeeded in resculpting him into a bird. His plumage was a few shades darker than before, but I didn't want to put him through the cleaning ordeal a second time, so I called it good.

He ended up in the flight cage with the head-injured bird, who had recovered to his full pesky glory by the following afternoon. I released them. They rejoined their siblings to return for handouts with decreasing frequency. We started seeing them on the ground vacuuming up ants or hunting bugs on tree trunks. Within a week, the woods had absorbed them. Occasionally we'd hear their *kleer* call in the trees.

Life without them became easier but duller—though not for long.

"How'd you guys like another baby dinosaur?" Peg asked. Before Linda could answer, she added, "This one isn't a flicker. It's a red-bellied woodpecker and very sweet."

I flew to my field guides for insights into the red-belly's personality. I came away empty except for an aside by Barrows in *Michigan Bird Life*. "In Florida, at least in some sections, this bird is know as the 'Orange Sapsucker' and 'Orange Borer,' owing to its fondness for eating oranges." If a love of oranges was Barrows's way of suggesting that the species was sweet, he could have stated it more directly.

But Peg had been right about his personality. "Big Boy," as Linda called him, won our hearts as soon as she installed him in the little cage in her study. Even though he resembled a flicker in general shape and proportions including a wickedly pointed beak—he lacked a flicker's pedal-to-the-metal philosophy of life. Instead of madly pecking our hands or gulping down the syringe at mealtime, he was almost oriole-like in his mannerliness. Sometimes Linda wouldn't even know he was hungry until she approached his mouth with the syringe. Then he'd snap open his beak and eat with excited squeaks. He was curious about his weird-looking parents. He tracked our movements with interest and enjoyed investigating our fingers with a tongue that felt as stiff as a toothpick.

He was slightly smaller than the two juvenile robins that she had put him in with, because she didn't want him to be alone. Linda never would have housed a frantic flicker with robins, but Big Boy sat contently in his margarine dish or clung to the side of the cage to taste the bars, never competing for food or territory. Some of the docility might have been due to his tender age. His head was prickly with pinfeathers that hadn't yet split their sheaths and blossomed into plumage. The gray incoming feathers lacked either the solid red bar from nape to beak that would distinguish a male or the broken red bar of a female. So she had named him prematurely but presciently.

Every day of his life, Linda's parrot Dusty liked to throw his seeds on the floor, and every time he threw them, Linda reacted as if a water main had burst. She would be the first to tell you that she wasn't a patient person. At mealtime, Bella stood on the countertop beside us, supposedly eating from her dish but mostly eying our plates. This low-key form of begging barely registered with me. It drove Linda crazy. "You've already got spaghetti," she'd tell the parrot. "I'm not giving you the rest of mine, thank you very much." These were disputes with family members, though. When it came to the little ones who were passing through our lives, her patience seemed limitless.

The day she told me, "Big Boy ate a worm," I knew this was a hard-won victory of love that didn't just happen by itself.

The robins would sit upon their perch and gape, so it was easy to sneak them a worm. Big Boy was more difficult, because he didn't wait open-mouthed for food to drop in. Taking advantage of his curiosity,

Linda held a mealworm just beyond his reach. He leaned forward, tapped the metal of the tweezers with his tongue, then the wriggling worm, then the metal. None of it registered as food. She kept trying, alternating the tweezers with the syringe and teaching him to lunge and grab. After a couple of days, he finally swallowed a worm and immediately wanted another. The same trick worked with the robins, and before long she had turned all three birds into worm snatchers.

When Linda moved them outdoors to the flight cage, it looked like she was going to have the same problem with Big Boy that she'd had with the flickers. He didn't want to eat on his own, ignoring worms in a dish on the cage floor as well as worms in a dish attached to Sherri's hanging bark. Buggy wood didn't tempt him either. After a few days, the robins began systematically emptying the floor dish, and Linda sent them winging away. But Big Boy remained dependent on hand feedings.

Lazy both by nature and by choice, I tended to leave the bird-parenting chores to Linda, though I made an exception when it came to Big Boy. He seemed to enjoy my company for its own sake, though when I joined him inside the flight cage I usually brought mealworms. I'd hold a jar lid of them near him, and with a volley of lisping baby squeaks and a few adult *chuck-chucks*, he'd snap up the worms with uncannily accurate beak strikes. There was no prodding impatience from him as I fumbled to replenish the lid, just a cocked head and happy noises as his bright eyes watched. He could have taught our parrots lessons in amiability. And they could have given him tips on independence.

A happy change occurred at the end of the week. I was arbitrating a quarrel between new cat, Frannie, and monarch of the upstairs, Agnes, when Linda called. "Quick, sweetie, come outside. Hurry!" She added something about Big Boy that I didn't catch as she rushed off. Fearful that we'd suffered another woodpecker disaster, I clomped down the stairs. My worry evaporated when I ran into her huge grin at the flight cage.

"Look what he's doing," she said.

It took me a moment to find him in the upper corner of the cage, then another moment to process the importance of what I was seeing. He was vigorously pecking at a block of suet that had been neglected by the flickers. This meant that it would be safe for Linda to release him. While Big Boy taught himself to bang on trees in search of insects, he could actually live off the fat of our land by frequenting our two suet feeders.

Our woodpecker followed the flicker path to independence by showing up on the same tree that they'd favored for refueling. But unlike those slurry guzzlers, he eagerly gobbled up mealworms. It became the highlight of Linda's day to listen for his *chuck-chucks* and rush outside. In honor of his vocalizations, I wanted to rename him Chucky, but she insisted on sticking with Big Boy. We knew now that he was indeed a boy. His feathers had started to reveal the ghost of a red racing stripe.

Linda would hold the jar lid filled with wrigglers close to the bark, which helped him associate trees with insects in case his instincts needed a boost. After making short work of the worms, he seemed to want to just hang out with her. This was a child who loved his mama. And he proved his devotion by accompanying us on walks.

More than half of the birds Linda released would wing away never to be seen again. The others would return to beg for handouts within sight of the flight cage, which they remembered as their place for happy meals. None of the babies had ever sought us out in the woods until the afternoon that we heard a red-bellied woodpecker calling overhead.

"Big Boy!" Linda called to him.

I started explaining to her that we often run into red-bellies when we're out and about and they all share the same vocalizations, when the bird zoomed down and landed on the trunk of a sapling beside her. No doubt about who it was. He clung to the bark, staring and chattering at us until we decided to follow the clumps of wild aster to a gently sloping spot that would take us down to the river. Before we got there, he zipped to another tree. He anchored himself at eye level and soaked up Linda's praises as she told him, "What a handsome boy you are."

"Didn't you feed him today?" I asked. "He must be really hungry to follow us."

"He wants to be with us and let us know that he's okay," she said.

I doubted that a desire for companionship motivated him to seek us out, and to prove it I brought his worms along when we went out again the next day. He repeated his tag-along performance, keeping with us tree-by-tree, blending into dark bark with a feather pattern that had earned him the nickname "zebra-back" in some of my older field guides.

When I offered him the jar lid of worms, he turned away, reaching out to peck the petals of a yellow daisy instead. I had obviously committed a faux pas equivalent to tipping a family member for dropping in. Generous to a fault, he forgave me immediately.

He became a familiar sight in the woods, and no hike felt complete without his enthusiastic participation. "Do you want to take a walk with the woodpecker?" I'd ask Linda, and somewhere between our house and the river Big Boy would show up. But as the red on his head grew brighter, his visits grew shorter. He might treat us to a flyby, or if we ran into him while he was foraging, he'd chuck a hello at us. He was becoming independent from mom and dad, and while it saddened us to lose him, few things pleased us as much as his transition into adulthood. And though we didn't know it at the time, he still had a small but important role to play in our lives.

Linda received another call from Peg. This time she didn't want us to raise a bird. She had been nursing an injured green heron back to health. "His wing is 90 percent healed," she said. "Normally we'd keep him until he's 100 percent, but he stopped eating and we don't dare keep him any longer. You guys have the perfect habitat, and you could keep an eye on him if we released him at your place."

I had fallen in love with green herons years earlier, back when I thought the only heron was the great blue heron until Linda spotted a half-pint greenie at Magee Marsh. It didn't even bother me that green herons weren't green. The older name "green-backed heron" came closer to the truth about this mostly brown and white bird, though the gray back only takes on a greenish sheen if the lighting is right and can just as easily appear blue or purple. Small at seventeen to eighteen inches long—from the tip of his beak to the end of his tail—compared to the forty-five- to forty-seven-inch great blue, the green has the cool shape-sifting trick of looking short and squatty until it suddenly sprouts a long neck when alarmed or hunting.

Peg once had a juvenile green named Forceps who startled me by landing on my shoulder and perching like an attenuated parrot. I stood statue still as he explored my ear with a stiletto beak. (She released the bird a few days later, after it had become curious about the human eye.) I barely breathed until Forceps flew back to his comfy towel bed on ancient wraith wings. Green herons made flickers seem like sensible modern birds in comparison.

The night of Peg's call, she showed up after dinner with her husband, Roger, who lugged a pet carrier down to the riverbank that weighed ten times more than the bird. He opened the front grate and tipped the container until the heron launched himself into wobbly flight close to the ground. With a tentative sounding *skee-yow*, the bird managed to glide to a low branch overlooking the river. After that he didn't stir.

"It's up to him now whether he makes it or not," said Peg. "At least we know that he can fly."

"We could get him some fresh smelt from the store to eat," Linda said.

"Anything's worth a try," said Peg.

When we took our walk the next day, we discovered that he hadn't moved an inch. Plodding back to the house, I returned with a few whole smelt and a few that I'd chopped up. I put some in a bowl of water in case he wanted to fish for them and the rest on the ground in case he didn't. But he didn't seem interested in us or in the smelt—and I confirmed this when I checked back after dinner and found everything exactly as it had been. If he didn't eat, he wouldn't last much longer. I didn't know how to help him.

In the morning while I was at work, Linda reluctantly made a trek to river, expecting to find the worst. "You won't believe what happened," she told me later. "I couldn't find the heron at first and figured he was probably lying dead somewhere, but I walked down the river path a little, and there he was standing on a rock in the water looking a whole lot perkier."

"His instincts must have finally kicked in."

"But you haven't heard the best part yet. Perched on a tree not too far from him was Big Boy! I called Peg and told her what had happened, and she said that the two birds knew one another. Big Boy was in a cage for a while right next to the green heron, and even though he was a baby at the time, he must have remembered him and wanted to cheer him up."

Stranger things than this happened nearly every day, and after living with animals for twenty years, I had learned not to underestimate them. If Dusty could tell an orphaned blue jay in a perfect imitation of my voice, "You're okay, sweetie," when the upset jay had started squawking, why couldn't a woodpecker comfort a green heron?

The next morning felt like a turning point to us. Either the previous day's progress had been a fluke, a last-ditch effort to escape the fatal gravity of the tree branch, or he had taken his first step toward a full recovery.

"I don't see him," Linda said when she spotted the rock that he'd occupied the day before. I couldn't decide whether his absence was a good thing, suggesting he had flown off to his destiny, or a bad thing, indicating he had keeled over and floated away. While I scanned the mudflats across the river through binoculars, Linda dashed ahead and called out, "There he is—on a stick."

I walked about fifty feet and picked out his rounded form near the water's edge. Turning to face me, he did the giraffe stretch with his neck to appear formidable in case I posed a threat. Realizing I was nothing at all, he reverted to an oval with a beak and shifted his attention to the shallows.

"I think he's going to catch a fish," said Linda, grabbing my arm.

He hunkered down on spindly legs and froze. Skates zipped past him. Then a lone minnow moved into his shadow. A dozen more drifted over. The water reflected a puffy white cloud that suddenly broke into rings as he struck.

"He's eating!" Linda said. "Wait until I tell Peg."

The next day, we found him snagging minnows fifty feet further down the river. The day after that, we couldn't find him at all. We figured that he had recovered enough to fly to a place of his own choosing where he could hunt and skulk away from prying eyes.

Over the years, thanks to help from experts and the occasional spurt of good luck, I had seen several spectacular birds. But none of them had satisfied me as much as the green heron that we didn't see. He may not have been rare, but when he suddenly made himself scarce, he defined a whole new category of "life bird" for me.

CHAPTER TEN

Anything Can Show Up Anywhere

Teetering on the edge of a railroad trestle with an angry mother osprey giving me the evil eye, I decided that the subtleties of birding weren't for me. Instead of beating my head against the elusive wall of coveted species, I should just relax and enjoy the birds that were close at hand—though relaxation seemed like a distant memory as I weighed my chances of avoiding the rocks below if the osprey came at me. As she hopped off her nest and swooped down, I can't say that my whole life flashed in front of me. I did treat myself to a brief rerun of the events that had brought me to the bridge.

On our way home from a dingy Chinese buffet in nearby Ionia a couple of weeks earlier, Linda had noticed an eagle-sized brown-and-white raptor plunging feet first into the Flat River in downtown Lowell.

"I think that was an osprey," she said. "Turn around!"

"Can't be," I replied. "They're only in the UP and the northern part of the state. It's probably a red-tail."

"Diving for fish? That wasn't any kind of hawk." By the time I made a U-turn, the bird had accelerated away.

I stuck to my guns that it couldn't be an osprey. One of the first breakthroughs I'd made years ago was learning to use the range maps in my *Peterson Field Guide to Birds*. The maps told me at a glance if a particular species could likely show up in West Michigan as a breeding, wintering, or migrating bird—or, more important, if it wouldn't show up here at all. This allowed my thumb to bypass tens of pages at a time and lessened the chances that I might mistake a frigid-weather northern shrike encountered in February for either a highly improbable, temperate-weather northern mockingbird or a downright impossible, mountain-dwelling Clark's nutcracker, since all three share plumage similarities.

Early in our marriage, Linda and I drove north out of the empty white southern Michigan osprey range map region of the *Peterson Field Guide* and into the deep pink map region of the Upper Peninsula, where some of these big raptors nest in summer. At Seney National Wildlife Refuge, we watched an osprey grab a fish from a pond with a mighty splash. A ranger told us that as the bird flew off with its catch, it would grip the fish in its talons with the head facing forward, tail backward—demonstrating an innate knowledge of aerodynamic principles. I didn't imagine that a bird with this many smarts would stray from pink to white and mistakenly end up in Lowell.

"If we've got an osprey, then anything can show up anywhere," I told Linda.

When I posted questions about this bird to my group, Jim Kortge replied. Beginning in 1998, Jim and more than fifty other volunteers had helped relocate osprey chicks from an established population in northern Michigan to former osprey territory in the southern part of the state. The Osprey Reintroduction Project of Southern Michigan was headquartered in Kensington Metropark in Oakland County and sponsored by the Michigan DNR, the Detroit Zoo, and DTE Energy. In addition to reintroducing osprey chicks to Kensington and Stony Creek Metroparks in the southeastern part of the state, the project also established ospreys at Maple River State Game Area north of Lansing—about forty miles away from Lowell as the osprey flies.

"It's possible that the Lowell osprey may have been a Maple River SGA-released bird or one of its offspring who nested there," Jim told me. He wondered if the presence of the bird indicated a nearby nest. I said I'd look into it, which was similar to promising that I'd start minting Spanish dubloons, since I had no idea how to proceed.

Linda knew exactly what to do. The next time she was at the Back Alley Bait Shop buying mealworms for her baby birds, she asked the owner about ospreys. He lit up with a smile and said, "Yeah, they've got a nest on the old railroad bridge, right out in the middle. You can barely make it out from the Jackson Street Bridge. You're better off getting a look at it in a boat."

One reason we would have been better off in a boat was the traffic on the pedestrian-unfriendly bridge. A pick-up truck brushed past so close it made me shiver. Scanning the dark hulk of the retired railroad bridge two football fields away, I had trouble locking my binoculars onto anything nest-like. Then Linda mentioned a bit of trash on top of one of the trestles. It resolved itself into a pile of sticks as I wrestled with the distant, jiggling view. I felt even more vehicularly exposed after I'd retrieved my telescope from the car and attached it to the tripod, whose leg extended toward the traffic lane. I clutched the railing as a van thundered by. The bald-headed fisherman on my right never flinched. He told me he'd been fishing in the same spot for years and didn't worry about any cars.

"I see her," Linda said, grabbing my arm. "Look and tell me if that isn't her head sticking out of the nest."

Even through the scope, making out the details was a stretch. After a few moments a bird's head surfaced above the sticks and rippled in the thermal currents. Linda told the fisherman about the osprey. He hunched his shoulders and didn't want to look. We took turns bending over the scope as the bird faced us in a beautiful profile. "If she can see fish swimming underwater, I'll bet she sees us," Linda said. Then a rattletrap truck sent us scrambling to our car. Linda tooted the horn at the fisherman's back as we passed.

We were so excited about the nest that without pausing to take my jacket off, I ran upstairs as soon as we arrived home and stabbed out an email to Jim Kortge. Jacketless, I read his reply an hour later asking if we could get close enough to discover if the mother had chicks. Out of all possible places for an osprey to nest, the exposed top of a train trestle struck me as a particularly bad choice. Jim said, "Ospreys won't nest in a tree unless it is a dead snag where there are no leaves. They want to be able to see in all directions so they are not attacked by larger raptors like bald eagles and great horned owls, who will prey on them if given the chance. The railroad trestle is apparently high enough for their liking with good visibility and no large raptor nests in the area."

I told Linda, "It's too bad there's no way of getting over there."

"Why can't we just follow the railroad tracks?"

"And get flattened by the Lowell Cannonball? No way."

Our friend Gary Dietzel happened to be doing handyman duties behind our barn repairing a poultry pen, and Linda happened to make her way outside to talk with him. He knew about the osprey nest—he'd been one of my birding mentors—and he described how to find the tracks that led to the bridge. "They don't use them anymore except to hold a

An internal compass error brought the penguin-like ancient murrelet from the far north to southern Lake Michigan.

few boxcars now and then," he said. "It's safe. I walk the neighbor's dog there."

I wanted to get the lay of the land on my own before committing both of us to a full-scale assault on the trestle. Following Gary's instructions, I pulled into the parking lot overlooking the Lowell dam, followed a chain link fence past an old mill wheel, and warily climbed up onto the track bed, keeping an eye out for locomotives sneaking up behind me. I'd seen too many black-and-white TV shows in my youth in which minor characters came to bad ends on trestles, and I didn't want to turn into one of them.

The old ties leaked black gobs of creosote, so I had to glance down with each step in addition to glancing around for a runaway caboose. Just as I approached an old granite marker inscribed with a "W" for "whistle" and leaning like an ancient gravestone, a thumping shuddered through the rails. I pivoted 180 degrees and hurried back the way I'd come, hoping to beat megatons of metal to a spot where I could safely scrabble down to ground level without breaking too many limbs.

Back in the parking lot, I spotted a train on the other side of the river headed in the opposite direction on a different set of tracks.

That was too close, I thought.

A few days later I returned with Linda, who would not be dissuaded from checking up on the nest. Pretending to reassure her but actually reassuring myself, I said, "We have a better chance of seeing a penguin than running into a train." I was so happy to be bolstered by her sunny presence as we trekked along the tracks, I would have whistled, if I knew how to whistle, even without seeing the "whistle" marker. Then as we rounded a curve, the leaning "W" and our way forward were blocked by a line of boxcars.

"Why can't we go around them?" Linda asked.

"*Fried Green Tomatoes*," I explained, but she kept on walking.

The sheer bulk of the railcars gave them an aura of menace. It seemed impossible that things so large could ever move, and once they did, that they could ever stop again. In case they were hell bent on reanimating, I edged as far away as possible, knocking loose gravel down a slope that was getting steeper the closer we came to the trestle. Soon we had even less room to maneuver. A massive turtle next to a boxcar stretched his neck and regarded us with malice. I didn't know if he was a snapper, but his beak appeared capable of taking a bite out of a two-by-four—or out of a five-foot-ten-inch person's ankle.

Linda was as cool as the fisherman on the bridge. "Aren't you a tough guy?" she told the turtle as she searched for a handful of grass. "We'll find you something to eat on the way back." I didn't like the way he fixed his greedy eyes on me when she mentioned eating.

Just as the turtle lost interest, the osprey found us. She emitted a series of keening twitters that might have come from high up in the clouds or from the limb of a dead tree on the opposite bank of the river. Her thin and distant-sounding protests didn't seem grounded in the untidy heap of braches on top of the flattened "M" of the bridge and may have been intended to distract from her actual location. But there was no mistaking the content. She was giving the alarm. The bird was alarmed, and she was alarming me.

"Is this a smart thing to do?" I asked. "Raptors are pretty ferocious."

"We're not going to bother her. We'll only keep going until we're able to see if she has babies in her nest." Mother-bird Linda couldn't resist another mother's brood.

But the bridge geometry defeated us when we reached the spot where the dirt ended and the ironwork began. The bird sat on top of the second trestle, which the first trestle blocked. We tried ducking and peering up from different locations, but the girders still blocked us. The solution was to stroll a few yards out onto the bridge for a clear view. It shouldn't have been a big deal. Then I noticed that the boards under the tracks were spaced widely enough apart to allow breathtaking views of the rushing water below. Under normal circumstances I could avoid these gaps. But if the mother osprey decided to launch herself at me in defense of her youngsters, my foot might fall through one of the openings or I might plunge sideways into the river. So I stayed put.

Linda chuckled at my cowardice until she discovered the gappy flooring on her own. This wasn't a bridge that allowed you to pretend it was anything but a skeleton of wood and metal stretched across a void.

She pointed to the riverbank alongside us. "Maybe we could see better from down there a little."

I held onto a girder and stepped down to a concrete footing, which was as far down the steep incline as I was willing to venture. As I leaned out like the "W" whistle marker, I succeeded in looking the osprey in her yellow eye, and she treated me to a glare so intimidating that I wanted to go back and hug my warm and fuzzy pal the snapping turtle. She stood up and with a hop swooped down on brown-and-white wings the size of police dogs while brandishing the jaws that bite and the claws that catch of the dreaded Jabberwock.

Two thoughts flooded my brain. First, this was far more exciting than chasing a warbler. Second—and far more important—how stupid was I to have put myself in such a precarious position?

I had good reason to be concerned about the osprey. In her book *Birdology: Adventures with a Pack of Hens, a Peck of Pigeons, Cantankerous Crows, Fierce Falcons, Hip Hop Parrots, Baby Hummingbirds, and One Murderously Big Living Dinosaur*, author and naturalist Sy Montgomery describes in hair-raising detail the ferocity of raptors. She told me recently, "Humans have rightly viewed raptors with caution for two million years. They once hunted and killed our ancestors. In college, I read about the famous fossil hominid, the Taung Child, discovered in 1924 by Raymond Dart, the first australopithicine. The child was rather recently discovered to have been killed not by a leopard, as had been thought, but by a raptor—an ancient relative of the crowned hawk eagle. In Mongolia, to this day, falconers hunt wolves with golden eagles, but must be careful that the eagles don't hunt near village children. One falconer's eagle killed his grandson."

Raptors, like good parents anywhere, will defend their nests with all they've got. "A friend of mine knew a guy who was killed this way," Sy said. "It was sort of a freakish accident, like poor Steve Irwin getting nailed by that stingray in the heart. The guy didn't realize he was near a goshawk nest, and one of the parents hit him exactly right in the back of the head. He died instantly."

In *Birdology*, Sy writes harrowingly about learning the highly dangerous art of falconry. She tells the story of her instructor, Nancy Cowan, who was once attacked by her husband's new goshawk, right in its mew (or aviary). "Nancy went to feed her, giving the bird her three delicious dead chicks. Everything had gone well until Nancy turned to leave—and felt talons going around her eyeball," Sy told me, recounting the story. "Her husband forgot to tell her that after feeding the third chick, he always used to fluff the goshawk's breast feathers. The change in routine was all it took to trigger the attack."

So what kind of quarter did I expect when I crowded a mother raptor at her nest? Fortunately, instead of flying in my direction, she glided across the river and settled on the limb of a tree, apparently unconcerned about a gnat like me.

As I clambered back up to the railroad bed, Linda emitted an osprey squeal of her own. "Two babies in the nest, and they're practically as big as the mother." Standing where I'd been standing a few moments earlier, she had pretzeled herself into a weird bent-down-but-upward-looking posture that gave her a clear view of the nest.

"You're going to wreck your back," I said.

"I don't care. You should see these big fat babies. They remind me of our grackles." She called to them, "Don't worry. Your mother's going to bring you back a fish."

Up until now, I thought I'd been searching for the nest for Jim Kortge. But Linda's joy was my reward. It made me wonder why I'd been so obsessed with seeking out rarities when ospreys, baby flickers, or a woodpecker hammering an exit through our barn brought me plenty of thrills.

I had been fascinated with birds for twenty years now and for the last ten had made a serious attempt to learn about them. But I finally seemed to have reached a plateau. I still suffered from poor visual processing that reduced unknowns to a single, usually misperceived feature, and I lacked the mental muscle to store any but the most elementary identification essentials in my head. Another factor was missing, too. I was bereft of the drive that fueled A-level birders, who didn't simply look for birds when strolling though the woods, as I usually did. Finding them was their life, and they were relentless about the pursuit. When they weren't traveling long distances in quest of rarities, they were checking and rechecking the same spots close to home, and it didn't trouble them if they came up empty 90 percent of the time.

Steve Santner is one of the top-gun birders on the listserv who has helped me over the years. During a winter trip to the Muskegon Wastewater System, I'd searched in vain for a reported snowy owl for eighty minutes and was about to head home when I noticed Steve and Darlene Friedman parked on the shoulder of the main facility road. They showed me not just one but six snowies in a field through their scopes.

A retired biologist who has been chasing birds for over fifty years, Steve is a county lister. His goal is to chalk up as many species as he can in each Michigan county. "Now that I have retired, I think I drive about forty-two thousand miles per year while birding. I have county lists for all eighty-three Michigan counties—and for all sixty-seven Pennsylvania counties as well," he told me. "I originally started county listing when I lived in Pennsylvania, because I noticed that I tended to go to the same spots at the same time each year. County listing forces me to bird more widely."

Covering the Lower Peninsula from Mackinaw City to Niles and Muskegon to Port Huron is challenging enough. The difficulty factor increases dramatically when you add the Upper Peninsula, which is larger than New Jersey, Maryland, Delaware, and five New England states. "It's about six hundred miles to either Ironwood in Gogebic County or Copper Harbor in Keweenaw County. This is about the same distance as driving to Atlanta, Georgia. It takes me at least a week to reach the western UP. I can't just spend a whole day driving, so I bird my way there."

Steve has seen a total of 365 species in Michigan, with 252 of them found in Monroe County, home to Pointe Mouillee State Game Area, a prime wetlands for rarities. "I generally stop birding hard in a county when my total reaches 200," Steve said. "My poorest county total of 162 in Oscoda County is far ahead of anyone else in the state. I'm trying to reach 200 in every county. I probably won't live long enough to accomplish this, but I'm still going to try."

I lacked anything approaching Steve's level of dedication. The fifty-three-mile trip to Muskegon Wastewater always felt like a continent-crossing haul, and I rarely subjected myself to that ordeal unless bolstered by Bill Holm's entertaining company. The wisest course for me was to continue soaking up crumbs of knowledge as I enjoyed birds close to home, leaving the pursuit of rarities to folks with more smarts and drive. Trying to compete with A-level birders led to increasing levels of frustration.

One major frustration was having to unlearn things I thought I knew after discovering that my faithful field guide range maps had been untrue. I could understand running into a rufous hummingbird from the Pacific Northwest in Michigan after Allen Chartier explained the bird's migration strategy. And the presence of ospreys on a railroad bridge in southern Michigan made sense once I'd learned about the Osprey Relocation Project. But when November rolled around and southwest Michigan birder Tim Baerwald announced finding in St. Joseph, Michigan, an Arctic bird from a family that the *Peterson Field Guide* calls "the northern counterpart of penguins," I decided that if anything could show up anywhere, finding rare species was an expert's game for sure.

Any Michigan birder worth his or her weight in binoculars can swoop down on the Florida Keys, the Rio Grande Valley in Texas, or other American hotspots to rack up dozen of life-list species that shun the Mitten State. Much more difficult is ferreting out unspeakably scarce birds in one's own backyard, like Tim with the ancient murrelet. Scarce hardly does justice to this member of the alcid family, whose best-known member is the puffin and which breeds mainly in the rocky islands of Alaska and British Columbia. I searched the Michigan Bird Records Committee database online and found only eight appearances of the ancient murrelet here since the earliest listed date of 1989. Seven of those occurred hundreds of miles north of us on Lake Superior in the UP's Chippewa County.

I wanted Linda to share this once-in-a-lifetime opportunity with me and hoped that her back problems would allow her to go. But the night before the ninety-nine-mile trudge to St. Joseph, near the bottom end of Lake Michigan, she told me, "My hip feels out, and if I sit in a car for a few hours it will get a lot worse."

I needed to go. Even though I hadn't yet been held by the ancient murrelet's glittering eye in person, I'd fallen under its spell. Unlike Steve Santner, I lacked the oomph to drive long distances on my own. I considered inviting Bill Holm, but giving him less than twelve hours notice for a half-day trip didn't seem respectful.

"Can't," said Bill when I reached him on his cell phone. "Did you forget that Marcia and I are in New York City? We haven't been birding yet, but we did go to Birdland—the jazz club—and some of the musicians were ancient. What's the call of the ancient murrelet? Does it say, *Awwketh?*"

"That's really good. Did you know it's an auk?"

"No, but it just goes to show the extent of my instinctual comic genius."

Slamming down the phone, I decided to make the effort to see the bird on my own and even scrambled to the store for an eggs-and-sausage "breakfast in a bowl" so that Linda wouldn't have to get up early to feed me. But when the clock beeped at 6:30 a.m., I lay in bed wracked by an escalation of my usual free-floating anxiety. According to my GPS, Tiscornia Park was a one-hour, forty-one-minute drive, plus I had to add fifteen minutes for a rest stop and for "Gypsy" to purposely lead me astray. Was this long trip worth taking? No one had found the murrelet on Friday, and I would feel foolish if I wasted a Saturday on a bird that had already flown when I could be spending my time in far more productive ways, such as staying under the covers.

I'd slept in the upstairs bedroom so as not to wake Linda, but as I adjusted my head on the pillow I heard her bumping around in the kitchen. "You sure picked a beautiful day for a drive," she said when I slunk into the room. "A high of fifty with sunshine."

"I'm not going," I told her. "My nerves are really bad."

"You always feel worse in the morning, and you'll be sorry if you stay home and then read emails from people who saw your bird."

My bird. Certainly not mine, but mine to see. And even if the murrelet never surfaced, birders had reported other rarities blown in by the same crazy winds that had delivered this flighted version of a penguin. So after spooning out the last morsels of egg product and a sausage-like substance from my breakfast bowl, I kissed Linda and hit the road.

If I had known what an odd experience awaited me, I never would have hesitated.

I wasn't encouraged about my chances of seeing the bird when I pulled into Tiscornia Park. Two stony-faced men were stowing their gear in the back of an SUV. I didn't need to ask, but I asked anyway. "Any luck with the ancient murrelet?"

"No one's seen it today," said Puffy Blue Parka. "We've been here two hours."

"But if you need a little gull, you can't miss it," Fishing Hat told me.

I could miss it. I had no idea what the little gull species looked like. I thanked them and left my spotting scope in the trunk. I didn't want to lug twenty-five pounds of scope and tripod four hundred yards down the pier when birders showing off their $3,900 Swarovski rigs would be happy to share a peek if the murrelet appeared. Otherwise, my binoculars gave me a better shot at tracking a swooping, wheeling gull, which I hoped more knowledgeable brains would identify for me.

I passed another disappointed soul and a few fishermen as I trekked along the cement. After ducking around a small lighthouse I ran into thirty or so birders scanning sky and water from the end of the pier. Before I could pop the caps off my binoculars, a guy in a headband gestured toward a compact flock of Bonaparte's gulls. Wearing nonbreeding plumage, the gulls had accessorized their gray-and-white duds with a dark smudge over the ear in place of summer's black hood. "We've got a little gull," the guy said. "He seems to have decided to stick around for a while."

Nodding sagely, I put the bins on the flock, then admitted defeat. "Which one?"

"He looks like the Boneys, but see how the underwing is darker?"

I concentrated, but even as I followed the little gull, I could barely tell him apart from the Bonaparte's gulls—though he was appropriately slightly littler.

Glancing at my watch, I resolved to give the murrelet an hour and not a minute more. Anything less seemed unreasonable after the drive. Anything more would challenge my ability to entertain myself on a slab of cement surrounded by water on three sides. To pass the time I asked a man with an enormous knapsack, "Would you say that the ancient murrelet is one of the rarest birds to ever come to Michigan?"

Without lowering his binoculars he said, "I wouldn't know. I live in Indiana."

I watched the little gull for another few minutes, finally clicking to his completely white-edged wings, compared to the Boneys with their black-edged wings. Whenever my concentration waned, I lost those distinctions along with the bird. Then I flinched away from the flock when a voice shouted, "I've got the murrelet!"

A great rustling of synthetic fiber jackets and a scuffling of feet took place. I hadn't noticed much conversation, but in the abrupt gasped silence that followed the announcement, I recognized a broken congeniality replaced by cries of "Where? Where?" A mood of tension contrasted with the dull gray rolling water that concealed the bird.

"Don't panic!" called the voice. "Everyone will get a chance to see it," as if the voice controlled the murrelet's movements, or as if it belonged to a cane-wielding carnival barker, or as if it had read desperation into a shove of tripods toward the edge of the platform. Remarkably, the voice had a calming effect. We collectively handed it our trust.

The voice belonged to expert birder and self-described "hawk watcher" Jeff Schultz, who had driven almost twice as far as I had from the southeastern part of the state. Under normal conditions, one birder could describe a specific spot to another by saying, "Look at the skinny maple that's in line with the utility pole on the hill. Go up to the third branch on the right. That's where the Clark's nutcracker is perched." Those kinds of landmarks didn't exist on the featureless plane of Lake Michigan—at least none that I could perceive. Jeff proved the superiority of his observational skills, however. "See where the patch of dark water ends and the light patch begins? Look straight out at the dividing line, at twelve o'clock from where I'm standing, about two hundred feet out. He's underwater, but watch for him when he surfaces."

Once the murrelet reappeared from the inky depths, Jeff pinpoint- ed the location even better. "See the Bonaparte's gulls on the water and behind them the little pod of northern pintails? He's right in the middle between those two groups."

Following Jeff's directions, I lit upon a black-and-white, penguin-like bird so small that the slightest swell of a wave concealed its body as ef- fectively as a mountain would have. There, not there—on, then off—he blinked in and out of view, bobbing like a cork. A mallard paddling lazily alongside the pier was a fierce warrior compared to this stubby, ten-inch- long bird as crazily out of place in Michigan as the names auk, alcid, and ancient murrelet. The foolishness or audacity that had brought him here to fend for himself all by himself rattled me. I thought of Julio Cortázar's short story, "Axolotl," about a visitor to the Jardin des Plantes in Paris who sees axolotls in an aquarium and empathizes so completely with the little salamanders that after several visits he becomes one of them.

The longer I held my binoculars on him, the sharper the sensation grew of being cast adrift in a foreign land—pretty much how I usually felt about life. I associated this thought with the murrelet, though, and I lost the edge of my wonder at seeing the bird as my identification with him strengthened. *I'm not really ancient*, I longed to tell the birders. *The white plume on my black head during breeding season isn't a patch of gray hairs.* Saving me from surrendering to a reverie about the sweet taste of krill, the voice rang out again.

"Black scoters coming in at two o'clock." Five bulky totally black ducks flew in perfect single file just above the water before landing a hundred feet past the murrelet. Someone else spotted a red-necked grebe flapping past the pier and achieving splashdown near the scoters. An escalating sense of strangeness deepened. I had never been in a place like this with nowhere to walk except to retreat to land, no new territory to explore, yet characters slightly removed from a Dr. Seuss book kept appearing. For a moment the world of birds revolved around me.

With an excited shout, Jeff conjured up another rarity, which he identified as a juvenile parasitic jaeger. Although birders were pleased by the arrival of this crisply patterned brown-and-white member of the skua family with an Arctic latitude address, the birds were not. When I'd studied its pictures in my field guides, this seabird had struck me as a kind of oversized gull. But in attitude it was closer to a raptor. It could just as easily been named "piratical" jaeger due to its dastardly means of appropriating food. I watched as it harassed a Boney until the harried gull regurgitated food from its crop, which the jaeger scarfed up as soon as it hit the water. Then it sought out another bird to bother.

Although no one had witnessed its departure, the murrelet—which had slowly been floating further from the pier—was suddenly nowhere in sight. The black scoters had also evaporated. I hung around another fifteen minutes, but the murrelet failed to reappear, and no new birds materialized, either.

I kept waiting for the voice to conjure up another rarity, but it had apparently lost its mojo.

I arrived home in the midafternoon bubbling over with so much excitement, I had trouble falling asleep that night. Retreating to the upstairs bedroom, I sat up reading for a while, flipping through field guides and staring at range maps for jaegers, scoters, alcids, and the little gull. I should have lulled myself listening to jazz instead. Eventually I fell into shallow sleep, neither sinking deeper nor surfacing until shallow dreams of the murrelet alone, adrift, and hungry jolted me awake around 3:00 a.m.

Until we started getting up close and personal with orphan baby birds, I had never thought about wild birds having unique personalities like our cats, bunnies, and parrots. I seldom glanced at a bird now without making a guess about its temperament—and I obsessed about the ones that seem to be in trouble. I worried that the ancient murrelet wouldn't survive.

This wasn't the farthest excursion by the species. On May 27, 1990, astonished British birders found one in breeding plumage paddling around the waters of Jenny's Cove on Devon County's Lundy Island, over forty-five hundred miles by a ruler-straight route from the bird's usual haunts. According to R. J. Campey in the *Annual Report of the Lundy Field Society*, 1990, the murrelet stayed nearly a month, only to return to the island on April 14 of the following year. It had been seeing leaving Lundy with razorbills and other auk species and had apparently spent the winter with them.

The Tiscornia ancient murrelet had no related species to join up with. No one to teach him what food to catch in southern Lake Michigan and no one to guide him to an Atlantic wintering site where he could find other auks.

I wasn't the only birder for feel concern for him, of course. In "Chasing the Ancient Murrelet," from his chapbook *The Ancient Murrelet*, Michigan poet and associate editor of the *Michigan Quarterly Review* Keith Taylor writes about the bird, which

> bobs in these choppy
> irregular fresh water swells,
> diving, often, after crustaceans
> that haven't lived here
> for a geologic epoch,
> but taking what minnows it can find
> to keep hunger off
> until it dies, here, in a place
> it doesn't belong, where it can't find
> the right food or mate,
> but where I find it, following
> clear directions on the internet

Our moments of pleasure seeing wildly out-of-place birds like this are often purchased at great expense. Something has to go dreadfully wrong for a bird to go astray by thousands of miles. It might become separated from its flock and blown off course by a storm—or have its judgment impaired by illness or injury. Under the best conditions, a lost bird might take on a few additional burdens in unfamiliar territory. But the bird could end up in mortal danger if it landed in a habitat incapable of sustaining the species. This was probably the case with the murrelet. Under those circumstances, I decided I'd much rather see a plump and healthy blue jay than the most spectacular rarity.

Not all Alaskan vagrants found themselves in such dire straits. On a cold March day, Caleb Putnam and Curtis Dykstra spotted a Barrow's goldeneye on the Grand River in downtown Grand Rapids. They discovered it with three hundred common goldeneyes, ducks so similar to the Barrow's you had to look closely to pick out the crescent-shaped (not oval) blaze on the black face and the white spots on the wings.

The Barrow's hadn't shot as far off course as the murrelet. While most of them winter in the Pacific Northwest, some choose the Atlantic coastline instead. Unlike auks, which are exclusively sea and ocean birds, the Barrow's nests on inland lakes. So it was at home diving for food on a Michigan river, where it also enjoyed the security of a flock.

Though the murrelet's location had been out of reach for Linda with her back problems, a mere twenty-five-minute drive separated us from the Barrow's goldeneye—or would have if I hadn't gotten pulled over by the cops for turning left at a red light on Ann Street NE. While the officer was hard at work humiliating me, from her bed of pillows in the backseat, Linda described the exotic duck in so much excited detail that he retreated without giving me a ticket.

"The next time you're in an unfamiliar part of town, be more careful what you're doing," he said, and it seemed best not to mention to him that I had grown up in this part of town.

As we headed for the river I took care to avoid left turns until we swung into a parking lot just east of the Leonard Street Bridge. I scanned the water south toward the Sixth Street Bridge. It took a few moments for the reality to sink in that the glinting white-and-black specks in my binoculars were ducks. The river was wider than I thought and goldeneyes significantly smaller. Then I located a few more directly opposite us—Caleb's flock of hundreds must have dispersed—and among them swam the Barrow's. He was farther from where I stood than the murrelet had been, but I'd gotten worse looks at rare birds before. I could see him well enough to distinguish him from the others.

"There he is," I told Linda. "See that tree all by itself on the other side of the river, and the male and female goldeneyes in front of it? Look for a lone duck to their left. That's the Barrow's goldeneye."

She didn't exhibit her usual enthusiasm. "I'm not seeing him very well."

"He's not exactly on top of us. But he's a Barrow's goldeneye, and that's a very rare duck for Kent County. We'll probably never see another."

The duck complicated viewing by diving and disappearing for several seconds at a time. Just when he started moving in our direction and it seemed like we'd get a decent look, the other goldeneyes flew off. After a brief hesitation, he tagged along.

Linda remained quiet when we climbed back into the car, not at all chatty like she had been on the way down. I mentioned again what an extraordinary bird we'd seen. "A very few might spend the winter on the Great Lakes, but they just don't come into Grand Rapids." I also reminded her how far the duck had come, but she still seemed unimpressed. "Aren't you glad you got a chance to see him?"

"I thought I was going to get a better look," she said. "I prefer to see them close up."

For all of my talk of having an intimate experience with birds, when it came right down to it—and despite all my protests—I was probably still a lister at heart. And now I could chalk up a brand duck, which I never, ever, under any circumstances could have ever found on my own. I just didn't have the right birding stuff.

CHAPTER ELEVEN

The Worm Turns

Just as I had reconciled myself to the fact that finding rare birds would never be a Tarte forte, the celestial bodies shifted just enough for a few minor miracles to occur. The miracles didn't happen all at once, and the shift caused a bone-jarring bump along the way, as celestial bodies will.

One Saturday morning in May, Linda and I sat on the bed drinking coffee while cats Maynard and Tina vied for a spot at the window. Massive Maynard—a propane tank covered in fur—easily dominated, and as he sniffed in great gulps of air through the screen, I feared that he might deplete the oxygen levels in our woods. Suddenly he stopped inhaling and started whining.

"What do you see, Maynard?" Linda asked.

"He's always watching the sparrows in the spirea bush," I said. But he wasn't staring in that direction. Leaning forward I found myself gazing into the shiny black eye of a blazing yellow prothonotary warbler perched on a twig less than eighteen inches from my nose. I called Linda over with barely coherent gasps that must have disheartened the bird, because he shot off before she made it to the window.

Although nowhere near as out of place as a penguin or Barrow's goldeneye, the prothon is primarily a creature of wooded southern swamps, not a cat-teasing Michigan window peeper like a chickadee or chipmunk. The species is rare enough in Kent County that when I hopped online to report it to eBird.com—a fantastic reporting tool and interactive database run by the Cornell Lab of Ornithology and National Audubon Society—the warbler didn't even show up in the checklist for my location. I had to tick a box for a list of rarities to appear, a process that caused my extremities to tingle.

A few days later a Michigan eBird reviewer emailed me requesting a detailed description of the bird that would rule out my having mis-identified another yellow bird for the prothon, such as a yellow warbler, pine warbler, blue-winged warbler, or even a goldfinch. Far from feeling inconvenienced by the query, I almost swooned to think that I had seen a bird worthy of official scrutiny.

My four-second glimpse of the prothonotary warbler that morning instantly changed the emotional tenor of a day that had started off downhill and had been rolling toward a hole. I had awakened at 5:00 a.m. unable to fall completely back to sleep, not worried this time about the fate of an ancient murrelet but gnawed upon by as many as five concerns. None of them on their own possessed enough oomph to disturb my slumber. But frets about cat Frannie's eye infection, an impending project deadline at work, a leak in the hallway ceiling, old age, and death formed the spokes of a wheel that turned fitfully at first. Then because I didn't stop the little dynamo right away, it gained enough momentum to jangle my neurons on a morning when I should have been sleeping in.

When I finally emerged from restless partial sleep a couple of hours later, I sat on the edge of the bed with Linda, awash in free-floating dread. But seeing that golden lightbulb of a bird flipped a switch and changed my polarity from negative to positive. It wasn't just the thrill of seeing the prothon that rerouted my faulty wiring. It was the promise that he carried of more visitors to our woods.

I wanted to fling myself downhill toward the river to search for him. In my bones I felt that other warblers had to be around. But first I had to herd the ducks, geese, and hens out to their pen, change their wading pool and bucket water, fill the feed dishes, dole out veggie treats, and top-dress their predator-proof sleeping room in the barn with fresh straw. It didn't take long, but I wanted Linda to come with me into the woods, and she had chores inside the house involving parrots, doves, parakeets, cats, and husband. Then we sat down for breakfast. By the time we'd eaten and completed a dozen little tasks, I figured that any stray warblers would have grabbed their own grub and moved on.

A sparse selection of species met us on the path. A song sparrow who had been showing off his repertoire shifted to "chip" calls and dove for cover as we approached. One lone red-winged blackbird flared his epaulets and launched into a stirring *conk-la-ree* while chickadees flitted

Proving he's a better birder than I am, our cat Maynard spotted a brilliant yellow prothonotary warbler through the bedroom window.

about. A few yellow-rumped warblers lingered in the trees, pecking at poison ivy berries they'd missed the previous fall. But the prothonotary warbler was nowhere to be found, and neither were his buddies.

"We could try Don's woods," Linda said. "He gets birds on his path that we don't get, and I want to walk there anyway."

Don's house was just across a gravel driveway from our property, and the bushier habitat pulled in catbirds that turned up their beaks at our more open woods. Twice we'd been buzzed at Don's by palm warblers hunting insects in the spring, and once and only once we had surprised a blue-winged warbler as it hung upside down from a branch. We'd been delighted to find these, because we usually experienced slim pickings even during the heaviest migration waves elsewhere in the state.

Each spring after reading listserv reports describing some southeastern Michigan spot as suddenly "dripping with warbler species," I'd comb our woods without finding even one. I didn't think that the returning migrants necessarily favored an eastern Great Lakes route, though it was possible. But "birdy" places like Nichols Arboretum in Ann Arbor are called migrant traps, and these green areas in urban environments attract birds because the surrounding cement, glass, and steel lack the appeal of trees and water. In the less built-up western part of the state where I live, migrating birds have many more green areas in which to pitch their little overnight tents, and for that reason they can be more difficult to find. The odds of a flock screeching to a halt in our patch of woods are almost as great as those of an ancient murrelet tagging along with a prothon.

Still, I couldn't think of a reason not to give Don's place a try. The simple act of going out and looking for birds kept my anxiety levels in check. I'd been nettled by nervousness ever since I'd spent a weird week at age seven certain that death loomed imminently, possibly as soon as I had finished watching the *Beany and Cecil* cartoon on TV. I hadn't examined the reasons behind that feeling at the time, but from then on some manifestation of nervousness or depression would periodically rise up like Cecil the Seasick Sea Serpent and chomp at me for days. As an adult I'd tried pharmaceuticals, mental tricks, and spiritual practices in hopes of keeping my reptile brain at bay. Nothing succeeded. When I went birding, though, I experienced a sense of inner quiet that was missing from other portions of my life.

I can't pretend that my attentiveness to birds made me one with all of nature. But Linda was naturally thus. As we traipsed along our neighbor's trail, she kept up a running commentary on things around her. "I bet you a horse that this is wild honeysuckle, though it doesn't have a honeysuckle scent," she said as I stood listening for cheeps, chirps, twitters, or snatches of song. "You'd think that there'd be morels here, since it looks like the place in our woods where they've been before. Don's in the nursing home, so he probably wouldn't mind if we kept any that we found, and maybe there's some way I could call him if we did."

When we reached the end of the path, just before it looped back toward Don's house, Linda noticed stirrings in the bushes. Then, for a few moments, it was as if a tiny piece of Magee Marsh had broken off and grafted itself onto our neighbor's thicket.

"There's an ovenbird!" she said, pointing to a chipmunk-colored bird on the ground.

Barrows in *Michigan Bird Life* writes that the ovenbird "has a habit when moderately disturbed of walking lengthwise along a branch with a deliberate slow step, like a chicken." I didn't get a chance to experience this nor to witness the spectacle of an ovenbird midsong. "The bird fairly quivers with the violence of his effort," Chapman notes in *Birds of Eastern North American*. "The result seems inadequate; we feel that he is striving for something better." In fact, I didn't even have time to wonder if a woven, dome-shaped, oven-like nest might lay nearby, because Linda had already spotted a gray-and-yellow Nashville warbler, which belies its name by refusing to nest anywhere in Tennessee. I almost mistook its leaf-obstructed form for a somewhat similar female common yellowthroat, but the yellowthroat was nearby, too, and unembarrassed by her lack of the Nashville's bold eye-ring.

These three were attractive, though by no means gorgeous. The "beautiful people" hung out higher in the thicket. Close to one another flitted a magnolia warbler with a brilliant yellow breast and black-striped necklace, a dandified gent in a charcoal gray suit with chestnut-colored cap and cravat known as a bay-breasted warbler, and a northern parula, who packed so much color into a small volume that he defied description. The bluish back and head and blue wings with two white wing bars are easily enough imagined. Paru-lyzingly difficult to do justice to is a band that posits a bluish stripe and a burnt-orange stripe between a yellow throat and a yellow breast. This little patch of complex brilliance almost overwhelms the eye.

We had never before encountered such a concentration of different species outside of Magee Marsh. Linda couldn't visit Magee any more unless her aching back called a truce for a few days and we had lined up a chiropractor in Ohio to line up her vertebrae. So I was thrilled that she had seen these six warblers with me—which abruptly vanished, as apparitions will. When we rounded the end of the trail, before my ganglia had recovered from the overstimulation, we ran smack dab into a bird who wouldn't content himself with simply wearing a restful shade of black. He added two splotches of orange to each wing and on the edges of his tail to give our brainstems a start.

"A redstart!" I told Linda. He lingered briefly before zooming away.

With this final warbler, we must have used up our quota of birds. As we headed back, not only didn't we discover any more warblers, but the song sparrow, red-winged blackbird, and chickadees had also abandoned the place. The woods still felt alive as we jabbered about our discovery, pausing only when Linda pointed out a painted turtle sunning itself on a log, a cluster of wild violets, or a conical crayfish mound.

As we talked, it struck me how differently we thought about the warblers. While I appreciated the eye-popping plumage, I was equally astounded that we had blundered into exactly the right place at exactly the right time, finding them in our homegrown version of a migrant trap—a micro-habitat of a thicket surrounded by less desirable bushes and trees. Linda was all about the beauty of the birds and didn't care how or why they had arrived. She considered their appearance to be a "gift from God," and that was that.

Tromping up the basement stairs, I remembered the Christmas card with the snow-covered log cabin on the front. She loved the card so much that it remained on top of her dresser long after winter had passed. I hadn't paid much attention to the card when it arrived. I'd opened it, glanced at the sender's name, and tossed it into a pile. But the illustration had struck a chord with Linda, who had seen more deeply into the rustic scene than I could. She had an eye for appreciating color, form, and art that I envied.

My obliviousness to things unrelated to birds hit home a moment later when I walked into the bedroom and noted that not just one but many Christmas cards poked out among her knickknacks. Her dresser was awash with them, and they'd been there for months unseen by preoccupied, self-centered me. One jolly portrait of a snowman peeked out from behind a framed photo of a church window at such a precarious angle, I couldn't figure out why it hadn't fallen over. Seized by a spasm of fussiness, I set it upright, which caused it to disappear behind the picture. No other vacant slot existed among her animal and angel figurines, so I stashed it in a drawer, figuring she wouldn't notice its absence.

When she sat down on the bed to change her shoes, she asked, "What happened? Where did my card with the snowman go?"

"I just thought you might want to switch over to a warm-weather theme."

She tucked the card back into its spot. "Are you kidding? I look at that picture and enjoy it every day."

Oh, how I wished I had her eye. My birding life—and my whole life—would have been so much richer.

I remained happy with my ears. They led us to another meaningful encounter with unusual birds close to home, though I almost missed it due to an even-worse-than-usual mood as I sat at my computer.

"Sweetie, there's a bird singing, and it doesn't sound like anything I've heard before," Linda told me from the stairs.

"You've said that before," I grumbled. "It's probably just a goldfinch or a titmouse."

"It has a really unusual song. Come outside and listen."

I should have welcomed the interruption, but I banged and harrumphed all the way down to the basement. I'd been writing a book called *Kitty Cornered* about our six cats, and a chapter spotlighting whiny Maynard wasn't coming together exactly as whiny Bob liked.

"You'd better wear your boots," Linda said. "It's wet after all that rain."

Fortunately for me she shot through the door and missed my ungentlemanly response. Zipping up my jacket as I walked, I hit my head on the bird feeder and felt my sock slipping down my ankle. By the time I reached Linda behind the barn, the ducks and geese were making such a racket, I couldn't have heard a helicopter landing. "I knew this would happen," Linda said when the quacks and honks died down. "Whenever I call you to hear a bird, it's gone by the time we come out."

Just as I was about to pivot on my heel and go back to staring blankly at chapter 10, a thin and distant sound stopped me. "C'mon," I said. Dodging puddles, we hurried up the neighbor's driveway toward the squeaking-hinge song. "That's the weirdest red-winged blackbird I've ever heard." I told her. "Or is it a grackle?" Frogs splashed into the pond as our shadows struck them. We rounded the corner past Don's house and followed the inner path, because the riverbank part of the loop was underwater after the recent flooding.

My crankiness dissolved. It belonged to a different world. As we drew close to the singer, I felt as if his song had plunged me into one of those dreams where a familiar place had been altered just enough to make it unrecognizable. We had floated off to a swampy sliver of primeval forest, a shadowy tangle of trees and overgrown bushes interrupted by a single line of utility poles. His call hadn't struck me as beautiful until I heard the repeated, short, shrill phrase as a kind of incantation. Then an unexpected musicality crept in, like a maestro coaxing Mozart out of a handsaw.

I found the singer on a branch in a wet thicket, head craned toward the sky as the creaking song flowed through him. About the size of a red-winged blackbird, black all over, he stood silhouetted against the glare. I caught his yellow eye, which looked right through me. All that mattered was the grip of the song that held him and held us and held our bubble of the woods. Jumping to a higher branch, he flared his tail without missing a beat. In the performance of a lifetime, he sang the history of his people. He crunched numbers, and he named names. He bent the air like a bow, twanging, rasping, squeaking his whole reason for existence, and I felt small beneath him.

The music remapped my neural pathways. It slid open the screen door to my heart, and though I remained totally focused on the bird, I thought of Linda and everything she had done for me. Instead of working at a job all day, I simply worked mornings, spending part of each afternoon writing books by fits and starts. Other women wouldn't have approved, considering the financial hit we'd taken. But she accepted the path I'd chosen, never complaining about this or any of my other quirks. She loved me with all of the power that the bird poured into his song, and I loved her just as much—though in a twanging, rasping, squeaking, complaining sort of way.

As the single-phrase symphony continued, Linda nudged me. I looked down among broken twigs and last year's dead leaves, where a dull brown bird skulked, acting cool to the ardor of her mate. Then, when the male dropped to the ground, she changed places with him, flying up to a branch and continuing his song with the same level of conviction. If I hadn't seen the change in performers, I never would have known that a different vocalist had taken over. It was as profound a declaration of devotion as I had ever witnessed, and I had seen bunnies in love.

We stayed and listened for a while. The mood dissolved when a crew team from a local high school rowed by with blaring bullhorns. The commotion didn't bother the birds, but it sent us trudging home.

"What were those?" Linda asked.

"Rusty blackbirds. I've never seen them before, or should I say I've never noticed them. This was the first time I've heard them singing, so

I probably always assumed they were grackles or red-winged blackbirds and never gave them a second glance."

"You never noticed *them*?" I might as well have said that I hadn't tasted the arugula lettuce from her garden in my salad or that I'd walked past her dresser without taking note of a new Christmas card.

"I'll definitely be looking for them now."

To birders, rusties are noteworthy but by no means rare. Flocks move through our state each spring on the way to their nesting grounds in New England and Canada. I decided to report it to the birding group but gave up after two attempts. I had no idea how to describe our experience. Usually the flashy appearance of a bird dazzled me. But not even the most brilliant warbler seemed as beautiful as the plain black male with the irresistible voice. Eventually it dawned on me why the encounter had seemed so unusual. For years I had been observing birds from the outside. But in this case we had wandered inside their world, witnessing a ritualized encounter between a pair that was packed with such deep meaning, we had felt its power.

It had been one of the most profound encounters with wild birds that I'd ever experienced, and I was glad that I could share the moment with Linda—just as we had shared my fateful first rose-breasted grosbeak so many years earlier. If she had known what a lunatic that grosbeak would turn me into, she might have distracted me with a woodchuck instead.

I didn't think any interaction with a wild bird could have a greater impact than our close brush with the rusties. They had made me deliriously happy for a stretch of minutes, more joyful than if I had scored a rare species—and that would happen sooner than I could have guessed. But first an enormous bird set his sights on me, scaring me even worse than the osprey had. It happened as I drove Linda home from the chiropractor.

Linda went to her regular back cracker at least three times a week and to a different doc when she needed a Saturday adjustment. The frequent visits kept her pain level manageable, but she still couldn't do activities that involved extended sitting. This kept us from eating at restaurants, going to the movies, or attending bullfights. Standing in one place was also a no-no. Walking around helped her feel better, which made birding an excellent activity for both of us.

As we rode back from Dr. Scott Robinson's office, Linda lay in her usual position in the backseat on a bed of pillows, feet propped against the side window, toes aligned with well-established scuffmarks on the glass. "Where do you want to go walking?" she asked.

"I just found out about a park in Ada we've never gone to before, Roselle Park. It's an eBird 'Birding Hotspot,' if you want to check it out."

Less than one half-mile away from home, a large bird cannonballed toward us out of the brush. For one brief moment that stretched into a decade, I stared into the eye of a wild turkey before it whomped the car. I swerved into the opposing lane, heading for an SUV that had fortunately been close enough to witness our collision with the turkey yet far enough away to slow down for me to cut back into our own lane. I waved my thanks as we passed, and then I swung into our driveway jolted by the disaster that we had narrowly averted. If the bird had struck the car a second or two earlier, he would have crashed through the windshield and plopped upon my lap like our great big fat cat, Maynard, but with a greater detriment to my health.

As we rolled to a stop, Linda wanted to know, "Is the turkey okay?"

I shook my head. "He's dead. I saw him in the rear view mirror lying on the shoulder."

As I hauled myself out of the driver's seat to survey the damage to Linda's Scion XB—a boxy car we called "the bread truck"—I winced in pain and clutched my side. At the moment of impact, I had tensed and jerked my torso slightly but sharply enough to cause a muscle cramp. The Scion had suffered a similar malady. The turkey had dented the passenger-side door. It had also broken off the mirror.

We felt terrible about what had happened. We'd once had turkeys as pets. A man had raised thirty-six of them in his garage and then released them into the woods under the illusion that a heavy, lumbering domesticated breed could survive as well as wild birds. After we found the four survivors of his Darwinian experiment wandering in the road, Linda tracked down the owner and received permission to take them home and spoil them. Each evening as "the judges" perched on stanchions in our barn, Linda went from bird to bird with an apple for them to peck. She switched to cut-up apples in a bowl after reporting that a turkey had conveyed its desire for chopped fruit via a penetrating stare.

Linda insisted that we check to make sure that the turkey had died instantly. If he was grievously injured, we'd have to find a way to put him out of his misery. One of our many vets had a practice just up the street, and he could euthanize him. I drove slowly, funereally, dreading what we would find. But when we rounded the curve, the only sign of Mr. Turkey was a single black feather on the gravel. Hitting Linda's car had apparently been the equivalent of a songbird banging into a window and winging off uninjured a couple of minutes later. He'd survived the accident with flying colors.

"You'll have to file a claim with the insurance company," I said. "And we may have to pay a deductible."

"I don't care about that. What matters is that the turkey is okay."

On Monday I discovered that Linda had as much of a rapport with insurance agents as she had with birds. "I talked to State Farm, and they kept me on the phone for more than twenty minutes. They asked so many questions, it threw off my whole morning."

"Wow, why did it take so long?"

"They wanted to know every little detail. The lady I talked to was real nice, though. She sounded young, maybe in her thirties, and she and her husband lived in Seattle and were going to move into a new house the next day, which she loved, because for the first time she was finally going to be able to have a garden. I asked her about Vachon Island, where Bette MacDonald lived, but she had never heard of her or *The Egg and I* and mentioned two other islands near Seattle. She said she didn't watch much television, but she did occasionally get to see *American Pickers* and seemed interested when I told her about *Building Wild* and *Down East Dickering*."

That explained the twenty minutes. Any insurance adjuster I'd ever met only spoke officialese, but Linda's chatting talents were formidable. Back when her spine behaved better, we had taken a second trip to Point Pelee National Park in Ontario. After dinner, she'd suggested that we stroll through the neighborhood behind our motel. Although the street was only two blocks long, covering that short distance ate up an hour as she struck up one conversation after another with residents who happened to be outdoors. Those encounters pleased her as much as our birding earlier in the day, and they became the standard by which she judged all other urban walks.

We postponed our trip to Roselle Park until the following Saturday, since it didn't seem like a good idea to drive around with her outside mirror dangling by its control cable. In a way, the unfortunate collision with the turkey turned out to be a stroke of luck. If it hadn't have been for the one-week delay, we might not have ended up in exactly the right place at exactly the right time for me to make the most significant discovery in my entire insignificant birding career.

I had discovered Roselle Park thanks to an app for my iPod called BirdsEye. Unlike other birding software that essentially consists of eBook versions of field guides with bird songs added, BirdsEye lists the bird species currently being reported in my area—or anywhere in the country. It draws its information from eBird.org, an unbelievably powerful online tool that shows "birding hotspots" worldwide—allowing you to click on a location and see a full roster of reported birds. You can also search hotspots, counties, and other areas by date. eBird will also generate bar charts for species occurrences according to any time frame that you choose: days, months, or even years. It links these charts to maps, allowing you to select a bird you want to see and determine when and where is the best place to find it in a given area. More interactive features are being added all the time, and as increasing numbers of birders report their sightings to eBird, it becomes increasingly valuable as a bird finding tool.

Using BirdsEye I noticed that several warbler species had been reported at Roselle Park. "How could there be a park this good for birds right under our noses, and we've never heard of it before?" I asked Linda.

As it turned out, Roselle Park had only been around since 2007. The 240-acre nature preserve encompassed fields, wetlands, prairies, forests, and river frontage that had formerly been owned by the Ada Beef Company. Two tall silos made the entrance easy to find. A girl wearing a bike helmet and two boys in shorts spider-crawled up climbing rocks set into the base of the silos. The park map showed an unusual arrangement of trails that mainly hugged the boundaries and kept the interior untouched, allowing plenty of undisturbed habitat for birds. I grew pessimistic when we started walking, though. The ultra-smooth, hard-surfaced paths drew bicyclists like a magnet.

"On your left," called a member of a wheeled family. A teen on a skateboard also whisked by us, then a woman on roller blades. Dog walkers, joggers, and a girl with a pet pig on a leash overtook us when we stopped to scan the cattails. Song sparrows and red-winged blackbirds were abundant, but I fretted that the rolling human traffic would keep other species at a distance.

A comical sound close by brightened our prospects. It called to mind a cartoon in which a dog, eager to rocket off after a cat, windmills his legs until his paws finally achieve traction and shoot him skidding forward. In a rare moment of understatement, Barrows describes the song as "a high-voiced rolling whinny," which hardly does justice to the strangeness.

"A sora!" I said.

"Are you sure that was even a bird?"

Using the BirdTunes app, I played the song on my iPod for her. Only yards away but hidden in the weeds, the sora answered. Rails comprise a family of highly secretive birds that are more often seen than heard, due to their cryptic coloration and shy demeanor. The expression "skinny as a rail" suits them to a tee. Their narrowness helps them slip through dense vegetation as they hunt for food and practice their secret yoga. Our skinny sora must have been facing us, because we couldn't find a sign of him no matter how closely we scrutinized the undergrowth, and he refused to treat us to his special-effects song again. Knowing he could stand in one place longer than Linda, we let him go about his ghostly rail business as we continued ambling toward the river.

I tuned out a throng of kids on bikes by homing in on a warbling vireo too high up in a tree to see and common yellow-throats calling *witchity-witchity* from deep inside a clump of willows. It was the park of hidden birds except for the red-winged blackbirds dropping down into the cattails or rising briefly above them across an expanse so wide that the marching ants on the other side turned out to be more cyclists.

I appreciated the beautiful park's potential for future birds as much as for the birds we were finding. We climbed a tower overlooking a wetland that was currently devoid of wet. "I'll bet in early spring when all of this is flooded, yellowlegs would show up," I said. Catbirds sang from bushes on the riverbank. "Imagine this spot during migration. It's probably jumping with warblers." The sun-flecked river seemed conducive to hosting exclusive species of ducks that would shun our almost identical stretch of water a few miles away. Not that long ago, I had learned that anything could show up anywhere, and Roselle struck me as being more anywhere than lots of other places we had visited.

Midway along the river path, we made a forty-five-degree turn and headed back on the diagonal path. I was imagining something exotic such as a yellow-headed blackbird materializing in a puff of smoke, when a *tick-tick-buzz* like an old rotary telephone rang my chimes. A sedge wren. It hadn't appeared on the BirdsEye list of reported species, so I had actually stumbled onto a bird termed "a rare and local migrant and breeder" by the *Birds of Michigan* field guide. The US Fish and Wildlife Service considers it a US migratory species of concern and has tagged the bird with endangered, threatened, or special-concern status in nine states. Fortunately the sedge wren's situation in Michigan isn't so dire, and I could rejoice at having heard it, even if I didn't hold out much hope of eyeballing the hide-and-go-seek singer—at least not until Linda saved the day.

"I see him!" she said. "Look on those weeds over there. He has one foot on one stalk and the other little foot on the other, and now he's singing!"

With some effort, I followed Linda's wagging finger and the *tick-tick-buzz* until I managed to separate his brown, white, and buffy yellow body from the weeds. The trademarked upraised wren tail clinched it.

"I can't believe we actually found a sedge wren," I told her when we had finished gawking and listening. "Without you, I never would have seen it."

Back at home, I took a few deep breaths, checked my punctuation and grammar, rechecked my punctuation and grammar, and then reported the sighting to the birding group. Within minutes I received three congratulatory messages—three more than I had ever received before—and I couldn't have been more thrilled.

"What year was it when we saw that grosbeak at your cabin?"

"I don't know, maybe 1987," Linda said.

It had only taken twenty-some years of on-again, off-again interest for me to learn to find and identify birds, including the last decade in which I had applied myself to the hobby with unusual vigor. Finally I had made the grade, graduating from a C-plus-level birder to an indisputably solid B-minus.

Goal reached, I could now slack off.

CHAPTER TWELVE

Back to the Beginning

My excitement over discovering the sedge wren lasted over a week. I flipped through pictures of the bird in books and on the Web. I read accounts of its life, which turned out to be slim, since little is known about the habits of this secretive bird that almost literally flies under the radar. Not a single sedge wren that's been caught and banded has ever been recaptured. Either the lifespan of the species is abruptly short, or the birds keep a stash of tools on hand for cutting off their leg bands.

At the same time that my sedge wren excitement was peaking, an opposing current pulled with equal vigor and eventually won out. It told me there were far more important things in life—such as making it through a day with all ten toes intact.

Linda's parrot Dusty was enjoying his morning out-of-cage time playing inside the closet at the bottom of the stairs, indulging in a favorite activity of biting a pair of shoes. He paid no attention to me as I padded stocking-footed down the steps to warm up a cup of coffee. I should have known better than to underestimate such a calculating bird. When I reached the landing he whirled around and launched himself at my feet, forcing me to vault over the back of our L-shaped couch, coffee cup in hand. Having reasserted his status at the top of the pecking order, he turned his attention back to the closet.

Once I'd reached the safety of the kitchen, I thought, *If I'm not chasing birds, I'm being chased by them.*

When the microwave beeped and I racked my brain to decide what species the beep reminded me of, I brooded about the effect that birding was having on my life. At one time I had imagined that my ability to find and identify birds would add an extra dimension to my personality. But instead of feeling that birding had broadened me, I wondered if I had turned into the rail-thin victim of an obsession. Whenever I stepped outdoors I went on the alert. It didn't matter whether I rushed out in the rain to retrieve the *Grand Rapids Press* or idled from the bunny display to the poultry building with Linda at the Kent County Youth Fair in Lowell. I was continually watching, listening, and sending out mental "bird-dar," distracted from everything else.

I didn't know whether to be happy or depressed that my coworkers thought of me as the bird guy. I was the person to ask about the "herring," "wobbler," or "crackle" they had seen, calling on me to attach a name to some impossible species of undetermined color and indeterminate size "with a perfect white rectangle on its back." I didn't feel this made me into David Attenborough. I was more like Wally Cox as Professor P. Caspar Biddle in "The Bird-Watchers" episode of *The Beverly Hillbillies,* and I fed into the stereotype by falling back on birds as a topic of conversation since I no longer had much to say about anything else.

Maybe I was being too hard on myself, since getting obsessed was the best way to learn about a subject. And talking about birds when I met new people was an improvement over mentioning the fact that I was an author within the first four minutes.

At least I had sense enough to hold back from expounding upon the sedge wren, which proved that I hadn't completely slipped my moorings. I was simply following the strange path of the heart, and for reasons beyond my control it led me to a local sewage pond.

Caleb Putnam—the Michigan Important Bird Areas program coordinator for Audubon and discoverer of the myrtle warbler x Audubon's warbler intergrade in my own yard—started an online birding group and invited me to join. Unlike Bruce Bowman's Ann Arbor–based birders@great-lakes.net, which caters to all levels of birders throughout the state, Caleb's Kent Listers Google group is more specialized. It's for Kent County rarities only, and it excludes ho-hum rare birds like sedge wrens that are known to nest in the area. Instead the group focuses on out-of-place vagrants such as a large, long-billed shorebird called a whimbrel, discovered waddling in the grass alongside the runway at the Gerald R. Ford International Airport by Gus van Vliet.

Caleb asked the group members to contribute a list of the birds that

I thought I'd died and gone to shorebird heaven when I stumbled upon a rare red-necked phalarope in Tawas City.

each of us "needed" for Kent County. I decided not to contribute, since my list would have included all but a paltry few of the 914 species of wild birds that naturally occur in the United States and Canada. I wasn't a county lister anyway, but I eagerly followed the reports, since any bird of interest to this elite group would be a to-die-for must-see species located within easy driving distance. Thanks to Caleb, I discovered that I no longer had to trek as far as the Muskegon Wastewater Treatment System to confuse myself with shorebirds. At a sewage pond in my own county I could gape at similar-looking species with barely a hope of telling them apart. It was like a dream come true.

The only way I had learned to identify warblers was by exposing myself to oodles of them at Magee Marsh, and I hoped that the same method would work with sandpipers and plovers. How hard could it be? The difficulty level flattened me as I flipped through two field guides dedicated to shorebirds. Most spring warblers are starkly different from each other, and putting a name to them is a matter of remembering a few bold field marks. Not so with shorebirds. I struggled to tell a semipalmated sandpiper from a least sandpiper, a greater yellowlegs from a lesser yellowlegs, and almost any juvenile shorebird from the juvenile shorebird alongside it.

When I arrived at the Kent County sewage ponds, I came bolstered by two plans for getting the jump on the birds. Both plans revolved around my new Nikon DSLR camera. Plan one consisted of shooting hundreds of photos through my 70-300mm telephoto zoom lens of every bird nearby and poring over the pics with my field guides later. Plan two consisted of attaching my Nikon, with its 18-55mm non-telephoto zoom lens, to my spotting scope via a special swiveling bracket and shooting hundreds of stunning close-up photos of distant birds through the scope—along with any planets that were visible in the daytime. Then, in the privacy of my home, I'd identify the birds and planets later.

I noticed a couple of hitches in my strategy while trudging up the long and winding asphalt road to the first of two gates at the treatment system. Lugging a telescope, a pair of binoculars, a DSLR camera, and a heavy tripod didn't harmonize with my chair-sitting lifestyle, and by the time I reached gate two, I was racking my brain for a plan three. Sweaty and borderline shaky, I unlatched the gate, gripping the tripod in front of me with both hands like a butter churn as I approached the pond. Once I had assembled my camera-telescope-tripod rig, it felt as clumsy and unbalanced as I did. No wonder most digiscopers who shoot photos through their spotting scopes use compact point-and-shoot cameras instead of clunky DSLRs.

Despite the trek, I liked the place at once. Not only was it closer than Muskegon Wastewater, but it was also much nicer—more like a park than a sewage treatment area, with expansive grassy areas and no discernible chemical smell. The grazing sheep made me a little nervous, though. As they lumbered slowly in my direction, I recalled a narrow escape from shirt-chewing sheep at a petting zoo in my youth and hoped that these hadn't acquired a taste for optical equipment.

A pair of shorebirds pecked on the grassy pond perimeter. They looked clear, if tiny, through my binoculars, and under normal circumstances my scope would have revealed a wealth of nearly identical feather details between them. But I was peering into the scope through the viewfinder of my camera, and because my camera adapter bracket had broken its promise of accommodating a DSLR, I could only with trial and error roughly align the telescope eyepiece and camera lens. By then the shorebirds had tired of waiting for their photo opportunity and winged away with complaining *peep-peep-peeps*.

More birds materialized on the pond edges. Finding them was simply a matter of getting used to seeing them. Smaller and better camouflaged than I'd expected, they were easily concealed by weeds and grasses. None of them sported obviously unique plumage, and I couldn't tell if I was observing more than one species or the same species over and over again. I eventually started noticing a few sparrow-size sandpipers with them, and they all appeared identical to one another. After shooting bursts of fuzzy, through-a-fishbowl photos with my ill-mated camera and telescope confabulation, I supplemented them with an equal number of distant but clearer pictures of specks with beaks using my camera and underpowered zoom.

Back at home, after studying the photos, I reached some solid conclusions. The large ones were definitely greater yellowlegs. Or lesser yellowlegs. Or solitary sandpipers. Or stilt sandpipers. Or possibly a few of each. I identified the tiny sandpipers sometimes known as "peeps" as least sandpipers, semipalmated sandpipers, or Baird's sandpipers. None of them was a walrus. I knew that much.

I made an encore visit to the sewage ponds the following week, determined to puzzle out the identity of at least one species. Accomplishing that, I could establish how another species differed and then move on to the next. No magic happened as I stood in roughly the same spot as before and peered through binoculars, telescope, and camera. I hadn't felt this clueless since my morel-hunting trip to Newaygo State Park with Linda an astonishing twenty years earlier. It seemed unfathomable that I had learned so little in two decades. I needed a mentor.

Right on cue, Caleb strode through the gate with his scope and tripod balanced on his shoulder as if the rig were no heavier than a pool cue. He was taller than I remembered—more weathered and tree-like owing to a job that demanded he subject himself to long hours of sunlight, rain, snow, cold, heat, humidity, mosquitoes, chiggers, ticks, biting flies, and ice pellets in marshes, dunes, grasslands, forests, and sewage ponds.

"Seeing anything interesting?" he asked.

"Lots of birds. But I don't know what any of them are. I can't tell a solitary from a yellowlegs." I described my plan of photographing them for detailed analysis later.

In one fluid motion he whisked his spotting scope from his shoulder, extended and locked the tripod legs, popped the cover off the lens, adjusted the height to a comfortable viewing angle, and showed me a bird at dead-center in his eyepiece. "Let me walk you through it," he said. "That's a solitary sandpiper, and you might in some circumstances confuse it with a yellowlegs. Its back is darker. And notice the eye-ring? A solitary is noticeably smaller than a yellowlegs and usually by itself instead of in a group. Now let's see what else we can find."

As easily as folding up an umbrella, he collapsed his tripod and returned it to his shoulder while I struggled to get mine to fold. Giving up, I lifted it as it was, holding it beside me and trudging slowly to avoid tripping over the legs. As we approached the solitary, the bird flew off with a *peet-weet-weet* whistle, which Caleb imitated. When we came upon a couple of tiny "peeps" he told me, "Okay, there are only a couple of possibilities right now. The timing isn't right for a Baird's, so that basically leaves semipalmated and least. A semipalm wouldn't have yellowish or greenish legs. Its legs are dark, so these are leasts." He grinned at the *kreet, kreet* flight call as the sandpipers bailed on us. "Definitely leasts."

Before my visits to the sewage ponds, the farthest I'd ever lugged my scope and tripod assembly was ten feet from the trunk of my car and back. I struggled to keep up with Caleb. Instead of following the perimeter of the pond, he took a few strides up an embankment and stopped. "The trick here is to pop your head up without flushing any birds in the grassy areas." Just over the embankment lay a flooded field—then another embankment and another flooded field. I hadn't realized that this large area even existed. "What I'm hoping for is a ruff. I know that may sound crazy, but the habitat is exactly right. It may take me ten or fifteen years, but I'm confident I'll eventually find one."

It only sounded crazy because I'd never even heard of this Eurasian wader, which according to the Michigan Bird Records Committee has only been recorded in Michigan a mere fifty-four times since 1959, and usually in lakeshore counties. Caleb's hopes for a Kent County ruff didn't cause me to suddenly think of him as any optimist, however. I already knew he was one from his attempt to teach me shorebirds.

He showed me a bird through his scope. "Hear that *chu-chu-chu*?

That's a lesser yellowlegs. The bill is about the same length as the depth of the head. A greater yellowlegs has a thicker bill that's one-and-a-half times as deep as its head, and it's slightly upturned, though you can't always see that."

With a clatter of wings, mixed flocks of birds lifted off the ground as we walked along the embankment. If the species were difficult for me to identify on the ground, I had no chance of parsing them while they were in motion and silhouetted against the sky. Even starlings, mourning doves, and killdeer turned into birds of mystery in the flapping chaos. Caleb had no trouble calling them out like an expert shooter taking down skeet.

"One spotted sandpiper, 6 solitaries, 9 leasts, 1 semipalm, probably 160 killdeer, 40 ring-billed gulls, 3 barn swallows, 200 starlings, 40 mallards—Canada geese, 10, 20, 30 . . . 150, I'd say, and a couple of mourning doves."

The birds wheeled in a vast circle, touching back down behind us as we arrowed down the embankment toward the first pond. Caleb had seen something in the distance and was bringing it closer with his focus knob while I dithered with the telescoping legs of my tripod, which had slipped and failed to hold my telescope upright.

"It's a dowitcher," he said. "Short-billed juvenile." Quicker than a sleight-of-hand trick, he attached his point-and-shoot camera to the eyepiece and blasted off a burst of photos. "This is a very good bird for Kent County. In fact, I need to call a friend of mine right now and tell him to get over here. I hate to bother him, because he's babysitting and supposed to be making dinner, but he's definitely going to want to see this. I'll buy them all a pizza later."

I felt modestly encouraged when I studied the short-billed dowitcher through my scope. It didn't look like anything else, with the exception of the long-billed dowitcher, which is so similar that long- and short-billed dowitchers were considered to be a single species until 1950. I figured I'd recognize the bird if I ran into it again. It was larger and plumper and had a significantly longer bill than most other shorebirds I would find.

In fact, the following June, I shocked myself by discovering twelve short-billed dowitchers at the sewage pond. I managed to shoot decent photos of four of them and deliriously submitted my report to the Kent County Listers group.

At the present moment, though, I thought Caleb was merely expressing his usual optimism when he shook my hand before striding off and said, "It's nice to have an extra set of eyes here." He might have been referring to the sheep.

In my year of the dozen dowitchers, Bill Holm and I made our third annual May visit to Magee Marsh for the Biggest Week in American Birding event. Pulling into the park drive from State Road 2, we witnessed an unusual phenomenon.

"Why's everybody leaving?" I asked.

"The Mayor of the Boardwalk has arrived."

"And his birder-hating friend."

Unlike on previous visits, no one stopped a car in the middle of the road to peer at a very important bird, backing up traffic in both directions. And for the first time ever, we managed to park in one of the coveted spaces directly opposite the portable toilets.

"Maybe there's a monsoon on the way."

"Somebody tweeted a report of a yellow-spotted cuckoo thrush at Metzger Marsh, and the birders believed it," Bill said.

"That was you?"

We had in fact been keeping tabs on #thebiggestweek postings on Twitter for breaking reports, but these had become vanishingly few. Once we hit the boardwalk, we understood why. Not just the birders had gone AWOL. So had the birds. Instead of being greeted by a multilayered symphony of song, we found ourselves enveloped by the Cone of Silence.

As he bustled past us, a man in a Cape May Bird Observatory cap paused to grumble, "This is the worst spring migration in twenty years."

"What happened?" Bill asked.

"I heard that the unseasonably cold weather in April is to blame. Instead of laying over in their usual spots, the birds are overshooting them and continuing north."

We had no idea if this was true, but we definitely found slim pickings in the warbler department. People were snapping photos of yellow warblers, which usually wouldn't have merited a glance. A far from uncommon Nashville warbler drew a crowd as it vacuumed up bugs from leaves. Even the lowly house wren earned attention. Further down the boardwalk, we gravitated toward a bubble of spectators, only to discover that they had been catapulted into delirium by a turtle.

The lack of warblers had an unexpected upside, which Bill brought to my attention. "Have you noticed how nice everybody is? The people who stayed behind are all in a good mood and grateful to be seeing anything at all. The birders are actually laughing and having a great time. They're not sour and serious like the typical Biggest Week crowd."

I immediately started searching the underbrush for a Connecticut warbler or another rarity. With Bill suddenly extolling the virtues of birders, anything seemed possible.

Improbabilities multiplied in August when I hit Tawas City on Lake Huron hoping to shore up my miserable shorebird identification skills. I had limped west from the Saginaw area after taking the Wildlife Drive auto tour at Shiawassee National Wildlife Refuge, wounded from having failed to identify wader after wader that populated the numerous ponds. They all looked like solitary sandpipers/greater/lesser yellowlegs to me, indicating that I hadn't processed Caleb's crash course from the previous year.

I made a disappointing stop at Nayanquing Point Wildlife Center en route to Tawas City, finding it both too wet and not wet enough to harbor shorebirds. The lagoon at the end of Tower Beach Road was too deep, while the surrounding fields were dried up. Adding insult to injury, every single flashy male yellow-headed blackbird had apparently streamed out of Nayanquing upon learning I was on my way.

Arriving at Tawas City around 4:00 p.m., I decided to wait until the next morning to misidentify shorebirds at Tawas Point State Park. I checked into the North Star Motel, tumbled into a short but deep nap, and then sauntered out to the pool area to admire a statue of a polar bear wearing an Uncle Sam hat and vest. The North Star Motel was my kind of place. The abnormally tall bear reminded me to investigate a children's slide shaped like a huge gull that I had seen less than a mile away on US-23. Reasoning that exotic gulls might fly in to worship the slide as a god, I made the short drive to Gateway Park.

A young mother pushed her child on a swing as I shot photos of four ring-billed gulls camping out in the shadow of the slide. Walking through weeds down to the beach, I found foraging peeps, which I knew to be least sandpipers by their greenish legs, and—miracle of miracles—I got close enough to a couple of birds to be able to confidently call them lesser yellowlegs with a *chu-chu*.

Then I died and went to shorebird heaven, as I assume all birders eventually will. A few feet from shore, a tiny white bird with a black-and-brown streaked back, sooty black cap, and black smudge behind the eye rode the lapping waves. Although only about the size of a sparrow, he appeared as much at ease in vast Lake Huron as the fattest walleye as he swam and spun, dipping his beak for food. The paleness, the delicacy, the elegance, and the downright cuteness knifed through my heart. A chorus of angels could have been belting out "Ode to Joy" overhead, and I wouldn't have heard a thing. My bird bliss overwhelmed me.

Even though I had never seen a juvenile red-necked phalarope before, I recognized him from having paged forward, backward, and sideways through the shorebird section of my field guides. If I had been in doubt, I could have almost bent down and picked him up. He seemed more concerned about maintaining his bearings in the surf than paying attention to a gawky, gawking hominid—assuming he knew what I was. Red-necked phalaropes nest far north in the Arctic where they aren't likely to come into contact with humans or birders and may genially allow a close approach during migration. They spend their winters in the Southern Hemisphere, as I have longed to do, and visit Michigan infrequently enough that the bird is considered a rarity.

I watched and watched and watched and watched and watched and watched and watched him swim until we were the only two creatures that existed in the world—except for the least sandpipers that paced back and forth in front of the phalarope's small stretch of beach and the yellowlegs, whose spindly legs and beaks demanded attention. Only for the thousandth time I wondered how, with so many other places where the phalarope and I might have been, we ended up here, together, at this particular time and place, out of all the gin joints in the world.

Nervous with excitement, I took a break and decompressed at the North Star Motel for about an hour. My head cleared as I sank into the chair next to the bed. Using my iPod I reported the bird to Mich-listers@envirolink.org, a statewide Michigan mailing list for rarities, in hopes that someone else would get a chance to see him.

After I felt calmer I returned to Gateway Park to spend a few more minutes with the swimmer/spinner. I photographed a medium-size gull, the sandpipers and yellowlegs, a miniature version of a killdeer that turned out to be a semipalmated plover, and the phalarope. I hated leaving him behind. As I pulled out of the parking lot, I could just make out a white dot riding the surf. I bade him and an amazing day farewell, heading to Big Boy for a Slim Jim® sandwich, an order of French fries, coleslaw, and a Coke.

The next morning I experienced an unexpected feeling of relief when I couldn't find him. The responsibility of being the sole witness to a bird of such delicate beauty would have weighed too heavily on me two days in a row. At Tawas Point State Park, while walking the Sandy Hook Trail, I ran into a woman with a scope who kindly pointed out least, stilt, semi-palmated, pectoral, spotted, and Baird's sandpipers, plus a trio of American golden-plovers. Another birder joined us as she was showing me a black tern.

"Did either of you see the red-necked phalarope?" he asked.

"Not today, but I saw him yesterday," I said. "Where was he?"

"On the beach south of town. I was an hour away in Gladwin, but when I read the post I rushed over and he was still there around eight o'clock. He flew off before I left."

I couldn't resist telling him that I was the person who had reported the bird. He thanked me and shook my hand. Nothing like that had ever happened to me before.

I sorted through my photos when I got home. I plastered my Facebook page with the better ones and was about to add what I figured was a shot of a juvenile Bonaparte's gull, but the bill shape didn't seem right. I posted it to the Facebook Bird ID Group of the World and instead of getting an immediate ID, an expert directed my attention to the eye-ring that didn't completely ring the eye. Using this and other hints, he guided me to identify it as a juvenile Franklin's gull.

I emailed the photo to Caleb, and he concurred. "Wow, juvenile Franklin's Gull! Excellent find, Bob, quite rare . . . I've found this species in Michigan only two or three times. Congrats!"

I had to pinch myself. After I submitted my Gateway Park report to eBird, Caleb forwarded an email from Joe Soehnel, administrator of the

Saginaw Bay Area Birding and Birding Trail website (saginawbaybirding. org). Joe asked Caleb, "Could you give me Bob Tarte's email address? I'd like to get his permission for the Franklin's Gull pic and to see if he got one of the Red-necked Phalarope from the other day. He's cashing in pretty well up there."

I had written a music column for the Los Angeles–based magazine *The Beat* for twenty years. One of my three books about our pets had become a *Wall Street Journal* bestseller. But nothing had ever made me prouder than seeing my bird photos on the cover page of the Saginaw Bay Area Birding website. For the briefest of fleeting moments, I had somehow managed to achieve a narrow sliver of greatness as a birder.

One final thing needed doing. With my new six-hundred-dollar pair of binoculars and fifty-some years of life experience, including twenty-some years devoted to some degree of birding, I returned to Aberdeen Park to search for birds behind the tennis courts—just as I had done back in 1962 when I was nine years old. I figured I'd cash in pretty well, just like in Tawas City.

Less impressive than what had changed—new fences around the tennis courts and fences removed from the playground across the street—was how much had stayed the same. The tennis court nets, which had probably last been replaced in the 1980s, appeared as bedraggled as the originals had looked to me as a child. I expected to find the twenty-first-century equivalent of a pseudo surfer dude aggressively slamming balls against the backboard, but the backboard had disappeared. In its place stood a brown metal utility building, which had already deteriorated enough to assume an air of antiquity.

The area behind the tennis courts had seemed like a small wilderness to me as a kid. It had changed more than any other part of the park. Someone had yanked out the wiry bushes and scrubby trees and leveled the undulating slope to ruler-flat blandness. It just about broke my heart. Standing behind the east end of the courts, I could see all the way to the west end as if staring down an alley. As I trudged along the path, I couldn't find a trace of human passage—not a single footprint or a Kit-Kat wrapper livened up the space. No one apparently used the path as a shortcut anymore or played behind the fence. Why would they, when not a single stick of scenery survived to fire up the imagination? It had all been fed into a wood chipper.

Keeping my ears peeled for birds, I heard a *tut-tut* call from somebody's backyard, a few sharp chirps, and finally a complaining squawk, and none of that came from me. So much for my impressive birding skills.

After I hauled myself back into the car, I glanced around hoping to find some small way in which the park had changed for the better compared to my memories from childhood. I only saw signs of aging and diminishment. Then, from a tree on the turnaround, the exuberant tootling of a house finch erupted—a bird that hadn't existed in Michigan when I was growing up. Cheered, I fished out a scrap of paper from my glove compartment and tallied up my report: "American robin. Blue jay. House sparrow. House finch." Not much of a list, but it was still four more species than I'd found as a nine-year-old. Take that, Terry Gray and Joan.

Now I could now head home and comb my hair like a surfer if I wanted to. As long as Linda gave the okay, of course.

CHAPTER THIRTEEN

The Redhead and the Redhead

I hadn't seen hide nor hair of a red-headed woodpecker since the spectacular pair that had buzzed Linda and me at Newaygo State Park so many years ago. The woodpecker wasn't rare in Michigan—not an improbable vagrant like an ancient murrelet or a secretive breeder like the sedge wren. It wasn't pathologically fussy about its nesting grounds like a Kirtland's warbler, whose habitat needed to be maintained by controlled burning and cowbird culling. Still, the woodpecker's numbers had taken a nosedive over the decades. I had never found one in our woods or in any woods in our area, and I wanted to see one while the woodpeckers and I were still around.

When my Facebook friend Vanessa Kaiser Birman posted a photo on her timeline of a red-headed woodpecker in Middleville, which was only about thirty miles away, I asked for particulars. She messaged me that she had found several on the Paul Henry–Thornapple Trail. Describing their location with the same precision she brought to her profession as a CPA, she said, "They are three-quarters of a mile in, where the dead trees are in the marsh area. They can be found on the right and left sides near the first metal bench, which is on the right. This is after crossing the two bridges."

The specificity confused me, of course. My leaky bucket of a brain started spilling data after "three-quarters of a mile." When I mentioned that I'd shoot over to the Paul Henry Trail at lunchtime the next day, she said that she didn't have any client meetings scheduled and could probably meet me there.

I didn't know if red-headed woodpeckers held any deep meaning for Linda, but to me they seemed emblematic of the early days of our marriage, when we were both vibrant and spontaneous—although, come to think of it, Linda still was, and I had never been. If Vanessa could take me to the birds, I'd take Linda the following the Saturday, or the Saturday after that, if her back allowed. That was my plan. But my budget cell phone had its own ideas. My service refused to function in Middleville, so I couldn't check in with Vanessa to find out if and when she would arrive.

I waited in my car until the lure of the woodpeckers grew too powerful to resist. Telling myself that she might already be looking for me, I studied a print-out of her directions one more time and hit the trail in search of bridges, metal benches, Vanessa, marshes, and birds. Just like at Roselle Park, cyclists and runners zipped by me as I walked and stopped, walked and stopped, scanning trees and bushes distant and far. I saw downy woodpeckers, a hairy woodpecker, and red-bellied woodpeckers. I even heard a pileated woodpecker across the river. But I couldn't locate a single redhead.

I lost heart once the marshes, ponds, and river receded and I reached a long straight stretch of the trail that seemed to ribbon out into infinity. I wouldn't find the bird in the sunlit fields ahead, so I turned around. Halfway back a woman approached with a DSLR dangling from her shoulder. It had to be Vanessa. When I told her about my lack of luck with the woodpeckers, she said, "There are lots of them here this year."

It was obvious through her Facebook posts and our conversation on the trail that Vanessa was an animal lover through and through. She and her family lived with a menagerie of indoor pets. Although she filled her days with clients and numbers, her passions were animals and photographing birds.

As we headed for woodpecker central, I couldn't help saying the names of the birds as I heard them, not so much to impress Vanessa but because it was what I did.

"So that's a blue-gray gnatcatcher," she said. "I've been calling it the screamie me-me. I'll remember it now."

I also showed her a singing common yellowthroat, pointed to the leafy canopy where a vocal red-eyed vireo bounced around, and then oohed and ahhed with her after a yellow warbler had given away its hiding place with a "chip" note. Vanessa was a natural. Although she hadn't been birding long, she had probably learned more over the past year than I had learned in five.

She led me to an area with a large pond on the left. I hadn't counted benches or bridges this time, but I was sure I had scoured this area ear-lier. "There's one," she said, shaming me by spotting it using her camera and telephoto lens when my binoculars had slid right past the bird. It wasn't until I found the woodpecker that I started noticing its spooky habitat of dead trees rising from the water, gnarled stumps like ruined monuments, wiry bushes, the steel gray pond itself, and a softening of greenery behind it. I wanted to come back on a foggy morning to watch the woodpecker fly out of the mists and then slice back into obscurity.

The red-head appeared different than I remembered, more like a bird going about its unhurried business flapping from trunk to trunk than the go-for-broke nest defenders that had spun and thrashed the air above our heads, scolding us for invading their territory. I didn't know wheth-er I preferred the long, lingering look that this distant bird allowed me or the explosive appearances at Newaygo State Park that had been too quick and chaotic to process but that had stuck with me all these years. The tranquil sighting reminded me of running into a high school friend decades later—the wild kid who always got into trouble—and listening as he tells me not about partying or girls or his close brush with the cops, but about remodeling his basement.

Vanessa wanted to keep birding. "Blue-gray gnatcatcher," she said when we heard the screamie me-me song again. "And that's an eastern phoebe, right?"

I needed to leave and for the second time headed back the way I had come. But she had given me the gift of red-headed woodpecker vision, and I easily found four more.

The further I got from the Paul Henry–Thornapple Trail, the propor-tionately larger my excitement about the woodpeckers grew, until I was bursting to share the experience with Linda. I felt like a little kid on Christmas morning when I hopped out of the car and zipped into the house. The one and only thing I wanted to do was sit down and show her the photos of the woodpecker on my camera screen. I hadn't even seen them yet—I was waiting until we could look at them together.

When I got inside the house I found her lying on a set of pillows on the living room floor. I knew exactly what it meant. Since she couldn't sit for any length of time, she would do this if we were watching television or if she was involved in an extended telephone conversation. The coiled

No bird amazed me more than the red-headed woodpecker like this one
who showed up for Linda just after I'd driven sixty miles to see one.

phone cord stretching in a taut line from the front of the couch to the wall of the dining room indicated she'd be occupied for a while. I considered transferring my photos to the computer, weeding out 50 percent, and then impressing her with the gems. This struck me as cheating. So I waited and I waited.

She mentioned somebody's daughter to the caller, but I couldn't figure out whether a friend or stranger was tethered to the other end of the line. Telemarketers feared our house. Linda would throw them off-script and induce them to reveal intimate details of their lives. She could have been talking to an agent from a charity, or she might have gotten back in touch with the insurance rep in Seattle from the turkey collision days. I flitted from room to room with as much patience as I could muster, and when she finally plunked the phone back in the cradle I decided not to ask about the call for fear that she would recount the conversation and delay the photos further. I knew I was being selfish, but outright joy seldom inhabited my frame, and I needed to discharge some of it.

"Two o'clock!" she moaned. "How did it get to be so late? I haven't even had my lunch." From the kitchen she asked, "Did you get to see your birds?"

"I'll tell you later," I said. While she ate her veggie-meat sandwich, I trekked out to the barn and did her outdoor chores for her. I changed the pool and bucket water and fed bread and lettuce treats to the ducks and geese. Finding a fat worm under a rock, I tossed it to our hen, Ginger, who muttered excitedly as she pecked it. I had timed my absence perfectly. When I reached the top of the basement stairs, Linda had finished eating and was cleaning her paper plate with a damp washcloth before stashing it next to the breadbox to use another day.

"You won't believe how beautiful those woodpeckers were," I told her as we plopped down on the couch. "I'll just skip to the good ones." I clicked through the first dozen shots in search of a standout. Then another dozen. Then fifteen or twenty more. Before I knew it, I had cycled back to the beginning and found myself scrounging for the least of the worst in a miserable batch. I settled on a fuzzy profile of a distant bird partially obscured by leaves and branches. I had nothing else to show her.

"Were they all that far away?" she asked. "We could practically reach out and touch them at Newaygo State Park."

"We can't go there anymore. It wouldn't be good for your back."

As we took our afternoon walk in our woods, instead of straining to hear birds or staying alert for movement in the trees or bushes, I tried to paint her the picture that I had failed to capture with my camera. "They definitely seemed much bigger through binoculars," I said. "Their heads were this amazing bright red when the sun hit them, and the setting reminded me of a haunted bayou. It wasn't like anything you'd expect to find in Middleville. We've really got to go there, since I know right where they are."

"I like seeing birds up close. It's too frustrating otherwise."

"You'll be able to see them just fine." Through no fault of Linda's I had suddenly grown defensive about an experience that, up until fifteen minutes earlier, had been the highlight of my month. And not only did a steadily developing bad mood dampen my excitement over the woodpeckers, but it was also keeping me from paying attention to the cardinals, song sparrows, Baltimore orioles, great-crested flycatchers, and other birds that I heard calling as we walked along the river.

A green damselfly crossed the path in front of us, vivid metallic emerald, and another fluttered just ahead of our feet. When a third landed on a sprig of weeds, I noticed that a white spot punctuated its black wings at the highest point of the curve. Maybe I'd begin learning damselflies, dragonflies, butterflies, katydids, and spiders to fill in the gaps between birds. Or I'd start appreciating the appearance of the river, which never looked the same two days in a row. Today it was busy bouncing back ripples of sunlight onto trees along the bank.

The brightest spot detached itself from the shadows and sailed to the edge of our path.

"Do you see that?" I asked Linda. "I can't believe I'm seeing what I'm seeing. Don't even move." I hardly dared to raise my binoculars. "Straight ahead. Look toward that X of branches, where the limb has broken off, then left to the biggest tree—climbing up the bark."

It took her a second. "How is that even possible?" she asked.

"It's the closest I've been to one all day."

Twenty-two years we'd lived in our house. If we knew any bird since day one, we knew this bird, and no red-headed woodpecker had ever shown up in our woods before. Like the red-breasted nuthatch, the pine siskin, and the white-winged crossbill, it had waited to come to me until

I had sought it out miles from home. This was the loop-back effect at its most powerful and its most mysterious. Stumbling onto a flock of brilliantly colored warblers in a tiny patch of brush during a single flickering moment of time was nothing compared to the mountain-cliff improbability of discovering a bird and then having it reflected back at me.

Who was the finder, and who was the found? Was I, in fact, the hare, not the hound? A bird dog dogged by birds?

If the phenomenon had any meaning, on this day the meaning seemed clear. I loved birds, and every bird was my favorite bird. But no bird was a better bird than a bird I saw with Linda. This had been true from when we had first met, and it was even truer now. Not counting, of course, the next sedge wren, Franklin's gull, red-necked phalarope, or ostrich I'd run into—totally by accident.

ACKNOWLEDGMENTS

Many thanks to my birder-hating birding friend Bill Holm, whose presence in this book almost guarantees bestseller status. Bill's companionship on birding trips has turned many a bad day out into a bad day out with laughs.

Thanks to all the experts who either provided material for the pages of *Feather Brained* or impressed me in the field by being outstanding in their field: Bruce Bowman, Allen Chartier, Darlene Friedman, Jim Kortge, Scott Manly, Peg and Roger Markle, Sy Montgomery, Stacey O'Brien, Caleb Putnam, Bill Rapai, Steve Santner, Jeff Schultz, Dave Sing, Sherri Smith, and Keith Taylor.

Other birders who influenced this book in some fashion include Tim Baerwald, Ric Brigham, Adam Byrne, Gary Dietzel, Brian Drake, Skye

Bill Holm, my nonbirder birding buddy, who may or may not have once been my boss at a weekly newspaper.

Haas, Janet Hinshaw, Cendra Lynn, Greg Miller, Keith Miller, Mark Obmascik, Elisabeth Paffhausen, Tom Pavlik, Ric Pedler, Dirk Richardson, Alan Ryff, John Smith, Kim Smith, Joe Soehnel, and Jerry Ziarno.

Special thanks to Marcia Davis, Bill Holm, Brian O'Malley, and Linda Tarte for reading chapters and providing helpful feedback and to my editor Scott Ham at the University of Michigan Press, project coordinator Elizabeth Frazier, copy editor Carol Sickman-Garner, and the rest of the excellent staff. Much gratitude to Cayr Ariel Wulff for feedback on my cover design. Huge indebtedness to Laura Kittens for her final proofing of the page proofs.

Lifelong thanks to my wife, Linda, who first introduced me to birds and then had to put up with my enthusiasm forever after.

ABOUT THE AUTHOR

Bob Tarte and his wife, Linda, live on the edge of a shoe-sucking swamp near the West Michigan village of Lowell. When not fending off mosquitoes during temperate months or chipping ice out of their pet ducks' plastic wading pools in the depths of winter, Bob fritters away his time scouring their woods for warblers. He ekes out a few minutes a day to write books about his two passions: his numerous pets and wild birds.

Bob is the author of three memoirs—*Enslaved by Ducks*, *Fowl Weather*, and *Kitty Cornered*—and his work has appeared in *The Beat* magazine, the *New York Times*, the *Boston Globe*, and the *Miami New Times*. He hosts a podcast for PetLifeRadio.com called *What Were You Thinking?* that's supposedly about "exotic pets" but often turns into a show about birding with Bill Holm.

Visit Bob's website at www.BobTarte.com to see excerpts from his three previous books plus scads of photos of his and Linda's pets.

I finally discover a birding student worthy of my skills.

FEATHER BRAINED BOOK CLUB
DISCUSSION QUESTIONS

If your book club slipped up somehow and decided to read *Feather Brained*, these 'no brainer' discussion questions may make your meeting less arduous.

- Did *Feather Brained* make you look at birds differently than before?

- What effect does birding have on Bob's life? Do you think it made his world wider or narrower in scope?

- Have any hobbies changed the way that you live?

- Would you ever agree to go to a location just because you liked its shape on the map? (Like Bob agreeing to visit Point Pelee.)

- What would you consider to be a really good bird? Would a birder agree with you?

- Did *Feather Brained* teach you anything about the "how" of finding and identifying birds? If so, what tip did you find the most valuable?

- Are there any hobbies that you feel you bumble at, but enjoy anyway?

- What would it take to get you to spend time at a sewage pond?

- What was the most interesting fact you learned from *Feather Brained*?

- Have you read any of Bob Tarte's other books? If so, how did they compare to *Feather Brained*. If not, shouldn't you buy them all right away?

- Bob says about his favorite bird, "No bird was a better bird than a bird I saw with Linda." Isn't he a prince? What is the extent of your injuries from swooning over this line?